ALAN WILLIAMSON
KIRK PEPPERDINE
JOEY GIBSON
ANDREW WU

W9-BHM-683

Ant

DEVELOPER'S HANDBOOK

SAMS 201 West 103rd Street, Indianapolis, Indiana 46290

Ant Developer's Handbook

International Standard Book Number: 0-672-32426-1

Library of Congress Catalog Card Number: 2002104736

Printed in the United States of America

First Printing: October, 2002

05   04   03   02   4   3   2   1

Trademarks

Warning and Disclaimer

Executive Editor
Michael Stephens

Development Editor
Songlin Qiu

Managing Editor
Charlotte Clapp

Project Editor
George E. Nedeff

Copy Editor
Mike Henry

Indexer
Heather McNeill

Proofreader
Linda Seifert

Technical Editor
Ben Hanner

Team Coordinator
Lynne Williams

Multimedia Developer
Dan Scherf

Interior Designer
Gary Adair

Cover Designer
Aren Howell

Page Layout
Michelle Mitchell

Contents at a Glance

Table of Contents

About the Authors

Alan Williamson is as much a veteran of the Java world as one can be with a language that is still very much finding its feet in the world. Alan has more than 15 years experience in the world of software development, graduating with full honors in computer science from the University of Paisley. Alan worked in mainly research and development roles until starting up the UK's first pure Java consultancy company five years ago, specializing in Java on the server side (http://www.n-ary.com/). Alan has also worked his way up to the dizzy heights of editor-in-chief of the world's largest Java magazine, *Java Developers Journal*, and can be found talking at various conferences all over the place!

Kirk Pepperdine has more than 15 years of experience in informatics. During that time, he has focused on applying object-oriented methodologies and technologies to the field of distributed computing, where Kirk has functioned as a researcher, developer, designer, architect, and consultant. Kirk has been heavily involved in the performance aspects of applications since the start of his career, and has tuned applications involving a variety of languages from Cray Assembler through C, Smalltalk, and on to Java. Kirk has focused on Java since 1996. He can be reached at kirk@javaperformancetuning.com.

Joey Gibson has been working in the technology industry since 1990. He is a Sun Certified Programmer for the Java 2 Platform and has been working with Java since early 1996. He is a Senior Consultant and instructor for BravePoint (www.bravepoint.com), located in Atlanta, GA, specializing in J2EE development. He is a "collector" of programming languages whose favorites include Java, Smalltalk, Ruby and Python. He can be reached at joey@joeygibson.com or jgibson@bravepoint.com.

Andy Wu has been involved in software development for more than five years. He is a software enthusiast who thrives on new technologies. Andy currently applies his Java expertise as a developer at n-ary consultancy in Scotland. Prior to joining n-ary, he worked in research and development roles, and achieved a full honours degree in software engineering from the University of Glasgow.

Dedications

Andy Wu: I'd like to dedicate my efforts to my parents who have been such an important influence in my life.

Joey Gibson: To my wife Tammy and our son Thomas for putting up with long hours spent writing and for encouraging me to put in the time necessary to produce an excellent book.

Kirk Pepperdine: Csodálatos felesé gemnek és két gyönyöru lányomnak— To my three girls who have consumed my heart, Anna, Szonja, és Andrea.

Acknowledgments

Alan Williamson: Working on this book has been a journey to say the least, and without the support and team effort from my co-authors, the journey would have been significantly harder. Kirk, Joey, and Andy, it was indeed a joy. I would like to thank all at Sams, particularly Songlin and Mike for their continued support and advice throughout. I would like to single out my co-author and friend Andy Wu for his non-stop nagging and overall moral boasting sessions. Finally, I would like to thank my wee boy Cormac for his continual entertainment that broke many a long night.

Andy Wu: My thanks go to Alan, Joey, Kirk, and the Sams Publishing team for making this a pleasurable experience.

Joey Gibson: I'd like to thank the Jakarta Ant team for producing such a great tool that has certainly made my life a lot easier. I'd also like to thank my co-authors for giving me such a wonderful book-writing experience.

Kirk Pepperdine: I don't know any other way to say this but Ant rocks! Mr. James Duncan Davidson, thank you for this wonderful tool. I'd also like to thank Alan Williamson for his great efforts to help make this book a reality. Beyond the authors of this book, Alan is responsible for assembling a great group of Java practitioners that get together in the Yahoo group, Straight Talking Java. What I've drawn from this group is incalculable. I'd also like to acknowledge the efforts of Art Griesser, Mike Boni, and L.C. Oliver, all of who have been very helpful. Last, but not least, I'd like to repeat Alan's thanks to the many people at Sams who have been able to endure my prose.

We Want to Hear from You!

As the reader of this book, *you* are our most important critic and commentator. We value your opinion and want to know what we're doing right, what we could do better, what areas you'd like to see us publish in, and any other words of wisdom you're willing to pass our way.

As an executive editor for Sams Publishing, I welcome your comments. You can email or write me directly to let me know what you did or didn't like about this book—as well as what we can do to make our books better.

Please note that I cannot help you with technical problems related to the *topic* of this book. We do have a User Services group, however, where I will forward specific technical questions related to the book.

When you write, please be sure to include this book's title and author as well as your name, email address, and phone number. I will carefully review your comments and share them with the author and editors who worked on the book.

Email: feedback@samspublishing.com

Mail: Michael Stephens
Executive Editor
Sams Publishing
201 West 103rd Street
Indianapolis, IN 46290 USA

For more information about this book or another Sams Publishing title, visit our Web site at www.samspublishing.com. Type the ISBN (excluding hyphens) or the title of a book in the Search field to find the page you're looking for.

INTRODUCTION

This book's goal is to help educate Java software developers in all aspects of the Ant tool: how to use it, how to integrate it into their current development environment, and how Ant can improve their current software development practices in such a way that both novice and experienced Ant users will be able to use it to streamline their builds and get more out of each build. This will enable developers to spend less time building software and more time developing it.

Intended Audience of This Book

Who should be reading this book? Well, if it were up to us, it would be a legal requirement to have this book taught in all computer science classes all across the land, due to its in-depth and unique look at this powerful tool from the Apache Group. However, in the unlikely event that our new legislation fails to get enough votes, let us take the time to explain the sort of developer we had in mind while writing the book.

To know who should be reading this book is to know how Ant can be used. We've written this book to highlight some of the problems facing the average Java developer. Contrary to popular belief, all is not rosy in the world of the IDE.

As Java developers, we hit problems daily that take us further away from actually solving the problem and more toward managing the solution. Our time is too valuable to be wasting it. Wrestling with compilation and deployment issues in addition to testing and debugging scripts over different platforms and potential varying development tools can be a headache for even the most astute project manager. Add to the mix the fact that many of the team members will use their own directory structure, and suddenly what should have been a simple task has ballooned into a full-time role.

It was for this very reason that Ant was brought into existence in the first place. James Duncan Davidson, marshaled with breathing life into what is now known as Tomcat, had major problems building his project. Instead of trying to shoehorn his project into an IDE, he wrote a tool that would take over all the management for him, enable him to run on any Java platform, and be extendable to nearly any task. That tool became Ant.

Ant creates a level playing field in terms of project management. Whether you're utilizing the most complex integrated developer tool or the simplest text editor, Ant ensures that everyone is building the same project consistently and accurately, irrespective of their platform.

If you're a developer facing any of these issues, which includes one-member teams right through to global open-source projects, Ant is the tool that you can't be without.

Approach of This Book

This book was written by a group of hardcore Java developers for another group of hardcore Java developers: you. This book was very much written to get you started with Ant as quickly as possible. You don't need to know every intrinsic detail immediately to start utilizing the power this tool has to offer. This book will get you up and running from the early pages of Chapter 1 and keep you running right through to Chapter 11.

We haven't employed the hypothetical situations that are too often found in other titles. We've placed Ant in the real world with ground-level running examples. Our purpose from the outset has been to give you examples that you can adapt for your own needs. We'll jump start your Ant infrastructure so that you can start using this tool from day one.

We don't intend you to read every word published in these pages. No Ant book should be read from start to finish. Ant is designed to save you time, not cost you time by investing significant portions of your valuable energy in reading a book about how to save time! That seems counterproductive to us, which is why the book was not written to serve as bedtime reading.

This book is arranged in such a way as to enable you to get to the answers quickly.

What's on the Web Site for This Book

All the code in this book is available for download on the Sams Publishing Web site at http://www.samspublishing.com/. Enter this book's ISBN (without the hyphens) in the Search box and click Search. When the book's title is displayed, click the title to go to a page where you can download the code.

Conventions Used in This Book

The following typographic conventions are used in this book:

- Code lines, commands, statements, variables, and any text you type or see onscreen appears in a `monospace` typeface.

- *Italics* highlight technical terms when they're being defined.

- The ➥ icon is used before a line of code that is really a continuation of the preceding line. Sometimes a line of code is too long to fit as a single line on the page. If you see ➥ before a line of code, remember that it's part of the line immediately preceding it.

CHAPTER 1

Introduction to Ant

Everyone in the developer arena seems to be talking about Ant. But what exactly is it? This chapter will give you an overview of what Ant is and will provide you with the scenarios to utilize this tool's unique development environment. We'll get you started quickly with a very straightforward example. This will lead us into the vocabulary of Ant where we'll explain the terms that Ant uses to manage its process. Finally, we'll look at some of the reasons for using Ant and illustrate the power that using this tool will bring to your everyday development tasks.

In the Beginning

Let's start by answering the most obvious question: What is Ant? The simple answer is that Ant is a Java-based make utility, although this definition covers only a small fraction of what Ant is capable of.

In this modern age of integrated development environments (IDEs), you might not be aware of what a make utility is. Before the advent of IDEs, code was developed using basic text editors, with custom-built shell scripts taking the source code and compiling it into the necessary executable. These shell scripts soon grew into a more formal approach methodology that was known as the *makefile*, which became associated with all variants of UNIX. The makefile enabled you to describe the necessary compilation logic that allowed your code to be compiled successfully. In the days when compilation order was important, makefiles allowed control over the processing order for the compiler. In essence, the makefile itself was just a series of commands, closely resembling a shell script. Ant is the Java version of this concept; it enables you to build compilation logic that operates over a variety of platforms.

Like many of the projects that are controlled by Apache, Ant grew out of necessity rather than luxury. Ant's creator, James Duncan Davidson—the man behind Sun's reference implementation of the Servlet and JavaServer Pages (JSP) specifications known as *Tomcat*—needed a reliable way to compile source files over a variety of different platforms. Because Davidson didn't use an IDE, shell scripts performed all compilation. Realizing this was introducing more problems than it was solving, he set out to write a tool that would enable him to easily control the process. This tool was introduced to the Apache group of projects in January 2000, when it was formally known as *Ant*. The first release of the tool as a standalone Apache project was the following summer in July 2000. From that point, Ant has grown to be enormously popular, with developers from all over the world contributing to its core feature set.

Ant is used in all areas of development and has become the de facto standard for working with multi-teamed projects, particular open source projects. Legend has it that Ant is an acronym for Another Neat Tool, which sums up the whole utility very nicely. After you've seen the power Ant can add to your development, you'll wonder how you ever worked without it. Ant is one of those tools you didn't know you needed until you had it.

What Makes Ant So Special

If you are involved in any one of the following, you need to be using Ant:

- Team development
- Large-scale projects
- Java 2 Enterprise Edition (J2EE) development
- Java Archive (JAR) file packaging
- Remote working
- Open source project

The actual compilation of a single Java class file isn't the most difficult task; simply throw it at the `javac` compiler and a `.class` file is easily produced. However, it doesn't take long for this process to become a little more complicated.

Add in package paths and dependent JAR files with external code, and before you know it, you need to create a custom shell script to speed up the whole process. Throw into the mix the fact you might need to do this in both Microsoft Windows and UNIX environments where the path name separator is different, and you need to start looking at supporting a whole suite of shell scripts. All this is before you even look at the problems that arise when someone decides to change the directory where all the source code lives or wants to build to another location or JAR file. Anyone who has been involved with J2EE development also knows the joys that building a WAR (Web Archive) file can bring, requiring a strict adherence to known pathnames and naming conventions.

You might argue that your present IDE takes care of all these problems, and for the most part, it probably does. However, in a team environment, you have to assume that everyone in the team is using the IDE in order for you to able share project files, which of course assumes that the actual IDE makes it easy for you to do so. But even if everyone in the team is using the same IDE, there is the problem that they might not be using the same directory structure to store their source files. Before you know it, each member of your team is building different-sized JAR files and you're unable to fully trust any of them to be the correct build.

These are the sorts of problems Ant can solve without introducing a huge administration cost to manage it.

What Ant Is

Ant is just a Java application. It can be used on any Java 1.1+ system, which makes it extremely portable to pretty much any operating system in use today. After the very easy installation (as described in Chapter 2, "Preliminaries"), you can use Ant immediately.

Ant is a command-line-driven program that uses an XML file to describe the build process. That XML file is known as the *build file*, and simply describes the various tasks Ant has to complete. If you leave off the filename, Ant defaults to looking for the file build.xml in the present directory.

The key to Ant's success is the fact it was built in Java. This enables developers from around the world to add to the rich array of tasks that Ant can do to make it even more useful. Even Davidson, the original creator of Ant, can't believe some of the things it is capable of doing today, and it hasn't stopped growing.

> **Note**
> Ant is an official Apache open source project that is freely available from Apache's main Web site: http://jakarta.apache.org/.

What Ant Is Not

When you refer to the development environment, you automatically think of an IDE. However, it is important to understand the distinction and that Ant is not an IDE. Ant is not an editor. It is not a compiler. It is not a JAR tool. It is not a version control system. In fact, Ant is the tool that is used to manage all those things, in much the same way that an IDE does, except that Ant doesn't provide any of the editing facilities that an IDE does.

In an ironic twist, nearly all available IDEs have the facility to call Ant from within their environment. In Chapter 11, "Tool Support for Ant," you will learn how to integrate Ant with some of the more popular IDEs and development tools. This is testament to the popularity and power of Ant-enabling your development.

The First Ant Project

Without much further ado, let's take a whistle-stop tour of a typical Ant project. In this section, we'll

- Download and install Ant
- Build a simple build.xml file for compilation and JAR file packaging
- Run Ant

This chapter will give you a feel for what Ant can do. Subsequent chapters will delve more deeply into the specifics, so don't worry if you don't understand everything to begin with.

Installation

The first thing you must do is retrieve the latest version of Ant from the main Apache Web site:

```
http://jakarta.apache.org/ant/index.html
```

Follow the Download link and select the correct binary for your system. Typically, this will be either a .ZIP or .TAR.GZ file. Installation is a simple matter of unpacking the downloaded archive into a directory and setting up two environment variables:

- ANT_HOME—This points to the directory you unpacked Ant to. It is also a good idea to add $ANT_HOME\bin to your system path. This enables you to easily call the ant script that encapsulates all the calls to Java.

- JAVA_HOME—This points to the directory in which you installed JDK. This is a very handy variable because it enables you to easily upgrade your JDK without having to change all your scripts.

That's it. To test your installation, simply enter the command `ant -version` and you should see something similar (actual version number may be different) to the following output should be returned:

```
C:\antbook_chapter1>ant -version

Apache Ant version 1.5
```

This verifies that Ant is correctly installed and is ready for you to use. If for any reason this doesn't work, make sure that you set your environment variables correctly. Failing that, see Chapter 2 for a more detailed study of the installation process.

Simple build.xml

Now that you have Ant installed, the next stage is to use it. If you simply enter `ant`, you'll discover the following output:

```
C:\antbook_chapter1>ant

Buildfile: build.xml does not exist!
Build failed
```

Ant gets its instructions from a build file, commonly named `build.xml`. You can specify a different name for your build file and simply pass it in as an argument to the script. However, for the sake of clarity for this first chapter, we'll work with the default `build.xml` file.

Before we have a look at this file, let's define exactly what it is we're attempting to achieve with this build file. Laying out the problem in clear, easy steps is halfway to solving it. Let's assume that we have a directory, `/src/`, that contains all our Java source files underneath the current directory. We want to keep the source files separate from the class files and, to make things easier, we want to compile into the `/classes/` directory that also sits within the current directory.

So, to complete a successful compile, we probably want to clean out the `/classes/` folder from any previous compiles, and then run the Java compiler (`javac`) on all the files in the source directory.

The build file is essentially an XML file with blocks of instructions that are defined to run in a specific order. The basic build file for our basic scenario is shown in Listing 1.1.

Listing 1.1   *Simple Ant Build File build.xml*

```xml
<project name="antbook" default="compile" basedir=".">

  <property name="src" value=".\src\"/>
  <property name="build" value=".\classes\"/>

  <target name="init">
    <mkdir dir="${build}"/>
  </target>

  <target name="compile" depends="init">
    <javac srcdir="${src}"
           destdir="${build}"
           optimize="on"
           debug="on">
      <classpath>
        <pathelement location="${build}"/>
      </classpath>
    </javac>
  </target>

  <target name="clean">
    <delete dir="${build}"/>
  </target>

</project>
```

Let's look at this from the inside out, by starting with the <target> blocks. Without going into too much detail, you'll probably get a feel for what each block is doing. As you can see, we name each target; for one of the targets, you'll notice the depends attribute. Each target represents a logical block of tasks that are treated as a single unit. The depends attribute controls the order in which these blocks are executed. For example, before you compile the source code, you might want to check that the output directory actually exists, and create it if it doesn't.

Near the top of the file, you'll notice the <property> elements, which define some variables that will be used throughout the build file. Here you're defining the source and output directories. This is a particularly powerful feature of Ant because you can easily change the output directory without manually editing the whole file for every occurrence.

So, let's run the file and see what happens:

```
C:\antbook_chapter1>ant

Buildfile: build.xml

init:
    [mkdir] Created dir: C:\antbook_chapter1\classes

compile:
    [javac] Compiling 1 source file to C:\antbook_chapter1\classes

BUILD SUCCESSFUL
Total time: 6 seconds
```

The first thing Ant printed was the name of the build file it was processing. Second, it started running through the targets. But how did it know which one to run first? Looking back at the build.xml file, you'll notice that in the top-level tag, <project>, there was an attribute, default, that defined which target was to be run first. default had the value compile, but init was the first target that was actually run. Why?

You've just witnessed the power of Ant and its ability to have dependencies with the order of how targets are run. If you look at the compile target, you'll notice it has the depends="init" attribute defined. This states that before this target executes, the target init should be run. That's good because in our example, we want to ensure that the output directory exists before we compile our Java source files into it.

As you can see from the rest of the output, the directory for the class files is created, and then the source file is compiled. But if you run the build file again, what happens this time?

```
C:\antbook_chapter1>ant

Buildfile: build.xml

init:

compile:

BUILD SUCCESSFUL
Total time: 2 seconds
```

Well, it starts out the same, but notice how the init target output has nothing written in it this time? This is because the default action of the <mkdir> task within the init target is not to do anything if the directory already exists. The next target that is processed is the compile target, which again has no output. This is because the timestamp on the class file is the same as the source file, so there is no need to recompile according to the rules of the `<javac>` task.

However, what if you want to force a compilation. How do you signal that? That is where the final target in the build file—the `clean` target—comes into play. As you can probably guess from its name, this target deletes the files in the directory defined by the property `${build}`. But how do you run it?

It's simple. You pass in the name of the target that you want to trigger to the `ant` script:

```
C:\antbook_chapter1>ant clean

Buildfile: build.xml

clean:
    [delete] Deleting directory C:\antbook_chapter1\classes

BUILD SUCCESSFUL
Total time: 2 seconds
```

This will override the default target defined in the project element and run the `clean` target. After you've done this, you can run the `ant` script again to compile. Alternatively, you could stack up the trigger targets in one call at the command line:

```
C:\antbook_chapter1>ant clean compile
```

This will run the `clean` target and then the `compile` target immediately afterward.

That's it—your first Ant project file. Ant is made up of a series of targets, each of which defines a sequence of tasks that make up the build process for a particular project. Depending on the circumstances, you can change the execution order of the targets, which in turn enables you to move around the building blocks of your development process.

The real power of Ant is in marrying the flexibility of its core/optional tasks with the framework that controls the overall flow. This book will take you through the more common tasks that are available to you for controlling and facilitating the development environment.

Ant Terminology

As you've already seen, Ant introduces some new terminology. Although you might be already familiar with these terms, it's always good to know what they mean in the present context. This section runs through the top-level terms.

Project

A *project* defines one or more targets and any number of properties. There is only one project block in any one build file. Table 1.1 details the attributes associated with this tag.

Table 1.1 *Project Attributes*

Attribute	Description
name	The name of the project.
default	The default target that will be run if none is specified in the command line. The default is main.
basedir	The directory from which all the relative paths are calculated. The default is the directory from which the script was run.

Properties

One of the most powerful features of the Ant framework is the ability to define properties inside or outside of the project file. These properties can then be used in any attribute throughout the project file. A property has a name and a value can be defined like so:

```
<property name="build" value="classes\"/>
```

Properties can then be accessed using the notation ${<propertyname>}; for example:

```
${build}
```

Be careful when defining and using properties because they are case sensitive. In addition, if a property is defined inside the main project element and outside a target, it is evaluated before any targets are executed.

As shown in Table 1.2, Ant defines a number of built-in properties that can be accessed just like any user-defined property.

Table 1.2 *Built-in Properties*

Property	Value
basedir	The absolute directory from which the ant script is running.
ant.file	The absolute path of the current build file.
ant.version	The present version of the Ant build.
ant.project.name	The name of the project as defined in the name attribute of the project tag.
ant.java.version	The version of the JDK from which this Ant session is running.

Some tasks can be triggered that will result in properties being defined. For example, `</tstamp>` results in the properties `DSTAMP`, `TSTAMP`, and `TODAY` being created with the current date and time.

In addition to the properties defined by Ant and the project, you can access any of the Java system properties by using the full property name:

```
${file.separator}
```

Target

The target is the key building block for Ant. A target defines a sequence or block of tasks that are to be executed. The target block is a very powerful piece of the Ant framework because it is from the target block that dependencies occur. For example, in the previous example, we wanted to make sure that the directories existed before we made any attempt to compile. Therefore, we made the `compile` target dependent on the `init` target for a successful run.

A project can contain any number of targets, thus giving any number of possible of combinations of target execution. It's important to note that no matter how many times a target is asked to run in any given pass, it's executed only once per session. Let's look at a slightly more complicated example adapted from the core Ant documentation; it's as good a way as any to illustrate the power of the dependency feature of Ant:

```
<target name="A">
  <echo message="I am Target A"/>
</target>
<target name="B" depends="A">
  <echo message="I am Target B"/>
</target>
<target name="C" depends="B">
  <echo message="I am Target C"/>
</target>
<target name="D" depends="C,B,A">
  <echo message="I am Target D"/>
</target>
```

If you choose to run `target-D`, what would be echoed out?

```
C:\antbook_chapter1>ant D

Buildfile: build.xml

A:
     [echo] I am Target A
```

```
B:

    [echo] I am Target B

C:

    [echo] I am Target C

D:

    [echo] I am Target D

BUILD SUCCESSFUL
Total time: 2 seconds
```

This is a *tiered dependency tree*. When it's traced back, you can see that every target ultimately needs A to be run, and then B, and so on until D is successfully run. Although this is very powerful, this is not the only way you can control the flow of execution through the targets.

In addition to the depends attribute, there are two more attributes that enable you to execute a target depending on the status of variables: if and unless.

The if attribute will look for a given property and, if it has been defined, the target will be triggered for execution. Conversely, if the property defined in unless is not found, the target will be triggered for execution:

```
<target name="B" if="somePropertyName">
  <echo message="I am Target B"/>
</target>
<target name="C" unless="somePropertyName2">
  <echo message="I am Target C"/>
</target>
```

Table 1.3 provides a complete list of attributes that can be associated with a target.

Table 1.3   Target Attributes

Attribute	Description
name	The case-sensitive name of the target.
depends	The comma-separated list of targets that must be executed before this target is executed.
if	If the given property has been defined, the target will be executed.
unless	If the given property has not been defined, the target will be executed.
description	The directory from which all the relative paths are calculated. The default is the directory from which the script was run.

The description of the target determines whether the target is defined as *internal*. An internal target is one that is not publicly available when queried from the script command line:

```
C:\antbook_chapter1>ant -projecthelp
```

Task

The task is where all the real work is performed. This is the actual command that is executed inside the target. A task can take any number of attributes, and can be any legally formatted XML tag. Ant has three different types of tasks:

- **Core tasks**   These are tasks that are shipped with the core distribution of Ant, and cover all common tasks that are normally associated with the core JDK and the build process in general. For example, <javac> is used for general compilation and <jar> is used for packaging JAR files (see Chapter 4, "Built-in Tasks").

- **Optional tasks**   These are official tasks that require additional JAR files in order for them to be executed. For example, <ftp> is used to upload and download files to a remote FTP server (see Chapter 5, "Optional Tasks").

- **User-defined tasks**   These are unofficial tasks that have been developed by users (see Chapter 6, "Extending Ant with Custom Tasks, Data Types, and Listeners").

Two later chapters are devoted entirely to both core and optional tasks, showing how you can best take advantage of the rich array of features within Ant. In addition, in Chapter 6, we take you through designing, building, and debugging your own custom tag to run within the framework.

Should I Use Ant?

We've touched on some of the major features of this framework, and hopefully you're already thinking of the power that Ant can deliver to your development process.

In the old days, when it was just one developer with a handful of source files, things were relatively easy and even the most basic IDE could handle the process without breaking a sweat. However, as the complexity of software grew, so did the management of the build. From checking out the software from CVS (control version system), to compilation, to final deployment in JAR, WAR, or even raw class file format, each step is fraught with problems. Add in two or more team members, possibly running on different platforms, and the whole process has suddenly become a project manager's worst nightmare.

Ant enables you to level the playing field by giving everyone the power to manage the process reliably from end to end. The build file that manages your project becomes as integrated and necessary as the very source files it is managing, finding a home within the CVS archive. No other tool comes close to the flexibility and power that Ant has to offer the developer in terms of sheer portability and ease of use.

> **Note**
>
> A common misconception is that Ant is restricted to only Java developers. This isn't so. Although it's fair to admit that the majority of the tasks were geared toward the Java developer originally, the rich array of tasks now considered core and optional to Ant enables developers in all languages to harness its power.
>
> Developers for the .NET platform can harness the power of Ant for developing C# applications. Developers can use Ant to automate uploads and downloads to remote servers, automate telnet sessions, and even send out e-mail. As you'll discover in later chapters, a wide range of tasks is available for you to experiment with, and if you don't find one that does exactly what you want, write it yourself!

Summary

In this chapter, we looked at the basics of Ant and touched on the power this tool can offer your development environment. We examined the problems associated with the build process, and the issues that can arise when trying unify the process across teams working in possibly different editors and IDEs. Although this chapter only touched on the simple compile process and key features, you'll discover from the following chapters that Ant has much more to offer.

The remainder of this book will dig deeper into the Ant world, detailing all its aspects and enabling you to get the most from Ant with minimal effort.

CHAPTER 2

Preliminaries

Now that you've had a bit of introduction to Ant, this chapter will take you through the acquisition and installation of Ant, and then through a development cycle to create a small Web application, using Ant for the build. After completing this chapter, you'll have a working version of Ant installed on your machine, and you should be able to write a build file and actually build a simple project using it.

How to Get Ant

There are basically three ways to get Ant for your system. The first and by far the easiest way is to download a binary distribution from the Jakarta Web site. The second way is to download a source bundle from the Jakarta site and build Ant yourself. The third way is to access the Jakarta Group's Concurrent Versions System (CVS) server, download the latest version of the source code, and build from that. Each method has its pros and cons, and we'll discuss each method in depth.

Downloading a Binary Distribution

As mentioned earlier, this is the simplest method of getting Ant. It is also the most foolproof because everything you need is included in the download. What does *foolproof* mean here? When you download source code and try to build it yourself, there are several configuration details that must be set, and several dependencies with other tools that must be met. Building Ant from source code, although not a truly difficult task, is much easier when you are more experienced with Ant.

Release Builds

The Jakarta site has two binary distributions of Ant that you can download: release builds and nightly builds. The release builds are stable and are probably the right version for the novice Ant user. There shouldn't be any surprises in terms of bugs popping up unexpectedly. The only caveat with release builds is that they might not have all the really nice features you've been reading about. The release build is based on the last released version, which at the time of this writing is 1.4.1. The latest source distribution is 1.5alpha. If you don't need the bleeding-edge features of the latest codebase and you're not willing to risk some instability, you should get the release build.

To get a release build of Ant, point your browser to `http://jakarta.apache.org/ site/binindex.html` and scroll down until you see the link with Ant in the name under the heading of Release Builds. At the time of this writing, Figure 2.1 is what you would see.

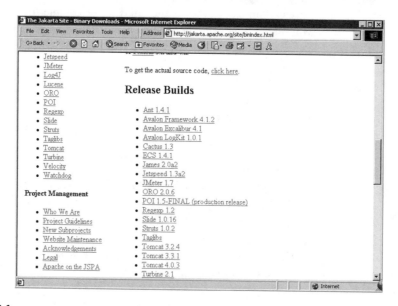

Figure 2.1
The Jakarta release build binary downloads page.

Click on the Ant 1.4.1 link (or whichever version is now current), and you should see something similar to Figure 2.2.

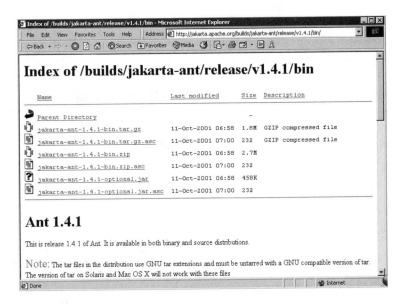

Figure 2.2
The available files for an Ant release build.

There are two versions of the standard build here: one is a compressed tar file and the other is a standard Zip file. If you are on a Windows box, you would probably opt for the Zip file; if you are on a UNIX box, you would probably go for the `.tar.gz` file. Click on the file of your choice, and save it to your local system.

There is a third file of interest, called `jakarta-ant-1.4.1-optional.jar`. Strictly speaking, you do not need this file. However, it provides several nice features that don't come with the stock version of Ant, such as integration with some application servers and source code management systems. You can skip the optional file for now, but know that you might need to come back and get it later if you start tinkering with some of the more advanced features of Ant, including some that will be described in Chapter 5, "Optional Tasks."

Nightly Builds

The nightly build is a distribution based on the code from the previous night. The archive at the Jakarta site keeps seven days of nightly builds, each in a directory identified by date. These distributions seem to be created between 5:00–7:00 a.m. the next morning. If you want the latest, go to `http://jakarta.apache.org/site/binindex.html`, scroll down until you see Ant listed under Nightly Builds, click on it, and then go into the directory named with the current day's date. There will generally be three binary downloads in each folder: one is a standard Zip file, one is a Gzip compressed tar file, and the other is a bzip2 compressed tar file. If you are on a Windows system, you will probably want to get the `.zip` file. If you are on a UNIX machine, go for the `.tar.gz` or the `.tar.bz2` file. Figure 2.3 shows what today's nightly build directory looks like.

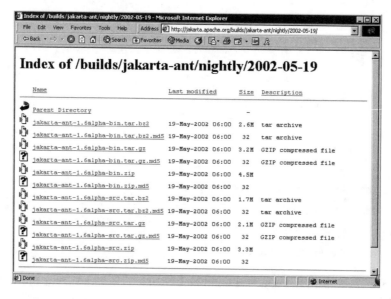

Figure 2.3
The available files for an Ant nightly build.

Notice that other files are in the directory as well, including nightly source bundles and checksum files. The files of interest are those containing -bin and ending in `.tar.gz`, `.tar.bz2`, or `.zip`. You can safely ignore the rest for now. Click on the link for the file that you want and save it to your system. Remember that you need to download only one file from this directory, unless you want the optional stuff.

Downloading a Source Distribution

Just as with the binary builds, there are two downloadable versions of the source: release and nightly. (Actually, there are three, the third being fetching the code directly from CVS, but that is covered in the next section.) The process of getting a source distribution is similar to that for the binaries.

Release Source Distribution

To get a release version of the source for Ant, point your browser to `http://jakarta.apache.org/site/sourceindex.html` and scroll down until you see the Ant 1.4.1 (or whichever is the current version) link under Release Builds. Clicking on that link should bring you to a screen similar to Figure 2.4.

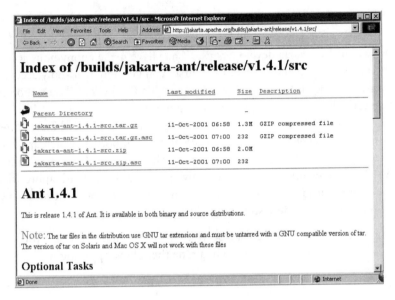

Figure 2.4
The available files for an Ant release source distribution.

There are only two formats available here: Zip and a Gzipped tar file. Pick the one that is most appropriate for your platform. Most Windows users will grab the Zip file and UNIX folks will take the .tar.gz file.

> **Note**
> I generally work on Windows, but I always take the .tar.gz file because it is almost always smaller than the Zip file. Of course, this requires you to have Gzip and GNU tar programs on your Windows machine. You can get excellent implementations of Gzip and tar with the Cygwin distribution, available from http://sources.redhat.com/cygwin.

Nightly Source Distribution

Just as with the binary releases, there are nightly source releases as well. The nightly releases are considered bleeding-edge and, as such, are not even guaranteed to compile. This can be a bad thing, but if you like to stay up to date with the latest features and you like to build the program yourself, this distribution could be for you. To get it, go to http://jakarta. apache.org/builds/jakarta-ant/nightly/ and then select the directory for the current date. You'll notice that you're in the same directory that you get to for the nightly binary build. The files of interest all have -src in their names. There are three formats you can download: Zip, .tar.gz, and .tar.bz2. Again, select the format that you prefer.

Getting the Source from CVS

If you want to be as up to date as possible, you need to fetch the source directly from the CVS repository that the Jakarta developers use. They have made anonymous access available to all the Jakarta projects, including Ant. Of course, you get only read-only access, but for building, that's all you need. First, you'll need to install a CVS client. You can obtain a command-line CVS client for most platforms by going to http://www.cvshome.org/downloads.html and getting the proper binary. There are also several other GUI CVS clients, such as WinCVS and jCVS, both of which are available from http://www.cvsgui.org. For the purposes of this chapter, we'll be using a command-line client on a Windows machine. The directions given are applicable (with appropriate platform-specific modifications to pathnames) to any system. If you want to use a GUI CVS client, you'll need to modify these steps accordingly.

The first thing to do is log in to the CVS server. Open a Windows console (or telnet session, or Xterm, depending on your platform). Then type the following to log in:

```
cvs -d :pserver:anoncvs@cvs.apache.org:/home/cvspublic login
```

When you execute this command, you'll be asked for a password. Simply type **anoncvs**, press Enter, and you'll be logged in. There is no real confirmation message; the fact that you don't get an error is the only confirmation that you get. A successful login should look like Figure 2.5.

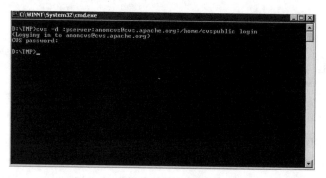

Figure 2.5

A successful login to the Apache CVS server.

Upon logging in, you are ready to download the Ant source code. To do a full download of the latest version, execute this command:

```
cvs -d :pserver:anoncvs@cvs.apache.org:/home/cvspublic co jakarta-ant
```

You should see several hundred lines go by that look vaguely like filenames and directory paths. This is a visual indication that the files are being downloaded to your system. Depending on the speed of your Internet connection, this process could take a few minutes. When you are returned to your command prompt, your screen should look something like Figure 2.6.

Figure 2.6
Successful download of the Ant source code from CVS.

You need to do this download only once. You can stay current with what is happening in the repository by performing updates with CVS. To perform an update, you use the CVS `update` command with a few options to control the download. To perform an update, change your working directory to the `jakarta-ant` directory, *not* its parent directory. Then execute the following command:

```
cvs update -P -d
```

You should see a much shorter list this time than when you did a full checkout.

Those are the three methods for getting Ant. Next, we'll discuss how to build and install Ant.

How to Install Ant

Depending on how you acquired Ant, these steps will change. If you downloaded a binary, all you need to do is unzip (or un-gzip or un-tar) the downloaded file onto your disk. The distribution will create a directory called `jakarta-ant-1.4.1` (or whatever the current version is). You can let this directory be created anywhere you want because you will be changing environment variables to set things up. We'll discuss those variables after we discuss building Ant from source.

Building Ant

Building Ant from source is not a big deal. In fact, in most cases, you can simply go into the jakarta-ant directory, execute build.bat (or build.sh for UNIX), and watch it build. The build process actually creates a stripped-down version of Ant, and then uses that to build itself! Figure 2.7 shows what you should see if Ant builds itself properly.

Figure 2.7
Successful build of the Ant source code.

After Ant is built, you'll obviously want to install it. This is easily accomplished by first setting the environment variable ANT_HOME to the full pathname of the directory in which you want to install Ant. If this directory does not exist, it will be created. After setting this variable, run the build.bat file again with the single argument of install. This will initiate a multi-minute process that will ultimately install Ant. You'll see several lines that look like errors; they are caused by JavaDoc not being able to find certain classes, but this won't affect the program at all. You should eventually see a BUILD SUCCESSFUL line as in Figure 2.8. Ant is now installed.

Environment Variables

There are only two environment variables that you need to set: ANT_HOME and PATH. The ANT_HOME variable is used by Ant to find its library, and PATH is used, obviously, to find the Ant batch file/shell script itself. If you have installed Ant to C:\Ant (/usr/local/ant, perhaps, on a UNIX system), you would set your variables like the following in the System control panel (or your *rc script on UNIX):

```
ANT_HOME=C:\Ant
PATH=%PATH%;%ANT_HOME%\bin
```

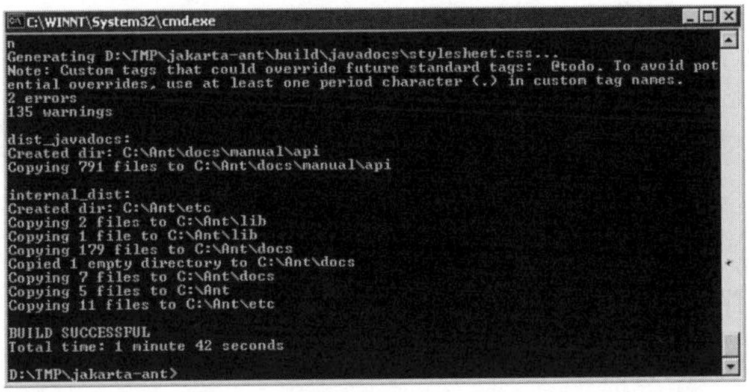

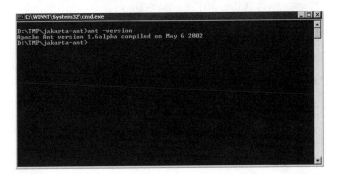

Figure 2.8
Successful install of Ant from source.

After you've set these variables, you'll need to exit this command shell and start another one to see the changes reflected. When you're in another command shell, just type **ant -version** and see what happens. You should see something like Figure 2.9. (Note that I'm using a *very* new version of Ant.)

Figure 2.9
If you see this, Ant is properly installed.

Strictly speaking, you don't have to set these variables. You can reference the full path to the Ant script each time, and add the ANT_HOME variable to the Ant script itself, but it's much easier just to make these changes to PATH and ANT_HOME directly.

A Tour of Ant with a Small Exercise

At this point, Ant is installed on your system and ready for use. In this section, we'll build a simple project using Ant. In keeping with the time-honored tradition of computer language textbooks beginning with a "Hello, World" example, we'll construct a "Hello, World" program and use Ant to build and assemble it for execution and distribution. We'll have two Java classes and a properties file involved just to make it slightly more interesting, and we'll end up with an executable Java Archive (JAR) file that is ready to run. Here's what we start with:

- HelloWorld.java

- HelloWorldClient.java

- Hello.properties

- MANIFEST.MF

The .java files will need to be compiled and placed in the proper package directory hierarchy. The properties file must be included with the .class files in the executable JAR, and the MANIFEST.MF file must be used as the manifest for the executable JAR because it contains the magic to make a JAR execute. All four of these files must be included in a source distribution JAR file. This is admittedly a contrived example, but it will give us a chance to see several of Ant's tags in action. So, let's get started.

The Component Files

As stated earlier, our application will consist of two Java classes, a Java properties file, and a manifest for our JAR file to make it executable. These files, which you can copy or type in yourself, can be downloaded from the Sams Publishing Web site. Because they are such simple files, we'll include the text of the files directly in the text of this book. We begin in Listing 2.1 with `HelloWorld.java`, our workhorse bean.

> **Note**
> Listing 2.1 is on the companion Web site for this book as HelloWorld.java.

Listing 2.1   *This Class Provides the "Logic" for Our Sample Program*

```
package hello;

import java.util.*;

public class HelloWorld
{
    private ResourceBundle bundle;
```

Listing 2.1   *(continued)*

```
    public HelloWorld()
    {
        bundle = ResourceBundle.getBundle("hello.Hello");
    }

    public String sayHello()
    {
        return bundle.getString("hello.text");
    }
}
```

Listing 2.2 is the driver, or client, program that will create an instance of our `HelloWorld` class and invoke its `sayHello()` method to get a string to present to the user.

> **Note**
> Listing 2.2 is on the companion Web site for this book as HelloWorldClient.java.

Listing 2.2   *The Client to Create and Use a HelloWorld Object*

```
package hello;

public class HelloWorldClient
{
    public static void main(String[] args)
    {
        HelloWorld helloWorld = new HelloWorld();
        String value = helloWorld.sayHello();

        System.out.println(value);
    }
}
```

Finally, we need our properties file. This is in the standard Java properties file format, and contains one string that will be presented by our program. This file must be called `Hello.properties`, and be in the `hello` package upon deployment. Listing 2.3 shows this file.

> **Note**
> Listing 2.3 is on the companion Web site for this book as Hello.properties.

Listing 2.3   *The Hello.properties File*

```
hello.text=Hello, World!
```

After you have these files, you need to create a directory for your project to live in. We'll call our project `helloWorld`, so something like `C:\SRC\helloWorld` would suffice. Inside this directory, create a directory structure that looks like this:

```
C:\SRC\helloWorld\
            src\
                hello\
            etc\
```

Put `HelloWorld.java` and `HelloWorldClient.java` into the `helloWorld/src/hello` directory, and `Hello.properties` into the `helloWorld/etc` directory. Here's what you should end up with:

```
C:\SRC\helloWorld\
            src\
                hello\
                    HelloWorld.java
                    HelloWorldClient.java
            etc\
                Hello.properties
```

Now that we have all our files, we'll start creating our build file.

Building the Build File

Our build file will be called `build.xml`. We'll step through the process of creating this file, showing fragments of the XML as we go. Using your favorite text editor (vi, Emacs, Notepad, and so on), create a file called `build.xml` in the `helloWorld` directory.

We first need the standard XML instruction that declares this to be an XML file and which version of XML is in use. Listing 2.4 shows this.

Listing 2.4   *The First Line of the build.xml File*

```
<?xml version="1.0"?>
```

You've seen this line in just about every XML file you've dealt with, and we need it here, too.

The <project> tag

Next is the `<project>` tag. This is the only top-level element that is allowed in a build file, aside from comments. The `<project>` tag should contain the name of your project, the base directory from which to create relative paths, and a default target. Listing 2.5 shows our `build.xml` after adding the `<project>` tag.

Listing 2.5   *The Growing Build File*

```
<?xml version="1.0"?>

<project name="helloWorld" default="jarfile" basedir=".">
</project>
```

If you set the base directory attribute to ".", you can omit the `basedir` property altogether. I prefer to leave it because it makes explicit where I intend the build file to live and work. The `default` attribute declares that if you don't specify a target to execute on the command line, the target listed here will be executed.

Setting Properties

Next, you'll want to set up properties that will be used throughout the build file. This is accomplished with a series of `<property>` tags that create key-value pairs. These `<property>` tags should be inside a target upon which all other targets, either directly or indirectly, will depend. You will generally define properties for the following keys:

- name
- src.dir
- etc.dir
- build.dir
- classes.dir
- deploy.name

There are others that you might want to define, such as libraries on which your project depends. The `name` property will be referenced by other properties to create things such as the deployed JAR filename. The `src.dir` property tells Ant where to find your source code. The `build.dir` property tells Ant where to dump the compiled files and where to create any JARs, Web Archives (WARs), or Enterprise Archives (EARs) that you specify. The `classes.dir` property is generally relative to the `build.dir`, and is where the compiled classes actually go. The `etc.dir` property is one that I use, but you may choose not to. I like to keep all my properties files and XML files in a single `etc` directory during development, and then copy them to their destinations at run-time. This works for me, but it might not work for you. Try it and see whether you like it. Finally, `deploy.name` is what we will call the WAR file that we will deploy. Listing 2.6 is the build file after adding the `init` target.

Listing 2.6   *The Build File with the init Target Included*

```xml
<?xml version="1.0"?>

<project name="helloWorld" default="jarfile" basedir=".">
    <target name="init">
        <property name="name" value="helloWorld"/>
        <property name="src.dir" value="src"/>
        <property name="build.dir" value="build"/>
        <property name="classes.dir" value="${build.dir}/classes"/>
        <property name="etc.dir" value="etc"/>
        <property name="deploy.name" value="${name}.jar"/>
    </target>
</project>
```

Notice that two of the properties reference other properties using the `${}` notation. Ant will interpret the value between the curly brackets to be a property name that has already been defined. It will then replace the whole construct with the value of that property, or the original string if it can't find the specified property.

> **Caution**
>
> If you do a build and see directories or files with names like this
>
> ${classes.dir}
>
> you have referenced a property before it has been defined. In this instance, we used the classes.dir property without defining it. This is an easy error to make, but also an easy one to correct.

This is very useful, especially when you copy a `build.xml` file from an old project to a new one. You can change the name in one place and the change will be reflected in several properties at once.

You could execute the build file at this point, but doing so doesn't make much sense because nothing it did would be persistent.

Preparatory Target

Next, you'll typically want a target that will do some preliminary setup before you actually start building things. This generally involves creating the `build` directory and the `classes` directory. It might involve other actions, but these are typical. It is customary to name this target prepare. Listing 2.7 shows our build file with the addition of the prepare target.

Listing 2.7 *The Build File with the prepare Target Included*

```xml
<?xml version="1.0"?>

<project name="helloWorld" default="jarfile" basedir=".">
    <target name="init">
        <property name="name" value="helloWorld"/>
        <property name="src.dir" value="src"/>
        <property name="build.dir" value="build"/>
        <property name="classes.dir" value="${build.dir}/classes"/>
        <property name="etc.dir" value="etc"/>
        <property name="deploy.name" value="${name}.jar"/>
    </target>

    <target name="prepare" depends="init">
        <mkdir dir="${classes.dir}"/>
    </target>
</project>
```

As you can see, we've created a target in our build.xml with a name of prepare. This target has only one action, which creates a directory hierarchy on our disk. We've combined the tasks of creating the directories into a single <mkdir> action because this task will create an entire hierarchy of directories at once. In other words, we don't have to create the parent directory and then create the child; the mkdir task handles that for us automatically.

If you execute this target by typing **ant prepare**, you'll end up with a directory called build in the current directory, and a directory called classes under that. Figure 2.10 shows the output from running Ant with our build file.

> **Note**
>
> If you type **ant** by itself without specifying the target to execute, you'll get the following error:
>
> BUILD FAILED
>
> Target 'jarfile' does not exist in this project.
>
> The reason for this is that we have not yet defined the jarfile target. We will get to that in a little while.

Notice that the target definition for prepare has an attribute called depends with a value of init. This can be a comma-separated list of targets that must be executed, in a specific order, before this target should be executed. In this case, the attribute tells Ant that before executing the `prepare` target, it should first execute the `init` target to set up the properties that it will need. You'll find that the dependency mechanism is a powerful feature of Ant.

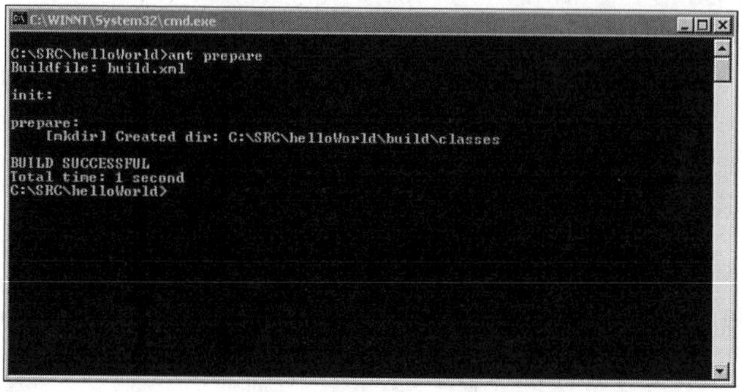

Figure 2.10
Running our prepare target.

Using the clean Target to Remove Old Build Artifacts

One target that every project needs is one to clean up after it's done. This target should be named `clean` and should delete any artifacts left behind by a build. This includes compiled classes, JARs, WARs, and so on. You would typically use the `clean` target when you've made changes to source code, and you want to delete all the `.class` files to make sure that everything is up to date. This target can be quite simple, as shown in Listing 2.8.

> **Note**
> For most of the rest of the examples, we won't include the entire XML document representing our build.xml. We'll include only the target under consideration, but not the surrounding text, unless we need to do so for special emphasis.

Listing 2.8   *The clean Target*

```
<target name="clean" depends="init">
   <delete dir="${build.dir}"/>
</target>
```

If you execute this target by typing **ant clean**, the directory described by `build.dir`, and all of its contents and subdirectories, will be deleted. This resets the game board, so to speak, for the next build. Figure 2.11 shows this execution.

Figure 2.11
Removing all build artifacts.

Compiling Java Source

If you want your Java classes to be at all useful, you need to compile them. This is accomplished using the built-in <javac> task. This task has many, many attributes, *all* of which are optional. Realistically, you need to include the srcdir and destdir attributes, but I will show you a few others that are useful. Listing 2.9 shows what our target called compile will look like.

Listing 2.9   The compile Target

```
<target name="compile" depends="prepare">
   <javac srcdir="${src.dir}"
          destdir="${classes.dir}"
          debug="true"
          deprecation="true"
          optimize="false"/>
</target>
```

Here we're specifying that the source code lives somewhere under the src.dir directory. The <javac> task will search recursively for .java files to compile. The destdir attribute tells the compiler where to place the binary files. In our example, this will be build/classes (with package directories created as needed).

The debug attribute tells the compiler whether to include debug information. This is analogous to passing the -g switch at the command line.

The deprecation attribute tells the compiler whether it should notify you if you're calling deprecated methods. This is useful if you are compiling against code that is changing and the developers use deprecation to alert their users to changes.

The `optimize` flag is similar to passing the `-O` command-line flag to turn on rudimentary optimizations. We are stating here that we do not want optimization turned on.

Each of these three properties can take "`true`", "`yes`", or "`on`" for positive values, and "`false`", "`no`", or "`off`" for negative values. I prefer "`true`" and "`false`", but you can take your pick.

Notice also that this target has the `depends` attribute set to `prepare`. This says that this target depends on those targets listed in the `depends` attribute. Here, we don't want to compile classes before we have a place to store the output. Therefore, we say that the `compile` target is dependent on the `prepare` target.

Executing this target by typing **ant compile** should result in output similar to Figure 2.12.

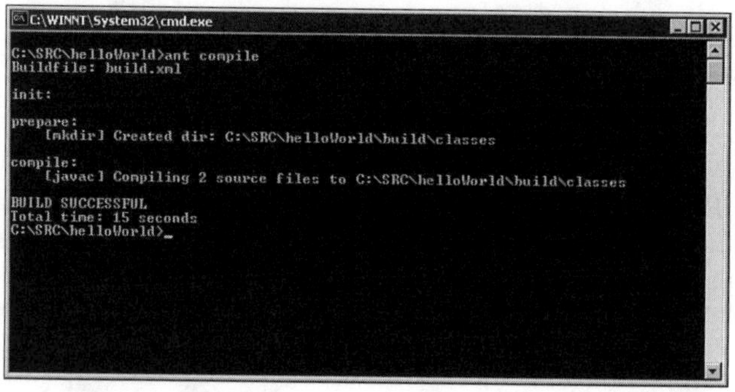

Figure 2.12
Compiling our Java classes.

Notice in the output that the targets being executed are listed along the left edge of the screen. The specific tasks within a target that are being executed are listed in square brackets and indented a little. You should end up with a BUILD SUCCESSFUL message and a total elapsed time for the build.

Building a JAR

Now that we have our compiled Java classes, we can package everything up into a JAR file for deployment. We'll call this target `jarfile` because it will be creating a JAR file that we can execute. Before creating our JAR file, we first need to copy our properties file from the `etc` directory to the `hello` package directory under `${classes.dir}`. We accomplish this using the standard `<copy>` task. Listing 2.10 shows our `compile` target so far, with just the copy step included.

Listing 2.10 *The jarfile Target with the copy Included*

```
<target name="jarfile" depends="compile">
    <copy file="${etc.dir}/Hello.properties"
          todir="${classes.dir}/hello"
          overwrite="true"/>
</target>
```

Now we'll use the built-in jar task to package our files into something we can use. Listing 2.11 shows our completed jarfile target.

Listing 2.11 *The Final Version of the jarfile Target*

```
<target name="jarfile" depends="compile">
    <copy file="${etc.dir}/Hello.properties"
          todir="${classes.dir}/hello"
          overwrite="true"/>
    <jar destfile="${build.dir}/${name}.jar"
         basedir="${classes.dir}"
         manifest="${etc.dir}/MANIFEST.MF"/>
</target>
```

The destfile attribute is the name of the JAR file to create. Notice that we are using two properties in creating this file: ${classes.dir} and ${name}.

The basedir attribute tells the jar tool where to start importing files. In this case, it will be in the build/classes directory and will include any file it finds in this directory or any subdirectory. You can filter which files are included, but we want everything, so the default works for us.

Finally, the manifest attribute tells the jar task that instead of using a default manifest for the JAR file, we want it to use our special one. If we omitted this line, a generic manifest would be used, and our JAR file would not be executable.

That's it! If you run Ant now by simply typing **ant** at your command prompt, you should see output similar to Figure 2.13.

Now you should have a JAR file named helloWorld.jar located in your build directory. You can run this JAR file by typing **java -jar build/helloWorld.jar**. You should see output as shown in Figure 2.14.

Listing 2.12 is the complete build.xml file that we've built up over the course of this introduction.

Note

Listing 2.12 is on the companion Web site for this book as build.xml.

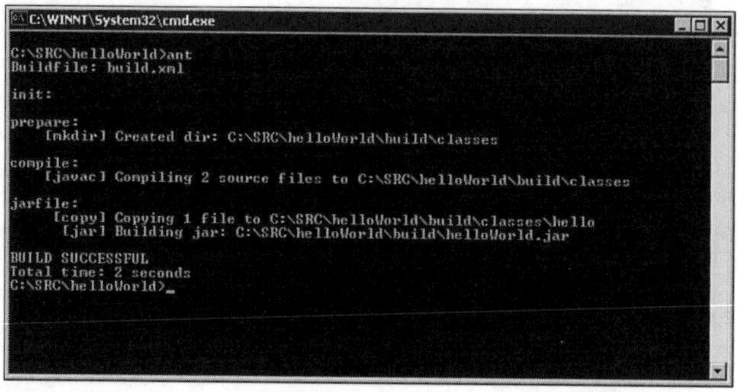

Figure 2.13

Building our JAR file.

Figure 2.14

Running our executable JAR file.

Listing 2.12   *The Complete Build File for This Example*

```xml
<?xml version="1.0"?>
<project name="helloWorld" default="jarfile" basedir=".">
    <target name="init">
        <property name="name" value="helloWorld"/>
        <property name="src.dir" value="src"/>
        <property name="build.dir" value="build"/>
        <property name="classes.dir" value="${build.dir}/classes"/>
        <property name="etc.dir" value="etc"/>
        <property name="deploy.name" value="${name}.jar"/>
    </target>
```

Listing 2.12   *(continued)*

```
    <target name="prepare" depends="init">
        <mkdir dir="${classes.dir}"/>
    </target>

    <target name="clean" depends="init">
        <delete dir="${build.dir}"/>
    </target>

    <target name="compile" depends="prepare">
        <javac srcdir="${src.dir}"
               destdir="${classes.dir}"
               debug="true"
               deprecation="true"
               optimize="false"/>
    </target>

    <target name="jarfile" depends="compile">
        <copy file="${etc.dir}/Hello.properties"
              todir="${classes.dir}/hello"
              overwrite="true"/>
        <jar destfile="${build.dir}/${name}.jar"
             basedir="${classes.dir}"
             manifest="${etc.dir}/MANIFEST.MF"/>
    </target>
</project>
```

Telling Ant What to Do

As you've noticed from previous sections, you can tell Ant to run a particular target by giving its name on the command line. You can also specify a series of targets to execute in a particular order by specifying them on the command line after the Ant executable. You can give one or more targets this way, and they will be run in the order given. For example, I frequently want to perform a clean before doing a build. I could run Ant twice like this:

```
ant clean
ant jarfile
```

But a nicer way to do this is to do it at the same time:

```
ant clean jarfile
```

Ant will first execute the `clean` target and then, assuming there were no errors, will execute the `jarfile` target. This is very handy for performing clean builds. Figure 2.15 demonstrates this. Notice that the `init` target is executed twice; once because of `clean` and again because of `prepare`. This is generally fine, but beware of targets being executed multiple times if they create or delete things.

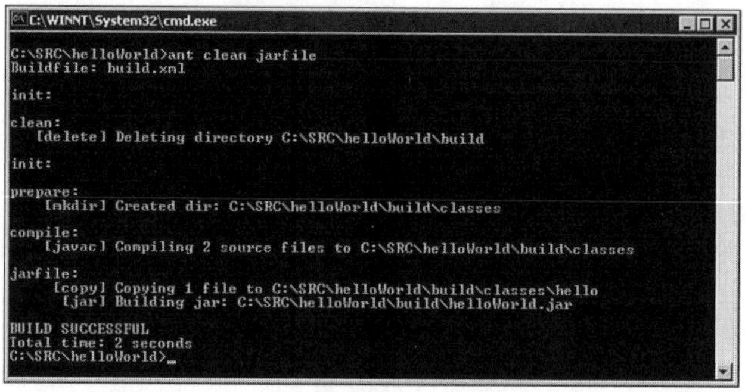

Figure 2.15
Running Ant with multiple targets specified.

Summary

This chapter presented quite a bit of information. We've covered the many different ways of getting Ant onto your system, including downloading binary distributions, downloading source distributions, and fetching source code directly from the Apache CVS repository. We then discussed building Ant from source and how to install it after you've downloaded a binary or built it yourself from source. We finished with a simple application that included a few components, and constructed a `build.xml` that can serve as the basis for future projects.

CHAPTER 3
Global Concepts

We'll begin this chapter with a description of a standard development directory structure. We'll show you what is generally used for different types of projects and explain why you should consider adopting it for your own projects.

> **Note**
> What we'll be showing you is a common structure, but there are other layouts that you may choose to use. Ant makes it easy to work with just about any layout you can dream up.

We'll then move on to more "standard" stuff. In this case, it's a discussion of what to call your targets. There are certain targets that just about every build file you run across will contain, and there are others that just make good sense. We'll discuss all of these.

Next, we'll discuss what are known as Ant *data types* including tags to generate sets of files matching certain criteria, path-like structures, and filters.

Moving on, we'll cover loggers and listeners. These facilities provide the capability to control how your builds are logged (loggers) and to trigger behavior when certain lifecycle events occur (listeners).

Finally, we will discuss those properties that are defined automatically by Ant, how they are useful, and the command line arguments that Ant accepts.

Note
Unlike most of the other chapters in this book, there are no Java source files that can be downloaded from the publisher's Web site, nor is there a working build file. The reason for this is the sheer volume of topics that will be covered and the near impossibility of devising a project incorporating all of them. You can, however, download a build file that contains each of the Ant snippets that will be presented so that you can paste them in to your own build files. This file won't be able to run by itself. Just think of it as a snippet repository.

Developing in a Standard Directory Tree

With a title like that for this section, you're probably thinking this sounds about as exciting as reading a dictionary, but hold on! This is stuff you need to know. In this section, we'll to cover a standard directory tree structure for your projects. Obviously, there isn't actually a standard for this type of thing yet, but this is a good starting point.

Directory Tree for Simple Projects

Let's begin by talking about the base structure for any type of project and then move into Web applications. For most applications, you'll have source code (otherwise, why would you need Ant?) that must be compiled, and you'll also have `.class` files that must go somewhere. You'll (probably) create some sort of archive file and it must live somewhere. If you're running unit tests on your code (you are, aren't you?), you'll want to store the output and subsequent reports someplace as well. If you use a custom `MANIFEST.MF` file, you'll want to store it somewhere, too. All these files and directories should live under a project directory. For example, if you have a project called "My Project," you would store everything related to this project in a directory called `myproject`. Where the project directory lives is up to you. I generally have all of my project directories under a `src` directory. We'll lay out a simple project called `myproject`. Listing 3.1 shows how you might lay this out.

Listing 3.1   *A Sample Directory Structure*

```
D:\SRC\ (or /home/jgibson/src on a UNIX box)
     myproject\
               src\
               build\
               reports\
               etc\
               doc\
               lib\
```

That's a good start. You can see that the src directory is under the myproject directory. The src directory will house all your source files, which, as you'll soon see, must be in their own directory structure, matching the package structure of the classes. Next is the build directory. You'll recall from Chapter 2 that we dumped our compiled Java classes under this directory in a subdirectory called classes, and that's where we built our JAR file. The reports directory is new. It's where you can have your unit tests write their output and generate testing reports. The next directory is etc, which is where your MANIFEST.MF file should live until you are ready to include it in a JAR file. The doc directory is where you should place any documentation for the project, such as use case documents and UML models. If you generate JavaDoc from your sources, you should have it generated in a subdirectory of doc called javadoc or api. (I've seen more instances of api than javadoc, and I actually prefer api.) Finally is the lib directory, which is where you should place third-party JAR files that your project depends on. You could leave these third-party JARs in their own install directories, but then you would have to worry about installing a new version and how that would affect this project. If you copy the JARs for the versions you are using to your lib directory, that concern goes away.

> **Note**
> An excellent paper by Steve Loughran, titled "Ant In Anger: Using Apache Ant in a Production Development System," is available in the doc directory of the Ant distribution (ANT_HOME/docs/ant_in_anger.html). In this paper, Mr. Loughran recommends having a bin and a dist directory. He recommends placing "common binaries [and] scripts" in this directory. You could also use the bin directory to store startup scripts or batch files that you'll used to start your finished program or if you have a C program that is the launcher for your Java program. The dist directory is where you would package everything for distribution. In other words, this is where you'd create a Zip file that would include all your source and support files so that others could download the kit and build your project for themselves.

When you get to Chapter 4, you'll read about the javac task that executes the Java compiler on your source files. One of the things that this task is capable of doing is an incremental compile. An *incremental compile* is one in which only those files that have changed since the last build will be compiled. This is a great feature, but there is a requirement for getting it to work. The requirement is that the source files must live in a directory structure that mimics the package structure defined in the classes, and that will ultimately be built on compilation. In other words, if your classes live in the chapter3.actions package, you must have a directory called actions under a directory called chapter3 in your src directory. Listing 3.2 shows this.

Listing 3.2   *The Requirement for Incremental Compilation*

```
D:\SRC\ (or /home/jgibson/src on a UNIX box)
      myproject\
              src\
                  chapter3\
                              actions\
                              dao\
                              utils\
              build\
                    classes\
              reports\
              etc\
```

If you have other packages, either under chapter3 or siblings of it, you must create those directories as well. This might seem like a hassle, but it really isn't that big of a deal. After you get used to it, you won't even think about. In addition, most of the current integrated development environments (IDEs) will create the source files in the package structure for you automatically, so you don't even have to think about it.

Now that the directory structure is laid out, let's populate it with a few files just to drive home what goes where. I've already mentioned the source files, the MANIFEST.MF, the unit testing reports, and the classes. Let's see where those files might fall in Listing 3.3.

Listing 3.3   *Files in the Directory Structure*

```
D:\SRC\ (or /home/jgibson/src on a UNIX box)
      myproject\
              src\
                  chapter3\
                              actions\
                                      MyAction.java
                                      MySecondAction.java
                              dao\
                                  CompanyDAO.java
                                  EmployeeDAO.java
                              utils\
                                      CacheManager.java
              build\
                    classes\
              reports\
                      TEST-chapter2.test.TestAll.xml
```

Listing 3.3   *(continued)*

```
                TESTS-TestSuites.xml
        etc\
            MANIFEST.MF
```

After you execute a compile, you'll end up with a directory structure inside the `build` directory that matches the directory structure under `myproject/src`. Listing 3.4 illustrates this for our example. (I've omitted everything but the build structure for brevity.)

Listing 3.4   *The Binary Package Structure*

```
myproject\
        build\
            classes\
                chapter3\
                        actions\
                                MyAction.class
                                MySecondAction.class
                        dao\
                            CompanyDAO.class
                            EmployeeDAO.class
                        utils\
                                CacheManager.class
```

Basic Structure for a Web Application

If you're building a Web application, you'll still need this basic structure, but you'll need to add a bit to it. For a Web app, you typically have some JavaServer Pages (JSPs) and/or Java servlets. You're required to have a file called `web.xml` and, depending on your Web container, you might have a vendor-specific file or two as well. Just like the `MANIFEST.MF` file, you can put your `web.xml` file and the vendor-specific file (if you have one) into the `etc` directory. You'll also need to create a Web archive, or WAR, file. If you have any images or tag library descriptors, you'll need to house them, too. Listing 3.5 presents the Web app structure. There's not much difference, just a few extra files.

Listing 3.5   *The Structure for a Web Application*

```
D:\SRC\ (or /home/jgibson/src on a UNIX box)
        myproject\
                src\
                    chapter3\
                            actions\
```

Listing 3.5   *(continued)*

```
                                MyAction.java
                                MySecondAction.java
                        dao\
                            CompanyDAO.java
                            EmployeeDAO.java
                        servlets\
                                MyServlet.java
                        utils\
                            CacheManager.java
                jsp\
                    index.jsp
            build\
                    mytest.war
                    classes\
            reports\
                    TEST-chapter3.test.TestAll.xml
                    TESTS-TestSuites.xml
            etc\
                    MANIFEST.MF
                    web.xml
            tld\
                    mytags.tld
            images\
                    banner.png
```

Using a directory structure like this will greatly help you in your development. One practice I've seen that I'd like to discourage is that of editing your source files in the same directories as your `.class` files. The problem this creates is that you have source and binaries in the same place. Why is this a problem? Because a typical `clean` target is defined as a `delete` task that just blasts the `build` directory. If your source as well as your binaries are in the `build` directory, you surely don't want to delete it. You would have to give filtering parameters to the `delete` task to avoid deleting your source. It's really much easier to keep your source and binaries separate from the beginning.

Creating Standard Ant Targets and What They Should Do

In every project that you do, and in just about every build file that you encounter, certain targets keep popping up. It helps to give these targets standard names so that everyone understands what the task does. Let's think about what you need to do in most projects. You need to set properties, create directories, compile, test, report on the tests, jar, perhaps war (if it's a Web app), generate JavaDocs, and deploy. You can name the corresponding targets accordingly. Here is a short list of common target names and what they do:

- init sets properties for the entire build

- prepare creates a build directory, test results directory, and so on

- fetch fetches your source code updates from a source code repository

- compile compiles, obviously

- test executes JUnit tests and generates reports

- jar creates a JAR file

- war creates a WAR file

- docs generates JavaDocs documentation

- deploy copies or FTPs the JAR/WAR/EAR to a deployment machine

Steve Loughran, in "Ant In Anger," also suggests the following targets:

- build performs an incremental build

- publish to "output the source and binaries to any distribution site"

- all performs an entire build from start to finish

- main performs a default build; generally just a build and test

- init-debug is called from init to set up properties for a debug build

- init-release is called from init to set up properties for a release build

- staging moves the complete project to a pre-production area

Let's discuss each of these targets and what they do.

Setting Properties with the init Target

The init target's duty is to set properties and not much else. So, it will basically be a bunch of <property> tags that set up all the properties you'll use in any target in your build file. Or, it could contain one statement that looks like Listing 3.6.

Listing 3.6   *Loading Properties from a File*

```
<target name="init">
    <loadproperties srcFile="build.properties"/>
</target>
```

As you can see, the `<loadproperties>` tag takes a `.properties` file and loads it up as Ant properties. This is equivalent to you setting them all in individual `<property>` statements. Chapter 4, "Built-in Tasks," has more information about this.

Another important thing to do in `init` is to set up a path-like structure that will be used as your class path. I cover this topic later in this chapter, but Listing 3.7 gives an example.

Listing 3.7   *Building a Path-Like Structure*

```
<target name="init">
    <loadproperties srcFile="build.properties"/>
    <path id="classpath">
        <pathelement path="${oro.jar}"/>
        <fileset dir="${struts.dir}">
            <include name="*.jar"/>
        </fileset>
    </path>
    <property name="classpath" refid="classpath"/>
</target>
```

If you heed Mr. Loughran's suggestion to have `init` targets set up things differently depending on whether you are doing a debug or release build, you would define `init-debug` and `init-release` targets. Each of these will either directly set properties that they need, or will load a different properties file. To determine which one will be called, you can make use of command-line properties and the `unless` and `if` attributes of Ant targets. Listing 3.8 shows an example of this.

Listing 3.8   *Using Discrete init Targets for Debug and Release Builds*

```
<target name="init">
    <property name="name" value="chapter3"/>
    <tstamp/>
</target>

<target name="init-debug" unless="release.build">
    <loadproperties srcFile="debug.properties"/>
</target>
```

Listing 3.8   *(continued)*

```
<target name="init-release" if="release.build">
    <loadproperties srcFile="release.properties"/>
</target>

<target name="prepare" depends="init, init-debug, init-release">
    <!-- other tasks -->
</target>
```

Notice the presence of an `unless` attribute in `init-debug` and an `if` attribute in `init-release`. These attributes conditionally execute a target *if* a certain property has been defined or *unless* a certain property has been defined. Here, if you execute `Ant` with `-Drelease.build=true` on the command line, `init-release` will be executed; otherwise, `init-debug` will be run. By putting both targets in the `prepare` target's `depends` attribute, the proper target will be called based on the presence or absence of the `release.build` property.

The listing also has an `init` target that could set up properties that will be useful regardless of the type of build being conducted.

> **Caution**
> In "Ant In Anger," Mr. Loughran suggests that to do this, you should define the two init-xxx targets, and then use the <antcall> task to execute them. This obviously worked in a previous version of Ant, but in the current releases, any properties set in a target that is executed via <antcall> will be visible only inside the target that is being called with <antcall>. This is definitely not what you want.

Preparing the Environment with the prepare Target

The `prepare` target doesn't generally do much, but it's important nonetheless. You'll typically want to create your `${build.dir}` and any subdirectories under it in the `prepare` target. If you'll be using the `<record>` task, this would be a good place to start it recording. `<record>` is covered in Chapter 5. Listing 3.9 shows a typical `prepare` target, turning on a recorder at the same time.

Listing 3.9   *A Typical prepare Target*

```
<target name="prepare" depends="init">
    <mkdir dir="${build.dir}"/>
    <record name="${name}.log" action="start"/>
</target>
```

Fetching Source Code from a Repository with the fetch Target

If you're on a project with more than a person or two, you'll most certainly store your source code in a repository of some sort, such as CVS or SourceSafe. You'll need a target to get the latest code updates from the repository so that you can ensure your code integrates with that of the rest of the team. The `fetch` target accomplishes this. You probably don't want to call this target every time you do a build because of the time it takes to get updates, but you do want it to be available when you need it. Listing 3.10 shows an example of getting source updates from CVS.

Listing 3.10   *Fetching Code Updates with the fetch Target*

```
<target name="fetch" depends="prepare">
    <cvspass cvsroot="${cvsroot}" password="${repo.pass}"/>
    <cvs cvsRoot="${cvsroot}" command="update -P -d" failonerror="true"/>
</target>
```

Compiling Your Classes with the compile Target

After you've set up the `build` directory it's time to compile your Java classes. The `<javac>` task makes building Java applications so much easier than doing it by hand. You generally don't need anything in this target other than `<javac>` itself. Listing 3.11 shows this.

Listing 3.11   *A Typical compile Target*

```
<target name="compile" depends="prepare">
    <javac srcdir="${src.dir}"
        destdir="${build.dir.classes}"
        classpath="${classpath}"/>
</target>
```

Testing and Reporting with the test Target

Unit testing and reporting on those tests are important steps that are too often left out of a development cycle. Ant automates everything but writing the tests themselves, so you really should try to utilize it. Putting both the `<junit>` and `<junitreport>` tasks in the same target is a good idea so that you don't forget to generate the reports from the raw output of `<junit>`. Listing 3.12 shows these two tasks in a `test` target.

Listing 3.12   *A Typical test Target*

```
<target name="test" depends="compile">
    <junit failureproperty="testsFailed">
        <classpath>
            <pathelement path="${classpath}"/>
            <pathelement path="${build.dir.classes}"/>
        </classpath>
        <formatter type="xml"/>
        <test name="chapter3.test.TestAll"
            todir="${reports.dir}"/>

    </junit>
    <junitreport todir="${reports.dir}">
        <fileset dir="${reports.dir}">
            <include name="**/TEST-*.xml"/>
        </fileset>
        <report format="frames" todir="${reports.dir.html}"/>
    </junitreport>
</target>
```

Creating a JAR File with the jar Target

Depending on what you're building, you might need to create a JAR file that contains your compiled classes. a JAR file can be easily created using the built-in <jar> task. Listing 3.13 shows a typical jar target.

Listing 3.13   *A Typical jar Target*

```
<target name="jar" depends="test" unless="testsFailed">
    <jar destfile="${build.dir}/${name}.jar"
        basedir="${build.dir}" includes="**/*.class"/>
</target>
```

The <jar> task here builds a JAR file with all .class files it finds under ${build.dir}. Also note that the target will not execute if the testsFailed property is present. This property is set by <junit> if any tests failed. This is a great way to conditionally execute targets.

Building a Web Archive with the war Target

If you're building a Web application, you'll most likely need to create a Web archive, or WAR file, out of it. A WAR file is just a JAR file with some special directories and file placement requirements. The `<war>` task is an extension of the `<jar>` task that makes creating WARs a simple matter. Listing 3.14 shows a sample war target.

Listing 3.14   *Building a Web Archive with the war Target*

```
<target name="war" depends="jar" unless="testsFailed">
    <war destfile="${name}.war" webxml="${etc.dir}/web.xml">
        <fileset dir="${src.dir}/jsp" includes="**/*.jsp"/>
        <classes dir="${build.dir}/web" includes="**/*.class"/>
        <lib dir="${struts.dir}" includes="*.jar"/>
        <webinf dir="${etc.dir}" includes="*.xml"
            excludes="web.xml"/>
    </war>
</target>
```

Generating Documentation with the docs Target

Because Java provides `javaDoc`, it is incumbent upon you as a developer to add JavaDoc comments to your code. The `javaDoc` tool takes these comments and creates excellent API documentation. Unfortunately, the options necessary to really tweak the generated documentation are lengthy and cumbersome. The built-in `<javadoc>` task makes it a piece of cake to generate JavaDocs exactly as you want them. Just look at Listing 3.15 for an example.

Listing 3.15   *Generating JavaDocs*

```
<target name="docs" depends="test" unless="testsFailed">
    <javadoc packagenames="com.mycompany.*" sourcepath="${src.dir}"
        classpath="${classpath}" destdir="${doc.api.dir}"
        author="true" version="true" use="true"
        windowtitle="MyProject Documentation">
        <bottom><![CDATA[<em>Copyright &copy; 2002</em></div>]]></bottom>
        <link href="http://java.sun.com/products/jdk/1.3/docs/api"/>
    </javadoc>
</target>
```

Notice that the docs target has an `unless` attribute. If there is a defined property called `testsFailed`, the documentation will *not* be generated because you generally don't want API documentation for broken code.

Deploying What You've Built with the deploy Target

After you've built a JAR or WAR file and generated your test reports and your JavaDocs, it's time to drop the JAR or WAR file somewhere for deployment. In the section in Chapter 8 called "Deploying What We've Built," you'll see an example of deploying to another box using FTP. Listing 3.16 is an example of a `deploy` target that uses the `<copy>` task to put the JAR file in a QA directory.

Listing 3.16 *Deploying the Project*

```
<target name="deploy" depends="jar" unless="testsFailed">
    <copy file="${name}.jar" todir="${qa.dir}"/>

</target>
```

Again, notice that this target depends on a previous target, and won't execute if any unit tests failed.

Turning again to "Ant In Anger," here are some examples for the targets that Mr. Loughran suggests. Notice that each of these targets makes extensive use of the `antcall` task to delegate work to other targets.

Performing an Incremental Build with the build Target

The `build` target could call the `compile`, `jar`, and/or `war` targets. Basically, it calls whatever it takes to do a build based on what you currently have on your system. However, it would not fetch source updates from your source control system. Listing 3.17 is an example.

Listing 3.17 *Building the Project*

```
<target name="build" depends="prepare">
    <antcall target="compile"/>
    <antcall target="jar"/>
</target>
```

Building and Testing with the main Target

A target called `main` would perform a build and test, generally, and not much else. It would not fetch source code from a repository, nor would it deploy anything. Listing 3.18 shows this.

Listing 3.18 *Building and Testing with the main Target*

```
<target name="main" depends="prepare">
    <antcall target="build"/>
    <antcall target="test"/>
</target>
```

Doing Everything with the all Target

A target named `all` does just what its name implies: calls all the relevant targets to get the project built. This would be a start-to-finish build, including removing all artifacts from previous builds, fetching source, building, testing, generating documentation, and deploying. You could leverage your existing `main` target by calling it instead of listing the compile and test steps directly. Listing 3.19 shows one possible implementation of this target.

Listing 3.19   *Doing It All with the all Target*

```
<target name="all" depends="prepare">
    <antcall target="clean"/>
    <antcall target="fetch"/>
    <antcall target="main"/>
    <antcall target="deploy"/>
</target>
```

If you use an `all` target, you should have an `unless` attribute on each target called by `antcall` to stop a build if a previous target doesn't complete successfully.

Publishing and Staging with the publish and staging Targets

Mr. Loughran recommends two additional targets: `publish` and `staging`. His concept of the `staging` target is essentially the same as the `deploy` target we've already discussed, in which our built and tested project is moved to a QA directory or machine. He differentiates the two targets by saying that the `staging` target is used for this purpose, whereas the `deploy` target actually moves the project into production. If you have a QA group, I think they will probably be the ones to move the final product into production, so having two different targets doesn't seem all that useful to me.

The `publish` target would essentially perform a build and test, and then zip the sources, binaries, and support files, and copy/FTP them to your distribution sites. This seems most useful for open source projects, such as Ant, in which you want to distribute binary versions of your product along with the source code.

This concludes our discussion of standard names for targets that you'll see in almost every `build` file.

Exploring Ant Data Types

Let's now move on to discuss the data types that Ant provides that aren't exactly tasks. If you are used to data types in programming languages, these are quite a bit different, but they provide services that you'll most certainly need. Specifically, we'll discuss the following:

- Description type—Describes a project

- PatternSet—Groups of patterns

- DirSet—Groups of directories

- FileSet—Groups of files

- FileList—Explicit list of files

- FileMapper—Translates filenames

- FilterReader—Custom class that filters out files

- FilterChain—Series of FilterReaders to further filter files

- FilterSet—Groups of filters

- Selectors—Provides more control over file selection

- Class FileSet—A FileSet for class files

- Path-like structures—A data type resembling a file system path

- XMLCatalog—Catalog of public XML resources

These elements will be used most often nested inside other tags. Some of them, the PatternSet for instance, are actually implicitly contained within other tags, such as FileSet, so you can use PatternSet tags inside FileSets. Confusing? It won't be in a little while. So, let's dive in and discover what these data types can be used for.

Description Type

The `<description>` tag is not used often enough. I have a hard time remembering to add it. There is only one place that a `<description>` tag should go, and that is at the top level of your project, directly under the opening `<project>` tag. Whatever you place between the open and close `<description>` tags will be printed on the console whenever Ant is invoked with the `-projecthelp` switch. Listing 3.20 shows this.

Listing 3.20   *The `<description>` Tag*

```
<project default="deploy" basedir=".">
    <description>You can build me using Ant!</description>
</project>
```

Don't confuse this tag with the `description` attribute of the `<target>` tag. They work together, but if you try to nest a `<description>` inside a `<target>`, all the text from the different `<description>` tags runs together, which is not what you want.

PatternSet

PatternSets are groups of patterns that enable you to easily filter files or directories based on certain patterns. Ant supports three wildcards that you use to create your patterns. They are

- ? matches a single character

- * matches zero or more characters

- ** matches zero or more directories *recursively*

These metacharacters (with the possible exception of the **) should be familiar to anyone who has ever worked at a file system command line. You can combine these wildcards in interesting ways to specify only those files or directories that you want or don't want. As we go along with PatternSets, you'll see examples of such uses.

As I said before, PatternSets are groups of patterns. They support four nested elements: `<include>`, `<includesfile>`, `<exclude>`, and `<excludesfile>`. The basic idea is that you nest these tags inside your `<patternset>` to filter out which files or directories are matched. Listing 3.21 shows how to get all `.class` files *except* those with `Test` in the name. This is recursive, by the way.

Listing 3.21   *Filtering .class Files for Test*

```
<patternset id="classfiles">
    <include name="**/*.class"/>
    <exclude name="**/*Test*.class"/>
</patternset>
```

The `id` attribute enables you to refer to this PatternSet later by using a `refid` attribute of some task.

The `<includesfile>` and `<excludesfile>` tags both take an `src` attribute that specifies a file containing patterns to match with. Specifying your patterns in the build file itself seems to be far more common.

All four of these nested elements have `if` and `unless` attributes that can be used to keep them from executing *if* a certain property is not present, or *unless* a particular property is present.

As you'll see, PatternSets are implicitly contained within several other tags.

It should be noted that each of those four nested tags of PatternSet (and FileSet, and so on) can also be specified as attributes rather than nested elements. Two of them change their names slightly: include becomes includes, and exclude becomes excludes. So, Listing

3.21 could be rewritten as shown in Listing 3.22 to the same effect. (I prefer the nested syntax because I think it is a little easier to read.)

Listing 3.22   *PatternSet Using Attributes Instead of Nested Tags*

```
<patternset id="classfiles" includes="**/*.class"
    excludes="**/*Test*.class"/>
```

DirSet

DirSets give you a way to specify directories by applying a pattern or patterns to a directory structure. Using these patterns, you can easily include certain directories while simultaneously excluding others. DirSets hold an implicit PatternSet, which means the four nested PatternSet elements appear as *attributes* of the <dirset> tag. You can also nest <patternset> elements, or <include> and <exclude>, and so on. Listing 3.23 shows the use of attributes, whereas Listing 3.24 uses a nested <patternset>. Listing 3.25 uses the PatternSet nested elements to gather those directories that contain the string classes, except for those with the word debug.

Listing 3.23   *A Sample DirSet Using Attributes*

```
<dirset dir="${build.dir}" includes="**/classes" excludes="**/*debug*"/>
```

Listing 3.24   *A Sample DirSet Using a Nested PatternSet*

```
<dirset dir="${build.dir}">
    <patternset id="classes">
        <include name="**/classes"/>
        <exclude name="**/*debug*"/>
    </patternset>
</dirset>
```

Listing 3.25   *A Sample DirSet Using PatternSet Elements*

```
<dirset dir="${build.dir}">
    <include name="**/classes"/>
    <exclude name="**/*debug*"/>
</dirset>
```

It should be noted that the <patternset> in Listing 3.18 has an id attribute. If set, this PatternSet can be referenced in other places in the build file. In our case, a task that works with references could have a `refid="classes"` attribute to reference the `classes` PatternSet.

FileSet

Similar to a DirSet is the FileSet, which, as you've probably already guessed, groups files based on a set of patterns. The `<fileset>` tag takes all the same attributes as `<dirset>` with one addition: `defaultexcludes`. This is a Boolean field that says whether to use its default list of files to exclude. This exclude list includes common files that you would want to filter out anyway, such as backup files, files inside CVS directories, and temporary files. The default is to use the default excludes; if you set this to "no", you will not get the benefit of the defaults.

Listings 3.26, 3.27, and 3.28 will look remarkably like the previous three listings because the syntax is almost identical. Like a DirSet, a FileSet contains an implicit PatternSet and works the same way. In these examples, we'll select those files that end in `.java`, and exclude any files with `Test` in their names.

Listing 3.26   *A Sample FileSet Using Attributes*

```
<fileset dir="${build.dir}" includes="**/*.java" excludes="**/*Test*"/>
```

Listing 3.27   *A Sample FileSet Using a Nested PatternSet*

```
<fileset dir="${build.dir}">
    <patternset id="sources">
        <include name="**/*.java"/>
        <exclude name="**/*Test*"/>
    </patternset>
</fileset>
```

Listing 3.28   *A Sample FileSet Using PatternSet's Elements*

```
<fileset dir="${build.dir}">
    <include name="**/*.java"/>
    <exclude name="**/*Test*"/>
</fileset>
```

FileList

Although FileSets enable you to dynamically select files based on patterns, sometimes it is easier to specify the files directly because you know up front exactly which files will be needed. The `<filelist>` tag enables you do this. This element can have an id attribute, and requires both a `dir` and a `files` attribute to specify which files (comma delimited) in which directory you care about. Listing 3.29 is a simple example.

Listing 3.29   *A Simple FileList*

```
<filelist id="xmlfiles" dir="${etc.dir}"
    files="poolman.xml, struts-config.xml"/>
```

Remember that wildcards are not allowed here. The `<filelist>` tag is for explicitly naming files. If you need to dynamically select files, you should use a FileSet.

FileMapper

The FileMapper transforms source filenames into destination filenames for tasks such as `<copy>`, `<junit>`, `<move>`, and so on. Several different types of mappers are included. Here's the list:

- identity—The target filename is identical to the source filename
- flatten—The directory structure is disregarded when the target filename is constructed
- merge—The target filename is the same for all source files
- glob—Glob matching is performed on the files
- regexp—Regular expression matching is performed on the files
- package—The transform is based on the Java package of the source files

The `<mapper>` tag has several attributes that can be specified. Exactly one of either *type* or *class* must be specified. The *type* attribute would be one of the mapper types listed in the preceding list. If you write your own mapper class, you would specify the full class name as the *class* attribute. If you do use the *class* attribute, you will most likely need to use either `classpath` or `classpathref` to give Ant access to the class. `classpath` takes a property value that works out to a path-like structure, and `classpathref` takes a reference to a path-like structure. The `from` and `to` attributes specify what to transform from and to, respectively. Depending on which mapper type you're using, you may specify neither, either, or both the `from` and `to` attributes.

Now, on to the types of mappers. The `identity` type performs no transformation at all from the source filename to the destination filename. This is the default mapper for `<copy>`, `<move>`, and a few other tags. You can change which mapper is used by nesting a `<mapper>` tag inside a task that uses a mapper.

The flatten mapper is useful if you have a directory structure and want all the files in all the directories to be copied to the same directory but *without* the directory structure. Listing 3.30 shows a copy operation that discards the directories and copies only the files.

Listing 3.30   *Copying a File Without the Directory Structure*

```
<copy todir="bar">
    <mapper type="flatten"/>
    <fileset dir="foo">
        <include name="**/*.java"/>
    </fileset>
</copy>
```

The merge type copies all files to the same filename. This could be useful for writing to a UNIX device such as a tape drive, or for creating a tar file (which is what the Ant documentation uses as its example). Listing 3.31 copies all files to a UNIX tape drive.

Listing 3.31   *Copying to a Tape Drive*

```
<copy todir="/dev">
    <mapper type="merge" to="mt0"/>
    <fileset dir="foo">
        <include name="**/*.java"/>
    </fileset>
</copy>
```

The ultimate destination is /dev/mt0, which is a typical name for a tape drive on a UNIX box.

Next is the glob type. This uses the filename-globbing wildcard *, and replaces the * in the from attribute with the * value from the to attribute. Listing 3.32 should make this clearer. It copies and renames all .java files to .java.save.

Listing 3.32   *Performing a "Backup" of All .java Files*

```
<copy todir="bar">
    <mapper type="glob" from="*.java" to="*.java.save"/>
    <fileset dir="foo">
        <include name="**/*.java"/>
    </fileset>
</copy>
```

Next is the regular expression mapper, regexp. It works just like the glob type, except that you have the matching power of regular expressions and more replacement abilities. If you put parentheses around interesting bits in the source filename, you can refer to these bits using standard naming, such as \1, \2, \3, and so on. Listing 3.33 demonstrates this using the same example as Listing 3.32.

Listing 3.33 *Copying with the regexp Mapper*

```
<copy todir="bar">
    <mapper type="regexp" from="^(.*).java$$" to="\1.java.save"/>
    <fileset dir="foo">
        <include name="**/*.java"/>
    </fileset>
</copy>
```

> **Note**
> It is important to note that for the regexp mapper to work, you must have access to a regular expression library. You essentially have three options. If you're using JDK 1.4, you have a built-in regexp library. If you're using JDK 1.3 or 1.4, you can use Jakarta Regexp or Jakarta ORO. Whichever one you choose to use, you must ensure that it is in the class path prior to execution. And, if you build from source, the regexp library must be in your class path before you build Ant. Otherwise, the Ant regexp support classes won't be built into Ant.

Finally is the package type. According to the Ant manual, this mapper will replace directory separators in the matched source files with dots. This would enable you to generate names based on the Java package scheme, which would be most useful in an uptodate or junit task. Listing 3.34 shows the example from the manual.

Listing 3.34 *Mapping Based on Java Package*

```
<mapper type="package"
    from="*Test.java" to="TEST-*Test.xml"/>
```

There is no definitive list of Ant tasks that use mappers. But if you think about those tasks that take a list of files and output files with similar names, but perhaps with different extensions, you should be able to figure out which tasks support mappers.

FilterReader and FilterChain

A FilterReader is a subclass of java.io.FilterReader. A FilterReader performs some sort of filtering on the stream of data coming from some source. In our case, the source will be files or directories. You can create your own FilterReaders simply by subclassing `java.io.FilterReader.`

FilterReaders can be used only when contained within a FilterChain, which is simply a chain, or pipeline, of FilterReaders. The basic duty of a FilterReader is to perform some sort of filtering on a file as it is read. Ant comes with several built-in FilterReaders. They are

- ClassConstants—Looks for constants defined in .class files and outputs them, one per line, in name-value pairs

- ExpandProperties—Expands Ant properties, such as ${build.dir}, contained in the input data

- HeadFilter—Returns only the top n lines from the head of the file

- TailFilter—The opposite of HeadFilter

- ReplaceTokens—Replaces tokens contained between delimiters

- StripJavaComments—Removes all comments from .java files

- StripLineComments—Removes lines that start with user-defined comment characters

- StripLineBreaks—Removes all end-of-line characters from the input file

- LineContains—Copies only those lines containing a specified string

- LineContainsRegexp—Copies only those lines containing a specified regular expression

- PrefixLines—Adds a specified string to the beginning of every line

- TabsToSpaces—Converts tab characters to a given number of spaces

ClassConstants

I'll demonstrate each of the FilterReaders using the `<copy>` task. We'll begin with the `ClassConstants` filter. This filter looks for all fields in a `.class` file that are constants (`public static final …`), and outputs those lines as key-value pairs. Listing 3.35 shows an example of this. Note that for this FilterReader to work, you must have the Jakarta BCEL package. Also, if you built Ant from source, you must have had the Jakarta BCEL package in your class path at the time of the build.

Listing 3.35   *Pulling the Constants from Binary Files and Storing Them in Text Files*

```
<copy todir="bar">
    <filterchain>
        <classconstants/>
```

Listing 3.35   *(continued)*

```
    </filterchain>
    <fileset dir="foo">
        <include name="**/*.class"/>
    </fileset>
    <mapper type="glob" from="*.class" to="*.txt"/>
</copy>
```

ExpandProperties

The `ExpandProperties` filter expands any Ant properties that are contained in the data it is processing with values that it knows about. This could be useful if you've specified a filename in the `.java` file with part of the path given as a property or you want to indicate which version of Java you built with (using the `java.version` property). Listing 3.36 shows how to use `ExpandProperties`.

Listing 3.36   *Expanding Ant Properties Using the ExpandProperties FilterReader*

```
<copy todir="bar">
    <filterchain>
        <expandproperties/>
    </filterchain>
    <fileset dir="foo">
        <include name="**/*.java"/>
    </fileset>
</copy>
```

HeadFilter and TailFilter

`HeadFilter` and `TailFilter` directly mimic the standard UNIX programs `head` and `tail`. `head` retrieves only the first *n* lines, whereas `tail` retrieves only the last *n* lines. `HeadFilter` and `TailFilter` are useful if you want to copy only a sample from a series of files rather than the entire file. Listing 3.37 copies the first five lines of each file, whereas Listing 3.38 copies the last five lines of each file.

Listing 3.37   *Copying the First Five Lines*

```
<copy todir="bar">
    <filterchain>
        <headfilter lines="5"/>
    </filterchain>
    <fileset dir="foo">
```

Listing 3.37 *(continued)*

```
        <include name="**/*.java"/>
    </fileset>
</copy>
```

Listing 3.38 *Copying the Last Five Lines*

```
<copy todir="bar">
    <filterchain>
        <tailfilter lines="5"/>
    </filterchain>
    <fileset dir="foo">
        <include name="**/*.java"/>
    </fileset>
</copy>
```

ReplaceTokens

You know how tools such as CVS and SourceSafe replace tokens like Id and Log with information about the current version and history of a file on checkout? You can get the same effect by using the ReplaceTokens filter when copying, moving, and so on. The way it works is that you specify a token to replace and what the replacement should be. You can also specify what the delimiters will be, using the begintoken and endtoken attributes, but the default is the @ symbol. Listing 3.39 demonstrates how to replace a token of @TODAY@ with a customized date.

Listing 3.39 *Demonstrating ReplaceTokens*

```
<copy todir="bar">
    <filterchain>
        <replacetokens>
            <token key="TODAY" value="${MY_DATE_FORMAT}"/>
        </replacetokens>
    </filterchain>
    <fileset dir="foo">
        <include name="**/*.java"/>
    </fileset>
</copy>
```

StripJavaComments

The StripJavaComments filter removes anything that resembles a comment in your Java source files. I'm not really sure why you would want to do this unless perhaps it was to remove commented-out sections that you didn't want to be seen by a customer, or something like that. StripJavaComments takes no parameters; all you have to do is specify it as in Listing 3.40.

Listing 3.40 *Removing Java Comments*

```
<copy todir="bar">
    <filterchain>
        <stripjavacomments/>
    </filterchain>
    <fileset dir="foo">
        <include name="**/*.java"/>
    </fileset>
</copy>
```

StripLineComments

This filter removes all lines that start with a user-specified comment string. This filter would be useful if you wanted to remove the comments from some SQL scripts or shell scripts. You can specify multiple comment strings by providing multiple <comment> nested tags as shown in Listing 3.41. Note that for a line to be stripped, the specified comment string must be the first thing on the line.

Listing 3.41 *Removes Lines Starting with the Specified Comment Strings*

```
<copy todir="bar">
    <filterchain>
        <striplinecomments>
            <comment value="--"/>
            <comment value="#"/>
        </striplinecomments>
    </filterchain>
    <fileset dir="foo">
        <include name="**/*.java"/>
    </fileset>
</copy>
```

StripLineBreaks

This filter removes all end-of-line characters, essentially joining the text into one big line. Unlike StripJavaComments, I can readily think of a good use for this one. If you're building a system in which you will be storing scripts (such as Jython, ECMAScript, or even HTML) in database cells, removing line breaks will save on storage. This filter has one optional parameter, linebreaks, that specifies what the end-of-line character is. The default is \r\n, which should have you covered. Listing 3.42 demonstrates how to remove line breaks using the default values.

Listing 3.42   Stripping Off Line Breaks

```
<copy todir="bar">
    <filterchain>
        <striplinebreaks/>
    </filterchain>
    <fileset dir="foo">
        <include name="**/*.java"/>
    </fileset>
</copy>
```

LineContains

This filter will copy those only lines that contain a specified string. Just as with the StripLineComments filter, you can specify multiple strings to match against; however, if you include multiple strings, the lines must contain *all* the strings. Listing 3.43 shows how to copy only those lines that contain foo and bar.

Listing 3.43   Copying Lines Containing foo and bar

```
<copy todir="bar">
    <filterchain>
        <linecontains>
            <contains value="foo"/>
            <contains value="bar"/>
        </linecontains>
    </filterchain>
    <fileset dir="foo">
        <include name="**/*.java"/>
    </fileset>
</copy>
```

LineContainsRegexp

This filter will copy those only lines that match a specified regular expression. Listing 3.44 shows how to copy only those lines that contain the word foo followed by the word bar after three spaces.

Listing 3.44 *Copying Lines Containing foo and bar with a Regular Expression*

```
<copy todir="bar">
    <filterchain>
        <linecontainsregexp>
            <regexp pattern="foo\s{3}bar"/>
        </linecontainsregexp>
    </filterchain>
    <fileset dir="foo">
        <include name="**/*.java"/>
    </fileset>
</copy>
```

PrefixLines

This filter will copy all lines, prefixing each line with the given string. This is another filter that doesn't seem all that useful, but Listing 3.45 shows an example anyway.

Listing 3.45 *Prefixing Each Line with Hello*

```
<copy todir="bar">
    <filterchain>
        <prefixlines prefix="Hello"/>
    </filterchain>
    <fileset dir="foo">
        <include name="**/*.java"/>
    </fileset>
</copy>
```

TabsToSpaces

Finally we come to the TabsToSpaces filter. As you can guess from its name, this filter replaces any tab it finds with an appropriate number of spaces. The single optional attribute, tablength, sets the number of spaces that each tab should be replaced with, but the default is 8 and that is probably a good value. Listing 3.46 shows how to replace each tab with four spaces.

Listing 3.46   *Replacing Each Tab with Four Spaces*

```
<copy todir="bar">
    <filterchain>
        <tabstospaces tablength="4"/>
    </filterchain>
    <fileset dir="foo">
        <include name="**/*.java"/>
    </fileset>
</copy>
```

Using Multiple FilterReaders Together in a FilterChain

Several of the FilterReaders we've just discussed are useful all by themselves. But the FilterChain enables you to string together multiple FilterReaders at one go. Listing 3.47 will copy all Java source files from the `${src.dir}` directory, strip all comments, expand Ant properties, and replace instances of the @TODAY@ token with the current date.

Listing 3.47   *Using Multiple FilterReaders at a Time*

```
<copy todir="bar">
    <filterchain>
        <stripjavacomments/>
        <expandproperties/>
        <replacetokens>
            <token key="TODAY" value="${DSTAMP}"/>
        </replacetokens>
    </filterchain>
    <fileset dir="foo">
        <include name="**/*.java"/>
    </fileset>
</copy>
```

FilterSet

The FilterSet is very similar to the `ReplaceTokens` FilterReader that was covered in the previous section. Using a FilterSet with a task such as `copy`, you can replace certain text tokens in each file with specified replacements. Just as with the `ReplaceTokens` FilterReader, the default token delimiter is `@`, but this can be changed using the `begintoken` and `endtoken` attributes. Specifying tokens to replace can be done either with a series of token tags, or by loading the filters from a file of key-value pairs. Listing 3.48 shows using the `copy` task with a FilterSet to replace instances of @TODAY@ with the current date, and Listing 3.49 loads the filters from a file.

Listing 3.48   *Copies Files Replacing @TODAY@ with the Current Date*

```
<copy todir="${dist.dir}">
    <fileset dir="${src.dir}" includes="**/*.java"/>
    <filterset>
        <filter token="TODAY" value="${DSTAMP}"/>
    </filterset>
</copy>
```

Listing 3.49   *Loads Replacement Tokens from a File*

```
<copy todir="${dist.dir}">
    <fileset dir="${src.dir}" includes="**/*.java"/>
    <filterset>
        <filtersfile file="${filters.file.name}"/>
    </filterset>
</copy>
```

Selectors

You saw in the discussion of FileSet that the decision of whether to include a file was solely based on a filename. But there are times when that approach is insufficient to creating an appropriate list. Selectors provide a means to select files based on factors *other* than filename. Although you can write your own selector, a number of them are included with Ant. They are

- contains—Selects files whose contents contain a specified string
- date—Selects files based on their modification date
- depend—Selects file that has been modified later than some other file that depends on it
- depth—Selects files at a certain directory structure depth
- filename—Selects file based on filename
- present—Selects file based on its presence or absence from a given directory
- size—Selects files based on the size of their contents

contains

The contains selector is much like the standard grep utility. It searches the content of a group of files for a specified string and returns those files that contain it. You could use `contains` to copy only those Java files that reference a certain class, for instance. Listing 3.50 demonstrates this usage.

Listing 3.50 *Copies Java Files Containing a Certain Class Reference*

```
<copy todir="${tmp.dir}">
    <fileset dir="${src.dir}" includes="**/*.java">
        <contains text="MyClass"/>
    </fileset>
</copy>
```

There is an optional attribute to the `contains` selector, called `casesensitive`, which determines whether differences in uppercase and lowercase letters matters. The default setting is true.

date

The `date` selector enables you to select files that have been modified before, after, or at the exact date and time specified. The optional attribute `when` controls the time matching. The possible values are `before`, `after`, and `equal`. The default is to select files before the date given. Listing 3.51 copies all Java files modified before noon of July 21, 2002.

Listing 3.51 *Copies Java Files Older Than Noon of July 21, 2002*

```
<copy todir="${tmp.dir}">
    <fileset dir="${src.dir}" includes="**/*.java">
        <date datetime="07/21/2002 12:00 PM"/>
    </fileset>
</copy>
```

depend

From its name, you might assume that the `depend` selector selects files on which some other file or files depend. Not so. It selects files that have equivalent files in a different location that are different. The example from the Ant manual shows a method for selecting those files that have changed between two versions of Ant. (I think this selector would have been better named `Diff` or something indicating that it deals with file differences, not file dependencies.) Listing 3.52 shows the example from the Ant manual.

Listing 3.52   *Selecting Files That Changed Between Versions of Ant*

```
<fileset dir="${ant.1.5}/src/main" includes="**/*.java">
    <depend targetdir="${ant.1.4.1}/src/main"/>
</fileset>
```

The `depend` selector has an optional attribute called `granularity` that takes a number of milliseconds to use as a cushion before deciding that two files are different. The default is 0 milliseconds.

`depend` also can use an optional mapper to define the mapping of source to target files. See the section about FileMappers earlier in this chapter for more details.

depth

The `depth` selector selects a file based on how deep in the directory structure it is. I don't really see this selector as being very useful, but Listing 3.53 shows an example nonetheless. This listing copies those files from `${src.dir}` that are two levels deep or deeper.

Listing 3.53   *Selecting Files Based on Tree Depth*

```
<copy todir="${tmp.dir}">
    <fileset dir="${src.dir}" includes="**/*.java">
        <depth min="2"/>
    </fileset>
</copy>
```

`depth` also has a `max` attribute that sets a limit on how deep the copy will go.

filename

It might seem odd to have a selector that selects files based on filename because that is how FileSets generally select files. However, if you combine the `filename` selector with other selectors inside selector containers (covered shortly), you can get very fine control over selection. You'll see an example of this shortly, but Listing 3.54 shows the basic usage of `filename`.

Listing 3.54   *Selecting Files Based on Filename*

```
<copy todir="${tmp.dir}">
    <fileset dir="${src.dir}" includes="**/*">
        <filename name="**/*.java"/>
    </fileset>
</copy>
```

present

The `present` selector selects files that are either in both the source and target directories or only in the source directory. This selector could be used to select only those files that exist in version 2 of your project but not in version 1. Listing 3.55 shows this.

Listing 3.55   *Selecting Files Based on Presence*

```
<copy todir="${tmp.dir}">
    <fileset dir="${v1.src.dir}" includes="**/*.java">
        <present present="srconly" targetdir="${v2.src.dir}"/>
    </fileset>
</copy>
```

The other possible value for the `present` attribute is `both`, which would select only those files that appear in both the source and target directories.

size

The `size` selector enables you to select files based on their size. Three attributes handle the file selection. The first attribute is `value`, which is the size you want to test against. The second attribute, `units`, determines what the size you specified in the `value` attribute represents. The default is bytes. Possible values for `units` include `Ki`, `Mi`, and `Gi` for power-of-2 kilobytes, megabytes, and gigabytes, respectively. Finally, the `when` attribute specifies to select whether files are `less`, `more`, or `equal` to the `value` attribute. The default is `equal`. Listing 3.56 copies only those files that are smaller than 1KB.

Listing 3.56   *Selecting Files Smaller Than One Kilobyte*

```
<copy todir="${tmp.dir}">
    <fileset dir="${src.dir}" includes="**/*.java">
        <size value="1" units="Ki" when="less"/>
    </fileset>
</copy>
```

There are also a number of container selectors. Such selectors can contain other selectors, including other containers, to make them work together. The included container selectors are

- and—Selects a file if all contained selectors select it
- or—Selects a file if any contained selector selects it
- not—Reverses its single contained selector

- majority—Selects a file if a majority of contained selectors select it

- none—Selects a file if none of the contained selectors select it

- selector—Useful for defining a reusable selector

and

The and selector will select a file only if *all* of its contained selectors select it. You would use this container if you wanted to apply several conditions to a file before selecting it. For example, if you wanted to combine selectors to select all those Java source files that contained the word Test in their name, were larger than 1KB, and were older than July 21, 2002, you could write something like Listing 3.57.

Listing 3.57   *Selecting Files Based on Multiple Selectors*

```
<copy todir="${tmp.dir}">
    <fileset dir="${src.dir}" includes="**/*.java">
        <and>
            <filename name="**/*Test*.java"/>
            <date datetime="07/21/2002 12:00 PM" when="before"/>
            <size value="1" units="Ki" when="more"/>
        </and>
    </fileset>
</copy>
```

or

The or selector is similar to the and selector except that it will select a file if *any* of its contained selectors selects it. If we change Listing 3.54 to use an or selector instead of an and selector, we'll get all Java files that contain Test in the name, *or* were modified before July 21, 2002, *or* are greater than 1KB in size. Listing 3.58 shows this.

Listing 3.58   *Selecting Files Based One of Several Selectors*

```
<copy todir="${tmp.dir}">
    <fileset dir="${src.dir}" includes="**/*.java">
        <or>
            <filename name="**/*Test*.java"/>
            <date datetime="07/21/2002 12:00 PM" when="before"/>
            <size value="1" units="Ki" when="more"/>
        </or>
    </fileset>
</copy>
```

not

The `not` selector can contain only one selector and it will reverse the condition. The single selector can be another container, so if we wanted to take Listing 3.57 and get only those Java files that do *not* contain the word `Test` in their name, are *smaller* than 1KB, and are *not* older than July 21, 2002, Listing 3.59 would work.

Listing 3.59   *Negating a Contained Selector Using the not Selector*

```
<copy todir="${tmp.dir}">
    <fileset dir="${src.dir}" includes="**/*.java">
        <not>
            <and>
                <filename name="**/*Test*.java"/>
                <date datetime="07/21/2002 12:00 PM" when="before"/>
                <size value="1" units="Ki" when="more"/>
            </and>
        </not>
    </fileset>
</copy>
```

majority

The `majority` selector is sort of a combination of the and and or selectors. It will select a file if a simple majority of contained selectors select a file. Turning once again to Listing 3.54, we can modify it so that files will be selected that meet two of the three criteria for selection by changing the and selector to the majority selector as shown in Listing 3.60.

Listing 3.60   *Selecting Files Based on a Majority of Multiple Selectors*

```
<copy todir="${tmp.dir}">
    <fileset dir="${src.dir}" includes="**/*.java">
        <majority>
            <filename name="**/*Test*.java"/>
            <date datetime="07/21/2002 12:00 PM" when="before"/>
            <size value="1" units="Ki" when="more"/>
        </majority>
    </fileset>
</copy>
```

none

The none selector will select only those files that were selected by *none* of the contained selectors. You could get the same effect by wrapping an and or or container inside a not. Listing 3.61 produces results identical to those produced by Listing 3.59.

Listing 3.61   *Negating a Contained Selector Using none*

```
<copy todir="${tmp.dir}">
    <fileset dir="${src.dir}" includes="**/*.java">
        <none>
            <filename name="**/*Test*.java"/>
            <date datetime="07/21/2002 12:00 PM" when="before"/>
            <size value="1" units="Ki" when="more"/>
        </none>
    </fileset>
</copy>
```

selector

The final selector, selector, is most useful outside of a task, with an ID assigned to it with the id attribute. It can be used later by referring to it with the refid attribute. Listing 3.62 demonstrates this by creating a selector in the init target, and then using it in the copy target.

Listing 3.62   *Creating a Selector for Later Use*

```
<target name="init">
    <selector id="copySelector">
        <and>
            <filename name="**/*Test*.java"/>
            <date datetime="07/21/2002 12:00 PM" when="before"/>
            <size value="1" units="Ki" when="more"/>
        </and>
    </selector>
</target>

<target name="copy" depends="init">
    <copy todir="${tmp.dir}">
        <fileset dir="${src.dir}" includes="**/*.java">
            <selector refid="copySelector"/>
        </fileset>
    </copy>
</target>
```

Class FileSet

There is a variation of the FileSet in the optional package called a Class FileSet. It is used in a similar fashion to FileSet, but it operates on classes. It provides the same attributes as a regular FileSet, but it has an additional one. Class FileSet works off the notion of a root file. After you've specified a root file, it selects all files on which the root class depends. You can specify multiple root files and you can specify a Root FileSet to get the dependencies for several files at one time. Listing 3.63 demonstrates copying all .class files that the class myproject.test.TestClass0 depends on.

Listing 3.63   *Copying the Dependencies of a Class*

```
<classfileset id="testClasses" dir="${build.dir.classes}"
    rootclass="myproject.test.TestClass0"/>

<target name="copy" depends="init">
    <copy todir="${test.dir}">
        <fileset refid="testClasses"/>
    </copy>
</target>
```

Notice that we defined a classfileset outside of a target. Class FileSets can be defined both in and out of a target. They can't be used inside another task, however. This seems odd because FileSets can be used inside another task. The way around this is to define your Class FileSet, give it an ID, and then reference this ID with a fileset tag as in Listing 3.63.

If you want to specify more than one root file, you can use the nested root tags. Listing 3.64 will copy all dependencies of the two classes listed in the root tags.

Listing 3.64   *Copying the Dependencies of Two Classes*

```
<classfileset id="testClasses" dir="${build.dir.classes}">
    <root classname="myproject.test.TestClass0"/>
</classfileset>

<target name="copy" depends="init">
    <copy todir="${test.dir}">
        <fileset refid="testClasses"/>
    </copy>
</target>
```

Finally, if you have several classes that you need to generate dependencies for, the nested rootfileset tag is the ticket. It looks just like a fileset tag and using it will result in the classes matching it to be used by the containing Class FileSet to generate dependencies. Listing 3.65 demonstrates selecting files that are depended on by all the test classes.

Listing 3.65   *Copying the Dependencies of Several Classes*

```
<classfileset id="testClasses" dir="${build.dir.classes}">
    <rootfileset dir="${build.dir.classes}" includes="**/Test*.class"/>
</classfileset>

<target name="copy" depends="init">
    <copy todir="${test.dir}">
        <fileset refid="testClasses"/>
    </copy>
</target>
```

Path-Like Structures

It sounds like an odd thing, but it is extremely useful and you'll be using them a lot. A path-like structure is essentially a platform-aware path or classpath. You can create these structures much more easily than setting up a system classpath, and then pass them to tasks that need them. You can create paths by specifying directories or JARs directly, but you can also nest FileSets or DirSets inside them to quickly add several jars or directories. Listing 3.66 shows a quick example of creating a classpath. Notice that we specify two JAR files directly, and then we add *all* the JARs in the ${lib.dir} using a FileSet.

Listing 3.66   *Setting Up a Classpath*

```
<path id="classpath">
    <pathelement path="${xalan.dir}/xalan.jar"/>
    <pathelement path="${castor.jar}"/>
    <fileset dir="${lib.dir}">
        <include name="**/*.jar"/>
    </fileset>
</path>
```

This block can live inside a target, such as init, or it can live outside of any target. I prefer to have it live inside init rather than floating around by itself. You can still access it from any target, which is what you want. You can reference this path inside another path using its refid, and you can pass it to javac and other tasks in the same manner. Listing 3.67 uses the path defined in Listing 3.66 as the classpath for javac.

Listing 3.67   *Using a Classpath*

```
<javac srcdir="${src.dir}" destdir="${build.dir.classes}">
    <classpath refid="classpath"/>
</javac>
```

You can also reference one path from within another and add more to it. For example, you may define a classpath in your init target that has the common classes that several tasks will need, but when you compile, you need to add another JAR file. This is easily accomplished and Listing 3.68 demonstrates this. It creates the initial classpath in init, and then adds to it at compile time.

Listing 3.68   *Using a Classpath*

```
<target name="init">
    <path id="classpath">
        <pathelement path="${xalan.dir}/xalan.jar"/>
        <pathelement path="${castor.jar}"/>
        <fileset dir="${lib.dir}">
            <include name="**/*.jar"/>
        </fileset>
    </path>
</target>

<target name="compile" depends="init">
    <javac srcdir="${src.dir}" destdir="${build.dir.classes}">
        <classpath>
            <path refid="classpath"/>
            <pathelement path="${oro.jar}"/>
        </classpath>
    </javac>
</target>
```

You can see from this simple example that path-like structures are quite powerful. They are certainly easier and less error-prone than trying to set your classpath either at a system level or in the Ant startup script.

XMLCatalog

The final data type is the XMLCatalog. It is used to create a repository of XML DTDs or entities for quick resolution without having to go to the Internet. This enables you to store DTDs locally, even though the public ID says they live elsewhere. This saves time when processing an XML document that needs the DTD or elements. The only tasks that currently work with an XMLCatalog are the `xslt` core task and the optional `xmlvalidate`. To create an XMLCatalog with a DTD in it, you must first copy the DTD to a local directory. Then you create the XMLCatalog in your `init` target and reference it later. Listing 3.69 creates an XMLCatalog with the DTD for the Enterprise JavaBeans deployment descriptor. It then references this catalog in an `xmlvalidate` task.

Listing 3.69   *Creates and Uses an XMLCatalog*

```
<target name="init">
    <xmlcatalog id="ejbDTDs">
        <dtd
        publicId="-//Sun Microsystems, Inc.//DTD Enterprise JavaBeans 2.0//EN"
        location="c:/DTDs/ejb-jar-2.0.dtd"/>
        <dtd
        publicId="-//Sun Microsystems, Inc.//DTD Enterprise JavaBeans 1.1//EN"
        location="ejb-jar-1.1.dtd"/>
    </xmlcatalog>
</target>

<target name="validate" depends="init">
    <xmlvalidate file="${etc.dir}/ejb-jar.xml">
        <xmlcatalog refid="ejbDTDs"/>
    </xmlvalidate>
</target>
```

Notice that the listing specifies two DTDs. The first uses a location with an absolute path, whereas the second uses a relative path. This relative path is relative to the `basedir` that you set in your project tag.

Listeners and Loggers

We need to briefly touch on two other concepts: listeners and loggers. A *listener* is a component that is alerted to certain events during the life of a build. A *logger* is built on top of a listener, and is the component that is responsible for logging information about the build.

Listeners are alerted to seven different events:

- Build started
- Build finished

- Target started

- Target finished

- Task started

- Task finished

- Message logged

These events should trigger some action in the listener.

For the most part, you really need to know about listeners and what they respond to only if you're trying to write your own custom task or logger. You can read about building such elements in Chapter 6, "Extending Ant with Custom Tasks, Data Types, and Listeners."

Loggers, however, are far more interesting and useful. You're using a logger whenever you run Ant, whether or not you specify one. If you don't specify a logger, you're using the DefaultLogger. In addition to the DefaultLogger, Ant comes with four standard loggers and one standard listener. They are

- DefaultLogger

- NoBannerLogger

- MailLogger

- AnsiColorLogger

- XmlLogger

- Log4jListener

Here's a rundown of what each one does, how you use it, and why you'd use it.

DefaultLogger

The DefaultLogger is used if you don't tell Ant to use something different. It is singularly unimpressive, but it does its job and does it well. Although you *can* tell Ant specifically to use this logger, there is really no good reason to do so. For the record, Listing 3.70 shows how to force Ant to use the DefaultLogger.

Listing 3.70   *Forcing Use of the DefaultLogger*

```
ant -logger org.apache.tools.ant.DefaultLogger
```

NoBannerLogger

The NoBannerLogger is very similar to the DefaultLogger, except it doesn't log anything from targets that don't log anything. When you run Ant, each target's name prints at the left-most column, followed by a colon, and then the name of each task contained inside it is printed in brackets. This occurs even if there is no useful output from any of the tasks.

If you want to suppress this output, use the NoBannerLogger. This logger still logs any useful information that is logged, but does not log anything for targets or tasks that don't make any "noise," so to speak. Invoke it as shown in Listing 3.71.

Listing 3.71 *Invoking Ant with the NoBannerLogger*

```
ant -logger org.apache.tools.ant.NoBannerLogger
```

MailLogger

The MailLogger logs whatever messages come its way, and then sends them in an e-mail. A group of properties must be set for MailLogger to do its job. These properties can be passed into Ant from the command line using the standard Java -D syntax or, more easily, in <property> statements in your init target. Or, easiest of all, by specifying a properties file. The properties are

- MailLogger.mailhost—Defaults to "localhost"

- MailLogger.from—You have to set this to a good "from" address

- MailLogger.failure.notify—Whether to send an e-mail on build failure; defaults to true

- MailLogger.success.notify—Whether to send an e-mail on build success; defaults to true

- MailLogger.failure.to—A comma-separated list of e-mail addresses to send to on build failure

- MailLogger.success.to—A comma-separated list of e-mail addresses to send to on build success

- MailLogger.failure.subject—The subject of the e-mail on build failure; defaults to "Build Failure"

- MailLogger.success.subject—The subject of the e-mail on build success; defaults to "Build Success"

- MailLogger.properties.file—The name of a properties file that contains properties for the logger

Just like before, to use this logger, you pass Ant the `-logger` command-line option and the logger's class name as in Listing 3.72.

Listing 3.72   *Using the MailLogger*

```
ant -logger org.apache.tools.ant.listener.MailLogger
```

AnsiColorLogger

If you're running Ant inside an XTerm window that supports color or a Windows *9x* command shell with `ANSI.SYS` loaded, the `AnsiColorLogger` can produce color output. Unfortunately, it won't work under Windows NT/2000 in the CMD shell. I also tested it using 4NT (a popular Cmd.exe replacement), but it didn't work there either.

You can specify certain ANSI color sequences for different types of messages based on severity. In other words, info messages are a different color than errors. You don't have to specify colors; you can just use the defaults. There are lots of codes that you can use to specify which colors you want. Consult the Ant documentation for the full list. Listing 3.73 shows the command line to use this logger.

Listing 3.73   *Using the AnsiColorLogger*

```
ant -logger org.apache.tools.ant.listener.AnsiColorLogger
```

XmlLogger

With XML being such a hot topic, and everything seemingly needing to import, export, and support XML, Ant comes with a logger that logs everything to an XML file. This logger behaves differently depending on whether it is invoked as a listener or a logger. In listener mode, the property called `XmlLogger.file` (set in your init target, at the command line with `-D`, or in a properties file), determines where the XML output goes. If this property is not set, the output goes to a file called `log.xml`. In logger mode, all output goes to the console unless the `-logger` command-line option is used and specifies a file to write to.

You can set a property called `ant.XmlLogger.stylesheet` to point to the XSL stylesheet of your choice. If you don't specify a stylesheet, the XML file will point to one called `log.xsl` in the current directory. If you don't want stylesheet support built into your XML file, set this property to an empty string. Listing 3.74 shows command lines for starting Ant with the `XmlLogger` in both listener and logger modes.

Listing 3.74 *Both Ways to Use XmlLogger*

```
ant -listener org.apache.tools.ant.XmlLogger
ant -logger org.apache.tools.ant.XmlLogger -logfile output.xml
```

Log4jListener

Finally, we come to the sole listener amongst the loggers, `Log4jListener`. You need to have `Log4j` installed and configured for this listener to work. What happens is that each listener event is delivered to `Log4j` with the class name of the sender of the event as the Log4j Category. All the start events are sent as INFO-level messages; finish events are sent as INFO if they succeed, and ERROR otherwise. Your `Log4j` settings will determine what gets sent to your log. You certainly have the most freedom and capability using this listener, but it would most likely be for very specialized uses. Listing 3.75 shows how to invoke Ant with the `Log4jListener` running.

Listing 3.75 *Using the Log4jListener*

```
ant -listener org.apache.tools.ant.Log4jListener
```

Predefined Properties

As you've seen already, the `property` task sets properties that can be referenced later. Ant provides a handful of predefined properties as well as making all the standard Java system properties available. The five Ant-defined properties are

- basedir—The value that you set in the basedir attribute of the project tag
- ant.file—The full path name of the build file being executed
- ant.version—The version of the currently executing Ant instance
- ant.project.name—The value from the name attribute of the project tag
- ant.java.version—The version of the Java VM that Ant detected at runtime

You can access any of these properties from your own targets. For example, if you wanted to name a JAR file with the same name as the project, you could write a property as shown in Listing 3.76.

Listing 3.76　*Referencing a Predefined Property*

```
<property name="jar.name" value="${ant.project.name}.jar"/>
```

Similarly, you can get to any property that would be returned by a call to `System.getProperties()` in your Java code. Some of these properties include:

- os.name—The operating system Ant is running on

- os.version—The version of the current operating system

- java.class.path—The classpath Ant is using

- user.home—The current user's home directory

Many more system properties are available. Consult the JavaDoc for `java.lang.System.getProperties()` for the full list.

The Ant Command Line

We've already discussed a few of the Ant command-line switches and arguments, but we need to spend a little time covering all of them. There really aren't that many, but they can fundamentally change the way Ant works.

The general format of an Ant command line looks like Listing 3.77.

Listing 3.77　*General Form of Ant Command Line*

```
ant [options] [target...]
```

Notice that you can specify multiple targets on the command line and they will be executed in the order you gave them. This is optional, and if no targets are given, the default target will be executed.

The options that Ant supports are

- -help prints a usage message.

- -version prints the version of Ant and exits.

- -projecthelp displays the names and descriptions of targets in the build file.

- -quiet suppresses most output messages to the console.

- -verbose displays more information about what the build is doing.

- -debug displays more information than you probably want about what the build is doing.

- -emacs prints console output in a format that Emacs can parse.

- -logfile <filename> sends all console output to the given filename.

- -logger <log class> uses the specified class to log messages.

- -listener <listener class> uses the specified class to process build events.

- -buildfile <build filename> uses the specified build file instead of build.xml.

- -find [build filename] searches for a build.xml file (or the specified filename.

- -Dkey=value sets a Java property for Ant to use.

- -propertyfile <filename> sets properties for every line in the specified file.

- inputhandler <inputhandler class> uses the specified class to process interactive user input.

We'll now discuss each of these with a bit of explanation. We'll begin with -projecthelp because -help and -version are self-explanatory.

-projecthelp

This switch is extremely useful, especially with a new project or if you've just gotten a build file from someone else. It will print the names and descriptions of each target in the file, indicating which target is the default. Listing 3.78 shows the output using the build file for Ant itself.

Listing 3.78 *Shows -projecthelp Output*

```
Buildfile: build.xml
Main targets:

allclean           --> cleans up everything
bootstrap          --> creates a bootstrap build
build              --> compiles the source code
clean              --> cleans up build and dist directories
dist               --> creates a complete distribution
dist-lite          --> creates a minimum distribution to run Apache Ant
distribution       --> creates the full Apache Ant distribution
interactive-tests  --> runs interactive tests
jars               --> creates the Apache Ant jars
```

Listing 3.78   *(continued)*

```
javadocs               --> creates the API documentation
main                   --> creates a minimum distribution in ./dist
main_distribution      --> creates the zip and tar distributions
run-single-test        --> runs the single unit test defined in the testcase
                           property
src-dist               --> creates a source distribution
test                   --> run JUnit tests
test-jar               --> creates the Apache Ant Test Utilties jar
test-javadocs          --> creates the API documentation for test utilities

Default target: main
```

You can see from the last line that if you do not specify a target to execute, the target called main will be run.

Notice that each of the targets has some descriptive text after the name. This is taken from the description attribute of each target. If you don't specify any description attributes, Ant will display all of your targets in response to a -projecthelp. As soon as you specify one target with a description attribute, Ant will display only those targets that have a description. So, after you start setting descriptions, you have to take it to completion if you want your project help to be useful. You can omit descriptions for targets that are purely internal to the build and should never be called by a user.

-quiet, -verbose, and -debug

These three switches control how much or how little information is sent to the logger or console. -quiet will output only errors, which is quite a bit less text than running Ant without -quiet. -verbose will print several hundred lines of information, showing properties, classpaths, and other settings; -debug prints an even more in-depth listing. If you're having problems with a build, try using one of these two switches to increase the amount of output. One interesting thing that will be displayed when using -verbose or -debug is that FileSets will display the files they are processing and whether or not they have been selected.

-emacs

If you are executing Ant from within Emacs, you must use this switch to cause Ant to alter its output so that Emacs can parse it. If you do this, Emacs will be able to take you to the source of errors in your source file. Otherwise, you'll have to manually navigate to these locations.

-logfile <filename>

By default, Ant logs everything to the console. You can redirect this output to a file by specifying the `-logfile` switch and giving a filename to log to. If there is already a file with that name, it will be overwritten.

-logger <log class>, -listener <listener class>

`-logger` enables you to replace the `DefaultLogger` with a different logger. `-listener` enables you to replace the event listener. Consult the "Listeners and Loggers" section earlier in this chapter for more details and a list of available loggers and listeners.

-buildfile <build filename>

By default Ant looks for a file called `build.xml` in the current directory. If you want to specify a different file, either in the current directory or elsewhere, pass it as the parameter to the `-buildfile` switch.

-find [build filename]

The `-find` switch is similar to `-buildfile` in that it lets you give an alternative build file to execute. However, instead of telling Ant specifically where the file is, the `-find` switch forces Ant to search for the alternative build file. If you don't give a filename, Ant will search for `build.xml`. The search rules are contrary to what you might expect, however. You would generally expect a find to start in the current directory and work *down*. The `-find` switch actually searches from the current directory *up*. In other words, it would first look for the build file in the current directory, and then it would move to its parent, and then its parent, and so forth, either until it found a build file or reached the drive root.

-Dkey=value

The `-D` switch is identical to the Java `-D` switch; it enables you to set properties from the command line. For example, if you had a target that executes only if the `release.build` property has been set, you could run Ant as in Listing 3.79 to set this property.

Listing 3.79 *Setting a Property from the Command Line*

```
ant -Drelease.build=true build
```

> **Note**
> It is important to note that properties set on the command line take precedence over those set by <property> tasks or in properties files. This is useful to occasionally change a property that needs to be at its default most of the time.

-propertyfile <filename>

This switch is equivalent to specifying a `loadproperties` task inside your build file. It will load all the key/value pairs from this properties file as properties that can be used in your build.

-inputhandler <inputhandler class>

This switch is a bit more esoteric than the others. Its purpose is to specify a different class to handle user input during the `<input>` task. This task enables you to prompt your user for input to answer build questions, and so on. The `input` task is covered in Chapter 4.

Summary

This chapter began with a study of a useful standard development directory tree. You'll find lots of projects that use this format or one very close to it. Whatever directory structure you choose, remember to keep your source files separated from your binary output, and to place your source files in package-structure directories under your source folder.

Next, we covered the basic targets that every Ant build file you create will most likely have. We discussed the common names for these targets and what each target does. Simple examples of each target were provided.

We moved on to discuss the data types that Ant provides for filtering and selecting directories, files, and text. Combining these data types with the built-in and optional tasks you will learn about in Chapters 4 and 5 will greatly help you in your development.

Next up, we moved on to cover listeners and loggers, which enable you to change the status output from your Ant builds. Listeners are geared more toward those who want to write custom tasks and loggers (with the exception being the `Log4j` listener), whereas loggers can be used by anyone. Several loggers are provided, and each supplies a different set of output data. We then briefly discussed the properties that Ant predefines for you and how to access Java system properties.

Finally, we discussed the Ant command line and the different options and arguments that enable you to control how Ant does its work.

CHAPTER 4

Built-In Tasks

Ant provides a large selection of tasks to use within projects that, as a whole, cover considerable ground. From the simplest task of creating a directory to querying a database, there are more than enough tasks for even the most complex of projects. Even more tasks are available through the optional tasks (see Chapter 5 for some optional tasks) and through building your own custom tasks (addressed in Chapter 6). This chapter, however, describes built-in tasks: the set of tasks that are immediately available when Ant is installed. By providing the details of the attributes of each task, nested elements that can be used, and examples of each attribute's use, this chapter should serve as an essential reference guide.

Note
This chapter is the longest in the book. It covers all the core tasks and gives you all the information you need to use them. It's not a chapter that requires you to read it from start to finish, but it's nonetheless a central chapter in your understanding of the power that the core Ant tasks offer you.

Common Attributes of All Tasks

Before we begin describing each of task and its unique attributes, you should be aware of a set of attributes that are common to all tasks. These (all optional) attributes are described in Table 4.1.

Table 4.1   *Table of Common Attributes*

Attributes (Optional)	Description
Id	The unique ID for this task instance, which allows it to be referenced from other tasks.
taskname	Specifies an alternative name for the task instance. This will be displayed in the task's output.
description	Allows you to comment tasks.

\<ant>

The \<ant> task enables you to run Ant on a given build file, which gives you the flexibility to use multiple Ant files within a project. Table 4.2 displays the attributes of the task.

> **Caution**
> It's important to note that properties set in the parent project will override properties set in the new project unless inheritall is set to false. Otherwise, it could be the cause of some bemusement.

Table 4.2   *Table of \<ant> Attributes*

Attributes (Optional)	Description
antfile	The name of the build file to use. Defaults to build.xml.
dir	The name of the directory to be used as the basedir for the new project. Defaults to the current directory.
InheritAll	If true, all the properties of the currently running project are passed to the new project. Defaults to true.
InheritRefs	If true, all the references of the currently running project are passed to the new project. Defaults to false.
Output	If specified, the output from the new project will be written to the supplied file. Defaults to the System output.
Target	The target to execute in the given Ant file. This defaults to the default target in the build file.

Nested Elements

You can nest \<property> elements to set properties for the new project. These override properties are set within the new task itself, regardless of the value of the inheritAll attribute.

Should you want to copy references into the new project, you can specify nested `<reference>` elements. See Table 4.3 for the `<reference>` attributes.

Table 4.3   *Table of <reference> Attributes*

Attributes	Description
Required	
Refid	The ID of the reference to be copied.
Optional	
Torefid	The ID to give the copied reference. Defaults to refid.

Examples

The easiest way to see this in action is using it to execute another task within the current build file. The following example will execute the `compile` task in the `build.xml` file in the current working directory, and write output to the `System` output (although `<antcall>` [see next task] will do the same thing).

```
<ant target="compile"/>
```

A more probable example is to use this task to run subproject tasks. The following example would run the default target in the project defined in the build file `ui.xml`, and set the property `someproperty` within the new project:

```
<ant target="" dir="" antfile="ui.xml">
  <property name="someproperty" value="yes"/>
</ant>
```

<antcall>

The `<antcall>` task allows Ant to be invoked from within a running Ant process. In other words, it enables you to call another target from within the current one. The restriction that makes this task fundamentally different from the `<ant>` task is that the target you want to call must be within the same build file. Table 4.4 shows the attributes of the `<antcall>` task.

This task offers more control than using `depends` to execute other targets and also facilitates modularization. For example, you can reuse a target by passing it different parameters.

Table 4.4   *Table of <antcall> Attributes*

Attributes	Description
Required	
target	The target to execute.
Optional	
inheritAll	If true, all the properties of the current running project are passed to the new project. Defaults to true.
inheritRefs	If true, all the references of the current running project are passed to the new project. Defaults to false.

Nested Elements

<param> elements can be nested in this task, allowing you to specify properties to pass to the called target. These elements share the same attributes as the property task.

Nested <reference> elements may also be used to copy references (refer to the <ant> task for attributes).

Examples

In the simple example that follows, the <antcall> will result in the execution of the echovar target. The echovar target will display the value of the property var, which has been set to yes by the <antcall>.

```
<target name="antcalltest">
  <antcall target="echovar">
    <param name="var" value="yes"/>
  </antcall>
</target>

<target name="echovar">
  <echo message="${var}"/>
</target>
```

<antstructure>

You can use <antstructure> to generate a DTD (Document Type Definition) for Ant build files. It contains information about the available Ant tasks and lists all the attributes associated to each task. However, it does not differentiate between required and optional attributes—all attributes are listed as `#IMPLIED`. Neither does it include any custom tasks added via the `<taskdef>` task. Michel Casabianca provides a solution to this problem at `http://www.sdv.fr/pages/casa/html/ant-dtd.en.html` although it should be noted that the solution is based on Ant 0.3.1.

One further problem with the `<antstructure>` task is that it does not necessarily generate a valid DTD. Due to the fact that Ant allows task writers to define arbitrary elements, name collisions can and will happen. Because DTDs do not provide a rich enough syntax to support this, the problem remains unsolved.

Table 4.5 provides a list of the `<antstructure>` attributes.

Table 4.5 *Table of <antstructure> Attributes*

Attributes (Required)	Description
output	The name of the file to output the DTD to.

Example

The following example results in the generation of the file `out.dtd`, which contains the Ant build file DTD:

```
<antstructure output="out.dtd"/>
```

<apply>/<execon>

The `<apply>` task is basically an extension of the `<exec>` task (as you can see by the similar set of attributes listed in Table 4.6), allowing for the provision of a set of files as arguments to the executable.

Table 4.6 *Table of <apply>/<execon> Attributes*

Attributes	Description
Required	
dest (if a nested mapper is specified)	The directory where the target files will be placed by the command when executed.
executable (if command not specified)	The command to execute.

Table 4.6   *(continued)*

Attributes	Description
Optional	
dir	The base directory in which to execute the command.
failonerror	If set to true, the build process will stop if the command exits with a return code other than 0. Defaults to false.
newenvironment	If true, the old environment will not be propagated when new environment variables are specified. Defaults to false.
os	The operating system(s) that support this command. If Ant is running on an operating system other than the one(s) specified, this task will not be executed. The name of the operating system is obtained from the os.name Java system property. Note that the match is case sensitive, and so must exactly match the format in which Java stores it. If a value is not given, the task is executed on all operating systems.
output	The name of a file for the output to be stored.
outputproperty	The name of a property for the output to be stored.
parallel	If true, all the files specified will be appended to the command as arguments. Otherwise, the command will be executed once for each file. Defaults to false.
relative	If true, filenames will be passed on the command line as relative paths as opposed to absolute. Defaults to false.
skipemptyfiles	If true, the command will not be run on empty filesets. Defaults to false.
timeout	Stops the command if it does not complete within the time specified (in milliseconds).
type	Valid values are file, dir, or both. Defaults to file.
vmlauncher	If set to true, the command will be run using the Java virtual machine's (VM's) execution facilities where available. If set to false, will be run using the underlying OS's shell, either directly or through the antRun scripts. Under some operating systems, this will give access to facilities not normally available through the VM; for example, under Windows, being able to execute scripts rather than their associated interpreter. Defaults to false.

Nested Elements

Nested <fileset> elements enable you to specify the files that will be passed to the system command as arguments.

`<arg>` and `<env>` elements can be nested as with the `<exec>` task to specify command-line arguments and environment variables.

Two further elements can be nested to indicate the desired position of the source files and target files within the command-line arguments. By default, all the arguments are listed first, followed by the source files, but target files are not listed. By positioning `<srcfile>` and `<targetfile>` elements, you can designate where in the command line they will appear. These elements are simply placeholders and so have no attributes. If you specify a `<targetfile>` element, you also have to set the destdir attribute and define a nested mapper.

Examples

This example, written to run on Linux only, will run grep passing the arguments -l someexpression logs/error.log logs/run.log (assuming the fileset includes error.log and run.log only). If parallel is set to false, this would result in grep being run for each of the two files; that is, grep -l someexpression logs/error.log and grep -l someexpression logs/run.log.

```
<apply executable="grep" os="linux" parallel="true">
  <arg value="-l"/>
  <arg value="someexpression"/>
  <fileset dir="logs" includes="**/*.log"/>
</apply>
```

The following trivial example illustrates how a nested `<srcfile>` argument can be used. For each .txt file in the fileset, the command somecmd will be executed with the name of the .txt file as the first argument, and the second argument being -p.

```
<apply executable="somecmd">
  <srcfile/>
  <arg value="-p"/>
  <fileset dir="." includes="*.txt"/>
</apply>
```

`<available>`

The `<available>` task enables you to check the availability of a resource, be it a class, file, directory, or a resource in the JVM. The result of the execution of the task is that a given property will be set (to a value of true by default) if the resource is accessible. Hence, you can execute other tasks on the condition of a resource being available.

Table 4.7 shows the list of attributes associated with this task.

Table 4.7   *Table of <available> Attributes*

Attributes	Description
Required	
classname (required if file or resource not given)	The name of the class to check the availability of in the class path.
file (required if classname of resource not given)	The name of the file whose availability is being checked.
property	The name of the property to set.
resource (required if classname or file not given)	The resource in the JVM whose availability is being checked.
Optional	
classpath	The class path to use.
classpathref	A reference to a PATH defined elsewhere that is to be used as the class path.
filepath	The path to use when checking the availability of a file.
ignoresystemclasses	If true, the Ant runtime classes will be ignored for the classname attribute. Defaults to false.
type	If looking for a file, this attribute should be used to specify whether you're looking for a file or dir. If this is not specified, the task will be successful if either a file or directory is found.
value	The value to give the property if the availability check succeeds. Defaults to true.

Nested Elements

Nested <classpath> and <filepath> elements are supported in this task to specify values for the classpath and filepath attributes.

Examples

This trivial example illustrates the use of <available> to check for the availability of a class. In this case, we're checking for the class that implements the <available> task. (Of course, we know it exists—otherwise we would not be able to run it!) The example will result in the setting of the property availableClass to true.

```
<available property="availableClass"
  classname="org.apache.tools.ant.taskdefs.Available"/>
```

`<available>` is useful in numerous situations. This example demonstrates how `<available>` can be used to decide whether a target should be executed. The execution of the target doSomething will take place only if the resourcesAvailable property has been set.

```
<target name="resourceTest">
  <available property="resourcesAvailable"
    file="data.xml"/>
</target>

<target name="doSomething" depends="resourceTest" if="resourcesAvailable">
÷
</target>
```

For more flexibility, look at the `<condition>` task, which enables you to set properties based on more complex conditions.

`<basename>`

The `<basename>` task can be used to determine the last element in a given path, be it relative, absolute, or just a simple filename. The specified property will be given this value. It is a simple task with only three attributes, as listed in Table 4.8.

Table 4.8 *Table of `<basename>` Attributes*

Attributes	Description
Required	
file	The full or relative path of the file from which the `<basename>` will be taken. Note that the file does not have to exist.
property	The property to set the value of.
Optional	
suffix	If the specified file ends with the specified suffix (with or without the "."), it will be removed.

Examples

The following example results in the property `filename` being set to `chapter4.doc`:

```
<basename property="filename"
  file="C:\Documents\Sams\AntHandbook\chapter4.doc"
/>
```

This example, in which just a simple filename (`build.bat`) is given, results in the `batchfile` property being set to `build`:

```
<basename property="batchfile" suffix="bat" file="build.bat"/>
```

<buildnumber>

The `<buildnumber>` task assists in the tracking of build numbers. It's a simple task that uses a file to get the current build number. The result of its execution is that the property `build.number` is set to the number read from the file, and the number in the file is incremented.

There is only one attribute as listed in Table 4.9. If the file specified does not exist, it will be created and the build number will be set to 0.

Table 4.9   *Table of <buildnumber> Attributes*

Attributes (Optional)	Description
file	The name of the file containing the build number. Defaults to build.number.

Example

In the following example, the file attribute is not specified, which will result in one of two actions. If the file `build.number` exists, the property `build.number` will be set to the value obtained from the file. The number in the file will subsequently be incremented. If the file `build.number` cannot be found, it will be created and the property `build.number` will be set to 0.

```
<buildnumber/>
```

<Bunzip2>

This task is the same as the `<gunzip>` task, except that the file is compressed with the BZip2 algorithm. See the "`<gunzip>`" section later in this chapter for more information.

<BZip2>

This task is the same as the `<gzip>` task, except that the file is compressed with the BZip2 algorithm. See the "`<gzip>`" section later in this chapter for more information.

<checksum>

The `<checksum>` task enables you to generate checksums for a set of files using a specified algorithm. Checksum verification can also be performed using this task.

For example, this can be used to generate checksum files for distributions. You'll see that you can download checksums for the Ant files.

Table 4.10 gives a rundown of the attributes for this task.

Table 4.10 *Table of <checksum> Attributes*

Attributes	Description
Required	
file (unless a nested fileset is specified)	The file to generate the checksum for.
Optional	
algorithm	The algorithm to use to generate the checksum value. Defaults to MD5.
fileext	The file extension to use for the generated checksum file. Defaults to the name of the algorithm being used.
property	The property to set with the checksum value. Use when specifying a single file.
provider	The provider of the algorithm.
forceoverwrite	If true, existing files will be overwritten even if the new files are more up-to-date. Defaults to false.
verifyproperty	If set, the task will be in verify mode. The property specified will be set to true or false if the generated checksum is equal to the checksum contained in the checksum file or property (if specified).

Nested Elements

Nested filesets are supported in specifying the files to generate checksums for.

Examples

The following example will generate a checksum for the file `chapter4.doc` using the MD5 algorithm. The `chksum` property will be set to the generated checksum. Omitting the `property` attribute would result in that same value being placed in a file `chapter4.doc.MD5`, assuming that it did not already exist.

```
<checksum file="chapter4.doc" property="chksum"/>
```

In the following example, a checksum will be generated for each file in the fileset (that is, `foo.txt` and `bar.txt`) and stored in the corresponding file with the MD5 extension (that is, `foo.txt.MD5` and `bar.txt.MD5`):

```
<checksum>
  <fileset dir="misc">
    <include name="foo.txt"/>
    <include name="bar.txt"/>
  </fileset>
</checksum>
```

Building on the previous example, you can verify a set of files given a set of corresponding files containing the checksum. In this example, the `<checksum>` task will verify that the checksum of the files `foo.txt` and `bar.txt` matches those within the files `foo.txt.MD5` and `bar.txt.MD5`. If successful, the `verified` property will be set to `true`; otherwise, it will be set to `false`.

```
<checksum verifyproperty="verified">
  <fileset dir="misc">
    <include name="foo.txt"/>
    <include name="bar.txt"/>
  </fileset>
</checksum>
```

The following example is similar, but demonstrates how to use the `property` attribute to verify a file. The checksum of the file `foo.jar` is checked against the value of the property `foo.MD5`. Again, if successful, the `verified` property is set to `true`; otherwise, it will be set to `false`.

```
<checksum file="foo.jar"
  property="foo.MD5"
  verifyproperty="verified"/>
```

\<chmod>

\<chmod> gives you the ability to change the permission of a file, directory, or set of files under UNIX. (It currently has no effect under other operating systems.) To that end, the permission attribute value is also specified in UNIX style; for example, ug+rwx. This attribute and the rest of the tasks attributes are detailed in Table 4.11.

Table 4.11   *Table of \<chmod> Attributes*

Attributes	Description
Required	
dir (required if file and fileset are not specified)	The name of a directory that holds the files whose permissions are to be changed.
file (required if dir and fileset are not specified)	The name of the single file or directory whose permissions are to be changed.
perm	The new permissions to apply.
Optional	
defaultexcludes	If false, default excludes will not be used. Defaults to true.
excludes	A comma-separated list of patterns of files to be excluded. The default is not to exclude any files (except default excludes).
includes	A comma-separated list of patterns of files to be included. The default is to include all files.
parallel	If enabled, all the specified files will be processed in a single chmod command. Defaults to true.
type	Specifies which types are considered in the chmod operation: file, dir, or both. Defaults to file.

Nested Elements

The \<chmod> task supports \<fileset> elements in specifying the files to operate on.

Example

This example adds the execute permission to the user and group permissions for the antbook.txt file.

```
<chmod file="antbook.txt" perm="ug+x"/>
```

<concat>

The `<concat>` task is used to concatenate a set of files, and produces a single output file. It also permits the concatenation of a string to a file (although not at the same time). The set of `<concat>` attributes is listed in Table 4.12.

Table 4.12 *Table of <concat> Attributes*

Attributes (Optional)	Description
append	If true and the destination file already exists, it will be appended to rather than overwritten. Defaults to true.
destfile	The destination file for the concatenated stream. The default is to output to the console.
encoding	The encoding for the input files. Defaults to the platform's default character encoding.

Nested Elements

`<fileset>` and `<filelist>` elements can be nested in specifying the files to concatenate. Filelists should be used in cases in which ordering matters because ordering cannot be guaranteed when filesets are used.

Examples

Executing the following example would result in the string `Testing Concat!` being appended to the file `build.log`. If `build.log` does not exist, it will be created and the string will be added to it.

```
<concat destfile="build.log">Testing concat!</concat>
```

The following example will result in the creation of the file `foo.txt`, which will contains the contents of all the `.txt` files in the `bar` directory. If the file already exists, it will be overwritten with the new file.

```
<concat destfile="foo.txt">
  <fileset dir="bar" includes="*.txt"/>
</concat>
```

<condition>

The `<condition>` task builds on the `<available>` task. It offers more flexibility when you want to conditionally set a property. Rather than specifying the condition as attribute values, `<condition>` is specified using nested elements as described in the next subsection. The attributes that can be specified are listed in Table 4.13.

Table 4.13 *Table of <condition> Attributes*

Attributes	Description
Required	
property	The name of the property to set.
Optional	
value	The value to give to the property if the condition evaluates to true. Defaults to true.

Nested Elements

The `<condition>` task supports a number of different nested elements as described in the following sections.

<not>, <and>, <or>

The `<not>`, `<and>`, and `<or>` elements behave as you would expect Boolean operators to behave, and they enable you to string together complex conditions.

Nesting a condition in the `<not>` operator will negate the result. The `<and>` and `<or>` operators accept an arbitrary number of nested conditions with the obvious behavior that the `<and>` condition will return true only if all its nested elements evaluate to true. The `<or>` condition will return true only if at least one of its conditions evaluates to true. The order of the conditions is important and can be used advantageously because the `<and>` and `<or>` operators behave lazily (that is, they behave like `&&` and `||` do in Java).

<available>, <uptodate>

The only difference in the use of the `<available>` and `<uptodate>` elements is that the `property` and `value` attributes are ignored.

<os>

The `<os>` element returns whether the operating system being used is the one specified. You'll notice in Table 4.14 that the `family` attribute is optional; however, the `<os>` element does not serve any useful purpose if `family` isn't specified.

Table 4.14   *Table of <os> Attributes*

Attributes (Optional)	Description
Arch	Specifies the architecture of the operating system to expect.
Family	The name of the operating system family to expect: windows, dos, mac, unix, netware, os/2, win9x, z/os.
Name	Specifies the name of the operating system to expect.
Version	Specifies the version of the operating system to expect.

<equals>

The <equals> element tests whether the two given strings are the same. Note that this match is case sensitive. Table 4.15 gives a full listing of the <equals> attributes.

Table 4.15   *Table of <equals> Attributes*

Attributes	Description
Required	
arg1	First string to test with.
arg2	Second string to test with.
Optional	
casesensitive	Indicates whether the match is case sensitive. Defaults to true.
trim	If true, whitespace will be trimmed from the arguments prior to the comparison. Defaults to false.

<checksum>

The <checksum> element is the same as the <checksum> task except that the property and overwrite attributes are ignored.

<isset>

A nested <isset> element can be used to test whether a property has been set. The property attribute is the tasks only attribute, as seen in Table 4.16.

Table 4.16   *Table of <isset> Attributes*

Attributes (Required)	Description
property	The property to check.

<istrue> and <isfalse>

The `<istrue>` and `<isfalse>` elements can be nested to test whether a given value is equivalent to true and false, respectively. `<istrue>` will succeed when the value is `true`, `yes`, or `on`. `<isfalse>` will succeed when the value is none of these values. Table 4.17 lists the attributes for both elements.

Table 4.17 *Table of <istrue> and <isfalse> Attributes*

Attributes (Required)	Description
value	The value to test.

<http>

Nested `<http>` elements can be used to test the response for a given URL. It is successful if the response code returned is less than 500. The element requires only the `url` attribute to be set, as seen in Table 4.18.

Table 4.18 *Table of <http> Attributes*

Attributes (Required)	Description
url	The full URL of the page to request.

<socket>

`<socket>` elements can be nested to check for the existence of a TCP/IP listener on a specified server port. Table 4.19 shows the attributes required for this element.

Table 4.19 *Table of <socket> Attributes*

Attributes (Required)	Description
port	The number of the port to check.
server	The name of the server to check.

<filesmatch>

This nested element succeeds if the two specified files match in a byte-by-byte comparison. The only attributes required (as seen in Table 4.20) are for specifying the two files to test.

Table 4.20 *Table of <filesmatch> Attributes*

Attributes (Required)	Description
file1	The first file.
file2	The file to match against.

<contains>

The <contains> element enables you to do the equivalent of str1.indexOf(str2) !=
-1 in Java. In other words, it succeeds if a specified substring is contained within another
string. Table 4.21 lists the supported attributes for <contains>.

Table 4.21 *Table of <contains> Attributes*

Attributes (Required)	Description
casesensitive	Indicates whether the comparison should be case sensitive. Defaults to true.
string	The string to search in.
substring	The string to search for.

Example

In the following example, the extModule property will be set to true if the file
${jars}/crimson.jar is available, the operating system is not UNIX, and the value of the
edition property is enterprise.

```
<condition property="extModule">
  <and>
    <available file="${jars}/crimson.jar"/>
    <not>
      <os family="unix"/>
    </not>
    <equals arg1="{edition}" arg2="enterprise"/>
  </and>
</condition>
```

<Copy>

The <copy> task enables you to copy files from one destination to another. By default, files
that already exist at the destination will be copied only if they are newer than the existing
version.

A full listing of `<copy>` attributes is given in Table 4.22.

Table 4.22 *Table of `<copy>` Attributes*

Attributes	Description
Required	
file (required if fileset elements are not specified)	The name of the file to be moved.
tofile (required if file is specified and toDir is not)	The destination file.
todir (required if toFile is specified)	The destination directory.
Optional	
failonerror	When a single file is specified, specifies whether to halt the build if the file does not exist. Defaults to true.
Filtering	If true, filtering is enabled in the move. Defaults to false.
flatten	If true, the directory structure is ignored; that is, all the files in the source fileset are moved to the source directory. Defaults to false.
includeemptydirs	If false, empty directories are ignored. Defaults to true.
overwrite	If true, existing files will be overwritten unconditionally. If false, existing files are overwritten only if older. Defaults to true.
preservelastmodified	If true, the copied files will be given the same last modified time as the original files. Defaults to false.
verbose	If true, the files that are being copied will be logged. Defaults to false.

Nested Elements

You can nest `<fileset>` elements to specify the files to copy, in which case the `toDir` attribute must be set. Nested `<mapper>` elements enable you to define the names of the destination files, whereas nested `<filterset>` and `<filterchain>` elements enable you to change the copied files.

Examples

The following example will copy the file `run.log` to the directory named `logs`:

```
<copy file = "run.log" toDir="logs"/>
```

The following example illustrates a more common task. Here, the `build.jar` file in the directory given by the `dist` property is copied to the `daily_builds` directory and the current date stamp is prepended to the filename. (See the `<tstamp>` section later in this chapter for more information about $DSTAMP.)

```
<copy file = "${dist}/build.jar" toFile="daily_builds/${DSTAMP}_build.jar"/>
```

This final example illustrates how the `<fileset>` and `<mapper>` elements can be used within a `<copy>` element. It will copy all the files with the `.java` extension in the `${source}` directory tree to the `${backup}` directory but without maintaining the directory structure. The copies will also have `.bak` appended to their names.

```
<copy todir = "${backup}" flatten=ótrueó>
  <fileset dir = "${source}">
    <include name = "**/*.java"/>
  </fileset>
  <mapper type = "glob" from = "*" to = "*.bak" />
</copy>
```

<copydir>

The `<copydir>` task has been deprecated. Use the `<copy>` task to copy directories.

<copyfile>

The `<copyfile>` task has been deprecated. Use the `<copy>` task to copy files.

<cvs>

This task gives you the ability within your Ant project to access a `cvs` repository, thus allowing you to automate version control tasks. It provides the capacity to use any valid `cvs` command, therefore you could use it to perform tasks such as tagging a release, pulling out a particular set of files, and generally maintaining a consistent way of doing these tasks throughout a project.

The prerequisite to using this task is to have `cvs` installed. You can get an installation from http://www.cvshome.org if you don't have one. Type **cvs** at the command prompt or terminal to see whether it is recognized.

Table 4.23 lists the supported attributes for the task.

Table 4.23   *Table of <cvs> Attributes*

Attributes (Optional)	Description
command	The command to execute. This can be any cvs command. Defaults to checkout.
compression	If true, compression will be used. This is equivalent to setting the compressionlevel attribute to 3. Defaults to false.
compressionlevel	The level of compression to use. Valid values are 1–9. Defaults to no compression.
cvsroot	The value for the cvsroot.
cvsrsh	The value for the cvs_rsh variable.
date	If specified, the most recent revision no later than the given date will be used.
dest	The name of the destination directory for checked out files. Defaults to the project's basedir.
error	The name of the file to direct any resultant errors to. Defaults to the Ant log file as MSG_WARN.
noexec	If true, only a report is given; that is, no changes are made to files. Defaults to false.
output	The name of the file to direct any resultant output to. Defaults to the Ant log file as MSG_INFO.
package	The name of the package/module to check out.
passfile	The name of the file to read passwords from. ~/.cvspass is the default.
port	The port number used to communicate with the server. Defaults to 2401.
quiet	Suppresses output from the executed command. Defaults to false.
tag	The name of the tag of the package or module to check out.

Examples

This simple example checks out the package com.sams.ant into the ${src} directory:

```
<cvs cvsroot=":pserver:andy@antbook.sams.com:/home/src"
  package="com.sams.ant"
  dest="${src}"/>
```

The following example updates the files previously checked out into the ${src} directory:

```
<cvs command="update" dest="${src}"/>
```

The next example shows how you could pull out a tagged set of files into a temporary folder, allowing you to use a particular release of your code:

```
<mkdir dir="tmp"/>
<cvs cvsroot=":pserver:andy@antbook.sams.com:/home/src"
command="checkout" tag="release-1_0_5" package="coms/sams/ant" dest="tmp"/>
```

Note that this is equivalent to the following:

```
<cvs cvsroot=":pserver:andy@antbook.sams.com:/home/src"
command="checkout -r release-1_0_5 com/sams/ant" dest="tmp" />
```

If you want a script for extracting a set of source files from a particular day, the following example specifies the Date attribute so that the most recent revisions with dates no later than March 28, 2002 will be checked out into the tmp directory:

```
<cvs cvsroot=":pserver:andy@muck.n-ary.com:/home/narysrc"
  command="checkout"
  date="2002-03-28"
  package="net/nary/datinguk" dest="tmp"/>
```

<cvschangelog>

The <cvschangelog> task will generate an XML file that reports the change log recorded in a CVS repository. Table 4.24 lists the <cvschangelog> attributes.

Table 4.24   *Table of <cvschangelog> Attributes*

Attributes	Description
Required	
destfile	The name to give the generated file.
Optional	
daysinpast	Specifies the number of days into the past that log information should be retrieved from.
dir	The directory from which the log command should be run.
end	Specifies the end date from which changes should be included.
start	Specifies the start date from which changes should be included.
usersfile	The name of a properties file containing a set of user-ID-to-name mappings corresponding to the way in which users should be displayed in the report.

Nested Elements

The role of nested `<user>` elements (see Table 4.25 for attributes) is to enable you to format the report so that, for example, user IDs will be replaced with a more meaningful name.

Table 4.25   *Table of `<user>` Attributes*

Attributes (Required)	Description
displayname	The name to display in the report in place of the specified user ID.
userid	The user ID from the CVS server that is to be replaced in the report.

Example

The following example will produce an XML-formatted report `changelog.xml` for changes that were made within the `src` directory over the past seven days. Where the user who made the changes has the user ID `wua`, the ID will be replaced with the value `Andy Wu` in the report.

```
<cvschangelog destfile="changelog.xml" dir="src"
  daysinpast="7">
  <user userid="wua" displayname="Andy Wu"/>
</cvschangelog>
```

`<cvspass>`

An alternative to using the login command via the `<cvs>` task is to add entries to a `.cvspass` file using `<cvspass>`. Details of the `<cvspass>` attributes are shown in Table 4.26.

Table 4.26   *Table of `<cvspass>` Attributes*

Attributes	Description
Required	
cvsroot	The cvs repository to add the entry for.
password	The password to be added to the password file.
Optional	
passfile	The name of the password file to add the entry to. Defaults to ~/.cvspass.

Example

This example creates and modifies a .cvspass file located in the user home directory with the cvsroot :pserver:andy@antbook.sams.com:/home/src and the password pass.

```
<cvspass cvsroot=":pserver:andy@antbook.sams.com:/home/src" password="pass"/>
```

<cvstagdiff>

The role of the <cvstagdiff> task is to generate a report listing the changes made to the files in a cvs repository between two dates or tags. Table 4.27 details all the attributes associated with this task.

Table 4.27   *Table of <cvstagdiff> Attributes*

Attributes* Required	Description
destfile	The name to give the generated report file.
enddate (required if endtag is not specified)	The end date from which differences are to be included in the report.
endtag (required if enddate is not specified)	The end tag from which differences are to be included in the report.
startdate (required if starttag is not specified)	The start date from which differences are to be included in the report.
starttag (required if startdate is not specified)	The start tag from which differences are to be included in the report.

*Also shares the compression, cvsroot, cvsrsh, failonerror, package, passfile, port, and quiet attributes of the <cvs> task.

Example

The easiest way to see this task in action is with the following example. It reports the differences between the files in the package jakarta-ant tagged ANT_14 and ANT_141.

```
<cvstagdiff cvsRoot=":pserver:anoncvs@cvs.apache.org:/home/cvspublic"
  destfile="tagdiff.xml"
  package="jakarta-ant"
  startTag="ANT_14"
  endTag="ANT_141"
/>
```

<delete>

The <delete> task gives you the ability to delete files and hence clean up after yourself. This is typically used to delete class files before a fresh build. The task uses the typical set of attributes (see Table 4.28) to specify the set of files to delete.

Table 4.28   *Table of <delete> Attributes*

Attributes	Description
Required	
dir (required if file and fileset elements are not specified)	The name of the directory to delete files from.
file (required if dir and fileset elements are not specified)	The name of the file to be deleted.
Optional	
defaultexcludes	If false, default excludes will not be used. Defaults to true.
excludes	A comma-separated list of patterns of files to be excluded. The default is not to exclude any files (except default excludes).
excludesfile	The name of a file that specifies a list of file patterns to exclude—one per line.
failonerror	If true, the build will be stopped if an error occurs. The error is reported to screen otherwise. Defaults to true.
includes	A comma-separated list of patterns of files to be included. The default is to include all files.
Includeemptydirs	If false, empty directories are ignored. Defaults to true.
includesfile	The name of a file that specifies a list of file patterns to include—one per line.
quiet	If true, no error is reported when a file or directory cannot be deleted. Defaults to false.
verbose	If true, the name of each deleted file will be output. Defaults to false.

Nested Elements

The <fileset> element can be nested to specify the files to be deleted.

Examples

This example shows how the `<delete>` task can be used to delete a file; in this case, `oldlog.txt`:

```
<delete file="oldlog.txt"/>
```

The following example illustrates the use of the `dir` attribute. It will recursively delete the `classes` directory; that is, all files and subdirectories within the `classes` directory will be deleted.

```
<delete dir='classes'/>
```

Finally, the following example shows how you could delete all the files that are not named `client*.bak` in a backup directory:

```
<delete>
  <fileset dir="${backup}" excludes="**\client*.bak"/>
</delete>
```

`<deltree>`

The `<deltree>` task has been deprecated. Use the `<delete>` task to delete files.

`<dependset>`

The `<dependset>` task is used to delete a set of files (target files) if any of a set of source files is more recently modified than any of the target files. So, for example, you could set up a dependency between the build file and a set of target class files to prevent changes in the build file from not being reflected in the class files.

Nested Elements

There are no attributes to set, but the `<dependset>` task must contain at least one nested `<srcfileset>`/`<srcfilelist>` and one nested `<targetfileset>`/`<targetfilelist>`. As you'd expect, the `srcfileset` and `srcfilelist` elements are used to specify the source files. Equivalently, the `targetfileset` and `targetfilelist` elements are used to specify the target files.

Note that in the case of the filelists (source or target), if any of the files do not exist, all the target files will be deleted.

Example

This example illustrates how you could delete a set of class files if the build file has been modified since the class files were produced:

```
<dependset>
  <srcfileset dir="classes">
    <include name="*.class"/>
  </srcfileset>
  <targetfilelist dir="." files="build.xml"/>
</dependset>
```

\<dirname\>

The \<dirname\> task complements the \<basename\> task. It returns the path up to, but not including, the last element in the path. So, you can set a property to the directory path of a file. Table 4.29 details the attributes of this simple-to-use task.

Table 4.29 *Table of \<dirname\> Attributes*

Attributes (Required)	Description
file	The file to find the directory path of.
property	The property to set.

Example

This example will set the `dirpath` property to the directory path of `C:\javadevelopment\misc\build.xml`, which is `C:\javadevelopment\misc`.

```
<dirname file="C:\javadevelopment\misc\build.xml"
  property="dirpath"/>
```

\<ear\>

Essentially a shortcut to a more complex \<jar\> task, the \<ear\> task enables you to create Enterprise Application archives (or EAR files). Thus giving you the ability to prepare a distribution for deployment using Ant.

Table 4.30 lists the attributes associated with the \<ear\> task.

Table 4.30   *Table of <ear> Attributes*

Attributes	Description
Required	
appxml	The deployment descriptor (application.xml) to use.
destfile	The name of the EAR file to create.
Optional	
basedir	The base directory the task will work from.
compress	If true, the data will also be compressed. Defaults to true.
defaultexcludes	If false, default excludes will not be used. Defaults to true.
encoding	The character encoding to use for filenames inside the archive. Defaults to UTF8. It is recommended that this attribute value be left as the default to avoid creating an archive that's unreadable for Java.
excludes	A comma-separated list of patterns of files to be excluded. The default is not to exclude any files (except default excludes).
excludesfile	The name of a file that specifies a list of file patterns to exclude—one per line.
filesonly	If true, only file entries will be stored. Defaults to false.
includes	A comma-separated list of patterns of files to be included. The default is to include all files.
includesfile	The name of a file that specifies a list of file patterns to include—one per line.
manifest	The name of the manifest file to use.
update	Indicates the choice of action if the file already exists. If true, the EAR will be updated; otherwise, it will be overwritten.

Nested Elements

You can use `<fileset>` and `<zipfileset>` elements within the `<ear>` tag to specify files to be included in the EAR file. In addition, the `<metainf>` element (basically a specialized fileset) can be nested to specify files to be included with the META-INF directory of the EAR file. The `<metainf>` element cannot be used to specify the manifest.mf to be used (it should be set using the manifest attribute), and attempting to include one will result in the file being ignored.

Example

The following creates an EAR file, myenterpriseapp.jar, containing the WAR and JAR files from the ${src} directory and of course, the application.xml sourced from ${misc}.

```
<ear earfile="myenterpriseapp.ear" appxml="${misc}/application.xml">
  <fileset dir="${lib}" includes="*.jar,*.war"/>
</ear>
```

<echo>

This task enables you to write a message to the System.out (which is typically the screen) or, optionally, to a file. Table 4.31 displays the <echo> attributes.

This task is particularly useful for providing additional information to the interactive Ant user and for logging additional information.

Table 4.31   *Table of <echo> Attributes*

Attributes	Description
Required	
message (unless the message is included in the body of the tag)	The message to be output.
Optional	
append	If true and a file attribute value is given, the output will be appended to the end of the file if it already exists. Defaults to false (that is, an existing file will be overwritten).
file	The name of the file to send the output to, instead of System.out.
level	Specifies the level at which the message will be reported. Valid values are debug, error, info, verbose, and warning. Defaults to warning.

Examples

The following example results in the message This is a test message being sent to the System.out:

```
<echo message="This is a test message"/>
```

This example shows how to specify a multiline message that will be written to the file nightlyBuild.log.

```
<tstamp/>
...
<echo file="nightlyBuild.log">
```

```
${TSTAMP} ${DSTAMP}
Completed compilation of ${src}
</echo>
```

<exec>

The <exec> task enables you to execute a system command. This task could potentially cripple the build file's machine independence, hence there is an attribute for specifying the operating system for this task. If an operating system(s) is specified, the command is executed only if Ant is run on that particular operating system(s). The full list of the <exec> task's attributes is given in Table 4.32.

Table 4.32 *Table of <exec> Attributes*

Attributes	Description
Required	
command (if executable is not specified)	The command to execute along with all the command-line arguments. This attribute is deprecated, and executable should be used instead along with nested <arg>s.
executable (if command is not specified)	The command to execute.
Optional	
append	If true, output will be appended to an existing file rather than the file being overwritten. Defaults to false.
dir	The base directory in which to execute the command.
failifexecutionfails	If true, the build will be stopped if the program can't start. Defaults to true.
failonerror	If set to true, the build process will stop if the command exits with a returncode other than 0. Defaults to false.
newenvironment	If true, the old environment will not be propagated when new environment variables are specified. Defaults to false.
os	The operating system(s) that support this command. If Ant is running on an operating system other than the one(s) specified, this task will not be executed. The name of the operating system is obtained from the os.name Java system property. Note that the match is case sensitive and so it must exactly match the format in which Java stores it. If a value is not given, the task is executed on all operating systems.

Table 4.32   *(continued)*

Attributes	Description
output	The name of a file for the output to be stored.
outputproperty	The name of a property for the output to be stored.
resultproperty	The name of a property for the return code to be stored.
timeout	Stops the command if it does not complete within the time specified (in milliseconds).
vmlauncher	If set to true, the command will be run using the Java VM's execution facilities where available. If set to false, the underlying OS's shell will be used, either directly or through the antRun scripts. Under some operating systems, this will give access to facilities not normally available through the VM. For example, under Windows, you would be able to execute scripts, rather than their associated interpreter. Defaults to false.

Nested Elements

Command-line arguments can be specified by nesting `<arg>` elements, whereas environment variables can be specified by nesting `<env>` elements (see Table 4.33 for `<env>` attributes).

Table 4.33   *Table of `<env>` Attributes*

Attributes (Required)	Description
key	The name of the environment variable.
file (required if path and value are not specified)	The value for the environment variable. (Ant converts this to an absolute filename.)
path (required if file and value are not specified)	The value for the environment variable where the value is a PATH structure.
value (required if file and path are not specified)	The literal value for the environment variable.

Examples

This example will result in the execution of the batch file `start.bat` in the `bin` directory, with the output written to the `run.log` file. This example will run only on Windows 2000; on other platforms, it will be ignored.

```
<exec dir="bin" executable="cmd.exe " os="Windows 2000" output="run.log">
  <arg line="start.bat"/>
</exec>
```

<fail>

The <fail> task serves the purpose of exiting the current build while also allowing you to specify a message to be displayed upon exit.

Table 4.34 lists the attributes of this task.

Table 4.34   *Table of <fail> Attributes*

Attributes (Optional)	Description
if	If specified, the build will fail only if this property does exist.
message	The message to be displayed when the build exits.
unless	If specified, the build will fail only if this property does not exist.

Examples

The following example will result in the build exiting and reporting the line number that the build exited at. For example, E:\javadevelopment\build.xml:190: No message.

```
<fail/>
```

The message can be set using either of the following two techniques:

```
<fail message="classpath property not defined"/>
```

```
<fail>
multi-line
message
</fail>
```

<filter>

The <filter> task enables you to set a filter for any of the tasks that perform file-copying operations through the Project commodity methods. A filter consists of a token and the value that will be substituted wherever it occurs. Note that the token matching is case sensitive.

The <filter> attributes are shown in Table 4.35.

Table 4.35   *Table of <filter> Attributes*

Attributes (Required)	Description
token (if no filtersfile is specified)	The token string to be replaced.
value (if filtersfile no specified)	The string value that should be substituted for occurrences of the token.
filtersfile (if token and value not specified)	The name of the file that contains a list of filters. This file must be formatted as a property file.

Example

The following example will result in the `.txt` files in the current directory being moved to the `newlocation` directory. In the process of the move, all occurrences of `@DATE@` will be replaced with the string `true`.

```
<filter token="DATE" value="29/01/99"/>
<move todir="newlocation" filter="true">
  <fileset dir="." includes="*.txt"/>
</move>
```

<fixcrlf>

The `<fixcrlf>` task converts files to adhere to the local conventions. More specifically, it enables you to bring a set of files to the same standard in terms of tabs, end-of-line characters, and end-of-file characters. This is particularly useful if members of the development team are working on different platforms. Table 4.36 details the attributes that enable you to specify the behavior of the task.

Table 4.36   *Table of <fixcrlf> Attributes*

Attributes	Description
Required	
srcdir	The name of the directory containing the files to be fixed.
Optional	
cr	This attribute is deprecated. eol should be used.
defaultexcludes	If false, default excludes will not be used. Defaults to true.
destdir	The name of the destination directory where corrected files will be placed. If not specified, the source files are overwritten with the corrected versions.
encoding	Specifies the encoding of the files. Defaults to the JVM default encoding.

Table 4.36   *(continued)*

Attributes	Description
eof	Indicates the handling choice for DOS end-of-file characters (Control-Z). Select from add: Adds an EOF if one does not already exist. asis: Leaves EOFs as they are. remove: Removes any EOFs. The default is platform dependent (UNIX: remove; DOS-based: asis).
eol	Indicates the handling choice for end-of-line characters. Select from asis: Leaves EOLs as they are. cr: Converts all EOLs to CRs. (carriage returns). lf: Converts all EOLs to LFs (line feeds). cr: Converts all EOLs to CR/LF pairs. The default is platform dependent (UNIX: cr; DOS-based: crlf; Mac: lf).
excludes	A comma-separated list of patterns of files to be excluded. The default is not to exclude any files (except default excludes).
excludesfile	The name of a file that specifies a list of file patterns to exclude—one per line.
includes	A comma-separated list of patterns of files to be included. The default is to include all files.
includesfile	The name of a file that specifies a list of file patterns to include—one per line.
javafiles	Set to true to indicate the fileset is a set of Java files. The result of this is that tab characters occurring within Java strings and character constants are never modified. Defaults to no.
tab	Indicates the handling choice for tab characters. Select from add: Sequences of spaces that span a tab stop will be converted to tabs. asis: Leaves tabs and space characters as they are. remove: Convert tabs to spaces. Defaults to asis.
tablength	Tab character interval (between 2 and 80, inclusive). Defaults to 8.

Example

The following example will convert a set of source files to the platform default and replace all tabs (other than those within the code elements) with two spaces. The existing file in the ${src} directory will be replaced with the corrected versions.

```
<fixcrlf srcdir="${src}" tab="remove" tablength="2" javafiles="true"/>
```

<genkey>

The <genkey> task is essentially a shortcut to keytool -genkey—the Java tool for creating private/public key pairs and adding them to the keystore. The attributes of the task are detailed in Table 4.37.

Table 4.37   *Table of <genkey> Attributes*

Attributes	Description
Required	
alias	The alias to use.
dname (if dname element is not dname)	The distinguished name for the entity.
storepass	The password for keystore integrity.
Optional	
keyalg	The algorithm to use when generating a name-value pair.
keypass	The password for the private key (if different).
keysize	An integer value corresponding to the size of the key.
keystore	The keystore location.
sigalg	The algorithm to be used when signing.
storetype	The type of keystore.
validity	An integer value corresponding to the number of days the certificate is valid.
verbose	Specifies whether verbose output is required.

Nested Elements

The <dname> element can be nested within the <genkey> tag acting as an alternative to stipulating a value for the dname attribute. The dname element does not have any attributes, but contains nested param elements—each param element is a name-value pair. So, for example, instead of specifying

```
Dname="CN=sams, OU=ant, O=authors"
```

the following will have the same effect:

```
<dname>
  <param name="CN" value="sams"/>
  <param name="OU" value="ant"/>
```

```
<param name="0" value="authors"/>
</dname>
```

Example

The following example will create a key in the keystore under the alias admin with the keystore password password:

```
<genkey alias="admin"
  dname="CN=Sams, OU=ant, O=authors"
  storepass="password"/>
```

<get>

The <get> task enables you to get a file from a given URL. One such example of how you could leverage this task is hitting a URL that in turn generates an SMS/email to notify someone something has gone wrong (or right). This task could also be used for something as simple as downloading an external resource.

Table 4.38 gives a list of the task's associated attributes.

Table 4.38   *Table of <get> Attributes*

Attributes	Description
Required	
dest	The destination for the retrieved file.
src	The source URL from which to get the file.
Optional	
ignoreerrors	If true, errors will be logged but will not stop the task executing to the end.
password	Specifies the password for basic HTTP authentication. Should be specified along with the username attribute.
username	Specifies the username for basic HTTP authentication. Should be specified along with the password attribute.
usetimestamp	If set to true, the file will be downloaded only if the timestamp on the remote file is newer than that of the local version. This option can be used only if you're using the HTTP protocol to download the file.
verbose	If true, a "." is displayed for every 100KB of the file downloaded. Defaults to false.

Example

This example will get the file at the given URL, and store it in the file named `data.xml`:

```
<get src="http://www.sams.com/ant/data/chapters.xml"
  dest="data.xml"/>
```

<gunzip>

The `<gunzip>` task is for extracting gzip files where the source file is gunzipped only if it is newer than the destination file. It is a simple task as illustrated by its table of attributes (see Table 4.39).

By default, the name of the destination file is the name of the specified source file minus the last extension—usually `.gz`. So, a source file of `somefile.txt.gz` will result in a gunzipped file called `somefile.txt` being output.

If, however, the destination is given, there are two possibilities. If the given destination is a directory, the naming rule described earlier applies, but this time the destination file is placed in the given directory. Otherwise, the destination file takes the name given by the `dest` attribute.

Table 4.39 *Table of <gunzip> Attributes*

Attributes	Description
Required	
src	The name of the file to be gunzipped.
Optional	
dest	The destination filename or directory.

Examples

```
<gunzip src="myarchive.tar.gz" />
```

expands the file `myarchive.tar.gz` to `myarchive.tar`.

```
<gunzip src=" myarchive.tar.gz" dest="myfile.tar" />
```

expands the file `myarchive.tar.gz` to `myfile.tar`.

\<gzip>

The \<gzip> task is used to gzip a file. It creates a gzipped version of the named source file, giving it the name supplied by the `zipfile` attribute. The file will not be created, however, if the zip file already exists and is newer than the source file.

\<gzip> was not been designed to gzip multiple files, as the lack of support for nested filesets suggests. The most practical use of \<gzip> is gzipping tar files—a common format of distribution.

A full listing of the task attributes is given in Table 4.40.

Table 4.40   *Table of \<gzip> Attributes*

Attributes (Required)	Description
src	The name of the file to be gzipped.
zipfile	The name of the destination file.

Example

The result of running the following would be the creation of a file named `distrib.tar.gz`, a gzipped version of `distrib.tar`:

```
<gzip src="distrib.tar" zipfile="somefile.tar.gz"/>
```

\<input>

If you need user interaction in a build, the \<input> task provides this facility. It enables you to supply a message to prompt for input, set some valid values so that validation may be performed, and provides a property that will be given the value entered by the user. Table 4.41 lists the attributes of this simple and useful task.

Table 4.41   *Table of \<input> Attributes*

Attributes (Optional)	Description
addproperty	The property to be set with the value input by the user.
message	The message to be displayed as a prompt for input.
validargs	A comma-separated list of values to accept as valid input. By default, there is no validation.

Examples

The message prompt can be set via the `message` attribute or nested within the input task as this example illustrates. This particular example could be used to pause the build until the user is ready or some external condition holds.

```
<input>Press enter to continue</input>
```

Using the validation options is easy, too. The following listing shows how you could extend the previous example to query whether to continue. It will continue to prompt the user until he enters **y** or **n** (followed by pressing the Enter key). On doing so, the `continue` property will be set to the entered value.

```
<input validarg="y,n" addproperty="continue">
Do you wish to continue?
</input>
```

`<jar>`

The `<jar>` task gives you the ability to create JAR files, which is useful when putting together distributions, backups, and so on. It is an implicit fileset that produces a JAR file from the files included in the set. The nested elements help to refine the set even further, as well as enabling you to specify the contents of the `META-INF` directory. Table 4.42 details the attributes of the task that makes creating JARs easy.

Table 4.42   *Table of `<jar>` Attributes*

Attributes	Description
Required	
destfile	The name of the JAR file to be created.
Optional	
basedir	The name of the directory from which the files to jar are located.
compress	Specifies whether the files will be compressed in the JAR file. Defaults to true.
defaultExcludes	If false, default excludes will not be used. Defaults to true.
duplicate	Specifies the behavior when a duplicate file is found. Valid values are create, fail, and skip.
encoding	The character encoding to use for filenames inside the archive. Defaults to UTF8. It is recommended that this attribute value be left as the default to avoid creating an archive unreadable for Java.

Table 4.42 *(continued)*

Attributes	Description
excludes	A comma-separated list of patterns of files to be excluded. The default is not to exclude any files (except default excludes).
excludesfile	The name of a file that specifies a list of file patterns to exclude—one per line.
filesetmanifest	Specifies the behavior when a manifest file is found in a zipfileset or zipgroup-fileset. Valid values are merge, mergewithoutmain, and skip. Defaults to skip.
filesOnly	If true, only file entries are stored. Defaults to false.
includes	A comma-separated list of patterns of files to be included. The default is to include all files.
includesfile	The name of a file that specifies a list of file patterns to include—one per line.
index	If true, an index list will be created (JDK 1.3+ only). Defaults to false.
manifest	The name of the file to use as the manifest. Alternatively, it can be the name of a JAR added through a fileset; in such a case, the META-INF/MANIFEST.INF file within that JAR will be used as the manifest.
update	Indicates what the choice of action if the file already exists. If true, the JAR will be updated; otherwise, it will be overwritten.
whenempty	Specify the behavior if no files match. Valid values are skip, create, and fail. Defaults to create.

Nested Elements

The `<jar>` task supports nested `<include>`, `<exclude>`, `<patternset>`, `<fileset>`, `<zipfileset>`, and `<zipgroupfileset>` (see the "`<zip>`" task section later in the chapter for more information) to specify the files to be included in the JAR.

Nested `<metainf>` elements, which are basically filesets, can be used to specify files to be included in the META-INF directory. However, `<metainf>` filesets cannot be used to specify the manifest.mf file.

Manifest files can be specified using nested `<manifest>` elements, however. This is identical to the `<manifest>` task described later in this chapter, but the file and mode attributes are ignored.

Examples

This example will create a JAR file named backup.jar that contains all the files in the classes directory. In this case, the default manifest.mf is used for the JAR file.

```
<jar jarfile="backup.jar" basedir="classes"/>
```

The following example demonstrates the use of a nested `<metainf>` element to specify the files to be included in the META-INF directory, and a nested `<include>` to specify the files for the JAR main directory.

```
<jar jarfile="distrib.jar"
  basedir="classes"
  manifest=".\misc\manifest.mf">
  <include name="com/sams/**/*.class"/>
  <metainf dir =".">
    <include name="*.xml"/>
  </metainf>
</jar>
```

`<java>`

The `<java>` task executes a Java class either running within the JVM used by the Ant process or in a forked JVM. It's a good idea to choose to fork another JVM when using the `<java>` task because a class that calls `System.exit()` will result in the termination of the JVM running the Ant process. It's also necessary to fork executable jars so that they can be run.

Note that Ant controls the standard input when using `<java>`, so you can't interact with your application via the keyboard.

Table 4.43 provides a full listing of the `<java>` attributes.

Table 4.43   *Table of <java> Attributes*

Attributes	Description
Required	
classname (required if jar is not specified)	The name of the Java class to execute.
jar (required if classname is not specified)	The name of the JAR to be executed (it must be an executable JAR; see footnote). Fork must be set to true if this option is used.
Optional	
append	If true, output will be appended to an existing file rather than the file being overwritten. Defaults to false.
args	The command-line arguments to be passed to the executing class. This attribute is deprecated; use nested <arg> elements.

Table 4.43   *(continued)*

Attributes	Description
classpath	The class path to be used. Defaults to the location at which Ant is executed.
classpathref	The classpath to be used, which is supplied as a reference to a PATH defined elsewhere.
dir	The directory location to invoke the forked JVM in (ignored if fork is disabled).
failonerror	If enabled, the build process will end if the executing Java class returns with a return code other than 0 (ignored if fork is disabled).
fork	If enabled, the class execution is performed in another JVM. This is disabled by default.
jvm	The command used to invoke the JVM. The default is java (ignored if fork is disabled).
jvmargs	The arguments to pass to the forked JVM (ignored if fork is disabled). This attribute is deprecated.
maxmemory	The maximum amount of memory to allocate to the forked JVM (ignored if fork is disabled).
newenvironment	If true, and fork is enabled, the old environment will not be propagated when new environment variables are specified. Default is false.
output	The name of a file to write output from the executed class to.
timeout	Specifies the maximum time (in milliseconds) to wait before stopping the command. Should be used only when fork is set to true.

An executable JAR is one that has a Main-Class entry in the manifest.

Nested Elements

To specify the classpath to be used, nested `<classpath>` elements are supported. Nested `<arg>` and `<jvmarg>` elements enable you to specify arguments for the class being executed and the forked JVM, respectively.

Nested `<sysproperty>` elements can be used to specify system properties required by the class. These share the same attributes as the `<env>` elements in the `<exec>` task. Furthermore, `<env>` elements themselves can be nested to specify environment variables to pass to the forked JVM (they're ignored if the JVM is not forked).

Examples

This simple example will result in the execution of the class `com.sams.ant.javaTest` with the supplied class path.

```
<java classname="com.sams.ant.javaTest">
  <classpath>
    <pathelement location="${build}"/>
    <pathelement location="${jarpath}jsdk.jar"/>
  </classpath>
</java>
```

The following example demonstrates the `failonerror` attribute. It's useful when you don't want to do something if the Java class fails to execute successfully. In the example, if `com.sams.ant.testClass` exits with a `System.exit(-1)`, the `echo` statement is not executed. If `failonerror` is set to false, the `echo` statement would be executed because the build continues regardless of the failure or success of the `<java>` task. On the other hand, if `fork` is set to false, a `System.exit()` in the `java` class will result in the build halting in all cases.

```
<java classname="com.antbook.testClass" fork="true" failonerror="true"/>
<echo message="Finished running class"/>
```

<javac>

A primary use of Ant is in the compilation of Java source files. `<javac>` is the task that gives you the power to do so. It runs the Java compiler on a set of Java source files within a specified directory (including subdirectories). The `<javac>` task works similarly to the `javac` executable in that it will compile only `.java` files that have no corresponding class file, and classes that are older than the corresponding Java file.

Note that because the source is not scanned, a class named `fooBar` in a file **not** named `fooBar.java` will always be compiled.

Table 4.44 lists the `<javac>` attributes, which include attributes that support all the options that you can pass to `javac` normally.

Table 4.44   *Table of <javac> Attributes*

Attributes	Description
Required	
srcdir (required unless nested <src> elements are used)	The name of the directory containing the source files to be compiled.

Table 4.44 (continued)

Attributes	Description
Optional	
bootclasspath	The path of bootstrap classes to use.
bootclasspathref	A reference to a path to use as the bootclasspath.
classpath	The class path to use.
classpathref	A reference to the class path to use.
compiler	Specifies the compiler to use, if other than the default compiler for the current JVM. This will override the build.compiler property.
debug	If true, info to aid debugging will be generated.
debuglevel	Valid values are none, or a comma-separated list of the keywords lines, vars, and source as per the javac -g flag (used by modern and classic). Defaults to none.
depend	If true, dependency tracking is enabled for compilers that support it.
deprecation	If true, information will be given where deprecated APIs are used. Defaults to false.
destdir	The destination directory for the generated class files. Defaults to current directory.
encoding	Specifies the source file encoding.
excludes	A comma-separated list of patterns of files to be excluded. The default is not to exclude any files (except default excludes).
excludesfile	The name of a file that specifies a list of file patterns to exclude—one per line.
extdirs	Specifies an alternative location of installed extensions that overrides the default.
failonerror	If enabled, the build process is stopped should the compile not complete successfully. Defaults to true.
fork	If enabled, the compilation is performed in another JVM. This is disabled by default.
includeantruntime	Specifies whether to include the Ant run-time libraries. Defaults to true.
includejavaruntime	Specifies whether to include the default run-time libraries from the executing VM. Defaults to false.
includes	A comma-separated list of patterns of files to be included. The default is to include all files.
includesfile	The name of a file that specifies a list of file patterns to include—one per line.
listfiles	If true, the list of files to be compiled will be displayed. Defaults to false.

Table 4.44   *(continued)*

Attributes	Description
memoryinitialsize	Specifies the initial size of memory for the JVM. Used only if javac is forked. Defaults to the standard VM settings.
memorymaximumsize	Specifies the maximum size of memory for the JVM. Used only if the javac task is forked. Defaults to the standard VM settings.
nowarn	If true, no warnings are generated. Defaults to false.
optimize	If true, the source will be compiled with optimization on. Defaults to false.
source	If set to 1.4, support will be enabled for assertions. Defaults to 1.3.
sourcepath	Specifies the source path to use. Defaults to srcdir.
sourcepathref	A reference to the source path to use.
target	Specifies the VM version to generate class files for (for example, 1.1 or 1.3).
verbose	If true, verbose output is enabled. Defaults to false.

Using Other Compilers

Ant enables you to specify an alternative compiler to use in the execution of the `<javac>` task. By setting the `build.compiler` property, the following choices are available to you:

- Classic (also javac1.1 and javac1.2)—The standard compiler of JDK 1.1/1.2.

- Modern (also javac1.3 and javac1.4)—The standard compiler of JDK 1.3/1.4.

- Jikes—The Jikes compiler. Note that you can set as Jikes as the default compiler by setting the JIKES_HOME environment variable to the location of the Jikes compiler.

- Jvc—The command-line compiler from Microsoft's SDK for Java and Visual J++.

- Kjc—The Kopi compiler (http://www.dms.at/kopi/).

- Gcj—The gcj compiler from GNU.

- Sj (also Symantec)—The Symantec Java compiler.

- Extjavac—Runs either classic or modern in a separate JVM.

You can also use a compiler other than one from the preceding list by writing a class that implements the `org.apache.tools.ant.taskdefs.compilers.CompilerAdapter` interface. The defined class is subsequently used by setting the `build.compiler` property to the full classname of the class.

However, if the `fork` attribute is set to true, the `build.compiler` property will be ignored.

Nested Elements

As an implicit fileset, the `<javac>` task supports the nesting of `<include>`, `<exclude>`, and `<patternset>` elements in the refinement of the set of files to compile.

In addition to those elements, nested `<src>`, `<classpath>`, `<bootclasspath>`, and `<extdirs>` (all pathlike structures) are supported in specifying values for the `srcdir`, `classpath`, `bootclasspath`, and `extdirs` attributes, respectively.

Finally, nested `<compilerarg>` elements can be used to specify command-line arguments for the compiler. These share the same attributes as command-line arguments (`<arg>` elements) with the addition of a compiler attribute (see Table 4.45). This extra attribute enables you to specify the compiler that this argument should be applied to.

Table 4.45   *Table of <compilerarg> Attributes*

Attributes	Description
Required	
file*	A file to pass as a single command-line argument. (This will be converted to an absolute file path.)
line*	A space-delimited list of command-line arguments.
path*	A string that will be treated as a pathlike string and as a single command-line argument.
value*	A single command line argument (which may contain spaces).
Optional	
compiler	The compiler this argument should be passed to. For other compilers, this argument will be ignored.

* One of these attributes must be specified.

Examples

The following example compiles the source files contained in the `${src}` directory, using `${build}` as the class path and storing the resultant files in `${build}`.

```
<javac src="${src}" destdir="${build}" classpath="${build}"/>
```

The following example is equivalent to the preceding one, and demonstrates how nested `<src>` and `<classpath>` elements can be put to use:

```
<javac destdir="${build}">
  <src path="${src}"/>
  <classpath>
    <pathelement path="${build}"/>
  </classpath>
</javac>
```

<javadoc> and <javadoc2>

First of all, note that the <Javadoc2> task is deprecated. The <javadoc> task enables you to run Javadoc on a set of source files. There are numerous attributes (see Table 4.46), but the attributes that are supported are dependent on which JDK you're running Ant with. For a more verbose description of some of these attributes, see the Javadoc home page at http://java.sun.com/j2se/javadoc/.

Table 4.46   *Table of <javadoc> Attributes*

Attributes	Description
Required	
sourcepath**	Specifies the location of the source files.
sourcepathref**	Specifies a reference to a PATH defined elsewhere that is to be used as the source path.
destdir (unless a doclet is specified)	The destination directory for the Javadoc output.
sourcefiles***	A comma-separated list of source files to be run through Javadoc.
packagenames***	A comma-separated list of packages with a terminating wildcard to put through Javadoc.
Optional	
access	Access mode: public, protected, package, or private.
additionalparam	For specifying additional parameters, as you would to the javadoc command line.
author	If enabled, author paragraphs will be included in the generated documentation.
bootclasspath	Sets the location of class files loaded by the bootstrap class loader.
bootclasspathref	A reference to a PATH defined elsewhere that is to be used as the bootclasspath.
bottom	Specifies the text for the bottom of every page.
charset	Specifies the HTML character set for the output documentation.

Table 4.46   *(continued)*

Attributes	Description
classpath	Specifies the location of the class files.
classpathref	A reference to a PATH defined elsewhere that is to be used as the class path.
defaultexcludes	If false, default excludes will not be used. Defaults to true.
docencoding	Specifies the encoding for the generated documentation.
doclet	The class file to be used that starts the doclet used in generating the documentation.
docletpath	The path to the doclet class file specified.
docletpathref	A reference to a PATH defined elsewhere that is to be used as the docletpath.
doctitle	Specifies the title to be placed at the top of the summary page.
encoding	Specifies the source file encoding.
excludepackagenames	A comma-separated list of package names to be excluded in the Javadoc output.
extdirs	Specifies a different directory to be used as the location of installed extensions.
failonerror	If enabled, the build process is stopped if the javadoc does not complete successfully.
footer	Specifies the footer text to be used for each page.
group	Specifies any grouping required on the overview page. This is a comma-separated list of arguments in which each argument is two space-delimited strings. The first string is the group's title, and the second one is a colon-delimited list of packages.
header	Specifies the header text to be used for each page.
helpfile	Specifies the name of a file that the help links on the page will refer to.
link	Specifies links to already existing Javadoc files.
linkoffline	Specifies two space-separated URLs. Link to docs at \<url> using package list at \<url2>.
locale	The locale to be used; for example, en_US (English, United States).
maxmemory	The maximum amount of memory to allocate to the Javadoc process.
nodeprecated	Specifies whether deprecated information will be included.
nodeprecatedlist	Specifies whether a deprecated list will be generated.
nohelp	Specifies whether to generate help links.
noindex	Specifies whether to generate an index.
nonavbar	Specifies whether to generate a navigation bar.

Table 4.46   *(continued)*

Attributes	Description
notree	Specifies whether to generate the class hierarchy.
old	Specifies whether to use JDK 1.1 emulating doclet to generate output.
overview	Specifies the name of a file that holds the text to be used for the overview page.
package	Shows package/protected/public classes and members.
packagelist	Specifies the name of a file containing the list of packages to run through Javadoc.
private	Shows all classes and members.
protected	Shows only protected/public classes and members (default).
public	Shows only public classes and members.
serialwarn	Specifies whether to generate compile time errors for missing serial tags.
source	Handles assertions in Java code. Setting this to 1.4 will document code that compiles with the -source 1.4 compiler flag. Ignored if a custom doclet is used.
splitindex	Specifies whether to split the index into multiple files, one file per letter.
stylesheetfile	Specifies the name of a file to use as the stylesheet.
use	Specifies whether to generate usage pages.
useexternalfile	If true, the source files will be written to a temporary file to make the command line shorter. Also applies to the package names specified via the packagenames attribute or nested package elements. Defaults to false.
verbose	Specifies whether Javadoc should operate in verbose mode.
version	Specifies whether to include version tags.
windowtitle	Specifies the title to be seen in the browser window when viewing the generated docs.

** At least one of the two are required or nested <sourcepath>.
*** At least one of the two are nested <source> or <package>.

Nested Elements

You can use nested `<fileset>` and `<packageset>` (a renamed `dirset`) elements in specifying the files to Javadoc. In both cases, the values of `packagenames`, `excludepacka-genames` and `defaultexcludes` have no effect on the files or directories specified.

Nested `<sourcepath>`, `<classpath>`, and `<bootclasspath>` elements are supported in setting the `sourcepath`, `classpath`, and `bootclasspath` attributes.

Similarly, nested `<package>` and `<excludepackage>` elements (see Table 4.47) enable you to specify packages individually rather than as a list in the `package` and `excludepackage` attributes.

Table 4.47   *Table of <package>/<excludepackage> Attributes*

Attributes (Required)	Description
name	The package name (wildcards permitted).

Rather than using the `sourcefiles` attribute to list the files, `<source>` elements can be nested, one per file (see Table 4.48).

Table 4.48   *Table of <source> Attributes*

Attributes (Required)	Description
File	The source file to document.

The `<doctitle>`, `<header>`, `<footer>`, and `<bottom>` elements enable you to specify the values of their respective attributes with the added bonus of being able to specify multiline values.

Nested `<link>` elements are supported to specify values for the `link` and `linkoffline` attributes. Table 4.49 lists the `<link>` element attributes.

Table 4.49   *Table of <link> Attributes*

Attributes	Description
Required	
href	The URL for the external documentation to link to.
packagelistloc (required if offline is true)	The directory containing the package list file for the external documentation.
Optional	
offline	Specifies whether the link is available online at the time of the Javadoc generation.

Nested `<group>` elements (see Table 4.50) enable you to specify multiple groups as well as allowing you to specify a group whose title contains a comma or a space character.

Table 4.50 *Table of <group> Attributes*

Attributes (Required)	Description
title (required if nested <title> is not specified)	The group title.
packages (required if nested <package> is not specified)	A colon-separated list of packages to include in the group.

The <doclet> element can be nested to specify the doclet that Javadoc should use to process the source files. The attributes of the <javadoc> task that apply to the doclet will be passed to it. Additional parameters to the doclet can be passed as nested <param> elements. The main attributes of the <doclet> element are listed in Table 4.51.

Table 4.51 *Table of <doclet> Attributes*

Attributes	Description
Required	
name	The doclet name.
Optional	
path	The path where the doclet class files are located.

An option that is available only with Java 1.4 is the facility to specify custom tags and taglets. This can be done using nested <tag> and <taglet> elements (see Tables 4.52 and 4.53, respectively).

Table 4.52 *Table of <tag> Attributes*

Attributes	Description
Required	
description	A tag description.
name	The name of the tag.
Optional	
enabled	Enables and disables the tag. Defaults to true.
scope	A comma-separated list from overview, packages, types, constructors, methods, fields, and all that specifies the scope for the tag. Defaults to all.

Table 4.53   *Table of <taglet> Attributes*

Attributes	Description
Required	
name	The full class name of the taglet class.
Optional	
path	The path to find the taglet class. Alternatively, this can be specified via nested <path> elements.

Examples

This simple use of the <javadoc> task will create Javadocs for all the packages in the com package subtree. The source files will be in the ${src} directory with the generated documentation stored in the ${docs} directory.

```
<javadoc packagenames = "com.*" sourcepath="${src}" destdir="${docs}"/>
```

Here's an example that goes a step further. This will generate Javadocs for all the publicly accessible classes within the com.sams subtree, but will not include any of the classes in the com.sams.net subtree. The docs will include the message Copyright © 2002. All Rights Reserved. at the bottom.

```
<javadoc sourcepath="${src}"
  access="public"
  destdir="docs"
  classpath="classes">
  <package name="com.sams.*"/>
  <excludepackage name="com.sams.net.*"/>
  <bottom><![CDATA[<i>Copyright &#169; 2002. All Rights Reserved.</i>]]></bottom>
</javadoc>
```

<loadFile>

The <loadfile> task offers the simple facility of loading the contents of a text file to a property. Table 4.54 displays the associated attributes for the task.

Table 4.54 *Table of <loadfile> Attributes*

Attributes	Description
Required	
property	The property to set with the contents of the file.
srcfile	The file to load.
Optional	
encoding	Specifies the encoding to use when loading the file. Defaults to the current locale.
failonerror	If true, the build will stop if an error occurs. Defaults to true.

Nested Elements

Nested <filterchain> elements are supported.

Examples

This example will load the contents of the foo.txt file to the bar property. If the file does not exist, the build will halt.

```
<loadfile srcfile="foo.txt" property="bar"/>
```

The next example demonstrates how nested <filterchain> elements can be used. Here, the header property will be set to the first line of the chapter4.txt file.

```
<loadfile property="header " srcfile="chapter4.txt">
  <filterchain>
    <headfilter lines="1"/>
  </filterchain>
</loadfile>
```

<loadproperties>

This task is an alternative to specifying the file attribute of a property task. The benefit of using this alternative is that it supports nested <filterchain> elements. For example, you can load only the properties from a file that match a given criteria (via a regular expression, for instance). On a negative note, you cannot use the <loadfile> task without a target, whereas you can do so with property elements.

<loadproperties> only requires one attribute to be specified, as detailed in Table 4.55.

Table 4.55 *Table of <loadproperties> Attributes*

Attributes (Required)	Description
srcfile	The name of the properties file.

Nested Elements

Nested <filterchain> elements are supported.

Examples

The following two lines are equivalent:

```
<loadproperties srcfile="mybuild.properties"/>
```

```
<property file="mybuild.properties"/>
```

However, in the first instance, it is possible to specify a <filterchain> element so that you could do something like simply loading the property server.jar.name.

```
<loadproperties srcfile="mybuild.properties">
  <filterchain>
    <linecontains>
      <contains value="server.jar.name"/>
    </linecontains>
  </filterchain>
</loadproperties>
```

<mail>

The <mail> task enables you to send SMTP email. This task is useful for notifying someone immediately if a job breaks in an overnight build. With the capability to include files in the message body and/or as attachments, logs, for example, can be sent in the mail.

Table 4.56 details the task attributes.

Table 4.56   *Table of <mail> Attributes*

Attributes	Description
Required	
from (required unless a nested <from> is used)	The e-mail address of the sender.
message (required if messagefile and <message> are not specified)	The message to send in the body of the e-mail. This is ignored if files is specified.
messagefile (required if message and <message> are not specified)	The file that contains the content for the email message body.
Optional	
bcclist*	A comma-separated list of e-mail addresses to BCC the message to.
cclist*	A comma-separated list of e-mail addresses to CC the message to.
encoding	The encoding to use for the email. Valid values are auto, mime, plain, and auto. Defaults to auto.
failonerror	If true, the build will stop if an error occurs. Defaults to true.
files	A comma-separated list of files to send as attachments to the e-mail.
includefilenames	If true, filenames will be included ahead of file contents. Defaults to false (valid only when encoding is plain).
mailhost	The hostname of the SMTP mail server. Defaults to localhost.
mailport	The SMTP server port. Defaults to 25.
Messagemimetype	Specifies the MIME type of the message. Defaults to text/plain.
subject	The value for the subject field of the email.
tolist*	A comma-separated list of email addresses that indicates the destinations of the e-mail.

* At least one of these, or an equivalent nested element, must be specified.

Nested Elements

The `<to>`, `<cc>`, `<bcc>`, and `<from>` elements can be nested to set their corresponding attribute values. Table 4.57 lists the attributes of these elements.

Table 4.57   *Table of <to>/<cc>/<bcc>/<from> Attributes*

Attributes	Description
Required	
address	The e-mail address.
Optional	
name	The display name for the address.

A nested <message> element can be used to specify the message for the body of the e-mail. Table 4.58 lists the <message> attributes.

Table 4.58   *Table of <message> Attributes*

Attributes (Optional)	Description
mimetype	Specifies the content type of the message.
src	Specifies the file to use for the contents of the message.

Nested <fileset> elements can also be used to specify files to be attached to the message.

Example

The following example sends an e-mail to three recipients, and contains the contents of the build.log file in the message body:

```
<mail from="andy@antbook.com"
  to="alan@antbook.com, kirk@antbook.com, joey@antbook.com"
  files="build.log"/>
```

<manifest>

The <manifest> task (see Table 4.59) aids in the creation or update of a manifest file.

Table 4.59   *Table of <manifest> Attributes*

Attributes	Description
Required	
file	The name of the manifest file to create or update.
Optional	
mode	Valid options are update and replace. Defaults to replace.

Nested Elements

You can nest `<attribute>` elements (see Table 4.60) to specify attributes for the manifest file. These can be nested within `<section>` elements.

Table 4.60 *Table of `<attribute>` Attributes*

Attributes (Required)	Description
name	The attribute name.
value	The attribute value.

`<section>` elements (see Table 4.61) enable you to specify sections within the manifest.

Table 4.61 *Table of `<section>` Attributes*

Attributes (Optional)	Description
name	The section name. Defaults to the main section.

Examples

The following example demonstrates how the `<manifest>` task can be used along with nested `<attribute>` and `<section>` elements to create the misc/manifest.mf manifest:

```
<manifest file="misc/manifest.mf">
  <attribute name="Build-Date" value="${TODAY}"/>
  <section name="common">
    <attribute name="Specification-Title" value="JDBC Specification"/>
    <attribute name="Specification-Version" value="2.0"/>
    <attribute name="Specification-Vendor" value="Sun Microsystems, Inc"/>
    <attribute name="Implementation-Title" value="jdbc"/>
    <attribute name="Implementation-Version" value="build101"/>
    <attribute name="Implementation-Vendor" value="Sams Publishing"/>
  </section>
</manifest>
```

The resultant manifest would look like this:

```
Manifest-Version: 1.0
Created-By: Apache Ant 1.5
Built-Date: May 19 2002

Name: common
Specification-Title: JDBC Specification
```

```
Specification-Version: 2.0
Specification-Vendor: Sun Microsystems, Inc
Implementation-Title: common
Implementation-Version: build101
Implementation-Vendor: Sams Publishing
```

<mkdir>

The <mkdir> task (see Table 4.62) enables you to create a new directory in the file system. All nonexistent directories in the provided path will be created, so there is no need to create each directory in the path separately.

A common use of <mkdir> in a project is as an initialization target to set up the project directory structure.

Table 4.62   *Table of <mkdir> Attributes*

Attributes (Required)	Description
Dir	The directory to be created.

Example

The following example illustrates how you use <mkdir> to create a directory named project/lib/ext in the base directory. If the project and lib directories in the path don't exist, they are created also.

```
<mkdir dir = "project/lib/ext"/>
```

<move>

The <move> task gives you the ability to move a file or set of files to a different directory. Either the file attribute or a fileset can be specified, but in both cases, if the destination file already exists, it will be overwritten by default. A more refined use is to set the overwrite attribute to false, in which case, an existing file will be overwritten only if the candidate to replace it is newer. A full list of attributes is given in Table 4.63.

<move> can also be used to rename a file using the file and tofile attributes. Furthermore, a nested mapper element can be used to rename sets of files.

Table 4.63 *Table of <move> Attributes*

Attributes	Description
Required	
file (required if fileset elements are not specified)	The name of the file to be moved.
tofile (required if file is specified and todir is not)	The destination file.
todir (required if tofile is specified)	The destination directory.
Optional	
filtering	If true, filtering is enabled in the move.
flatten	If true, the directory structure is ignored. That is, all the files in the source fileset are moved to the source directory. Defaults to false.
includeemptydirs	If false, empty directories are ignored. Defaults to true.
overwrite	If true, existing files will be overwritten unconditionally. If false, existing files are overwritten only if older than the new files. Defaults to true.

Nested Elements

Nested <fileset> elements are supported in this task in specifying the files to be moved, and <mapper> elements allow for the naming of the destination files. Nested <filterchain> elements are also supported.

Examples

The following example will move the run.log file to the directory specified by the repository property:

```
<move file = "run.log" todir = "${repository}"/>
```

This next example will move the files contained in the directory named destination/directory to the source/dir directory and maintain the directory structure:

```
<move todir = "destination/directory">
  <fileset dir = "source/dir"/>
</move>
```

The final example, as well as moving all the files with the .log extension from the logs directory to the old directory, renames them by appending .old to the filename in the process.

```
<move todir = "old" >
  <fileset dir = "logs" >
    <include name = "**/*.log"/>
  </fileset>
  <mapper type = "glob" from = "*" to = "*.old" />
</move>
```

<parallel> and <sequential>

The <parallel> and <sequential> tasks are container tasks that enable you to run sets of tasks in parallel or sequence. Each task nested within a parallel task is executed in its own thread. On the other hand, the tasks nested within a sequential task are executed one after another. Combining these elements enables you to run groups of tasks in parallel with each other. But, as is the case whenever threads are involved, care should be taken to avoid race conditions.

There are numerous examples in which these elements can be taken advantage of. They can be used to make the most of resources by running independent tasks in parallel, thus reducing build time.

Example

A very noteworthy example of the parallel task being put to good use is in testing servers. A server can be run in one thread while the test harness is run in another. One such example of how this might be done follows:

```
<parallel>
  <antcall target="startserver"/>
  <sequential>
    <sleep seconds="10"/>
    <antcall target="testserver"/>
    <antcall target="stopserver"/>
  </sequential>
</parallel>
```

<patch>

The <patch> task enables you to apply a diff file (a file produced by the diff utility) to a file, thus producing a patched version. This task requires patch to be installed.

Table 4.64 lists the <patch> task attributes.

Table 4.64   *Table of <patch> Attributes*

Attributes	Description
Required	
patchfile	The name of the diff file.
Optional	
backups	If true, backups will be kept of the original files. Equivalent to -b.
dir	The base directory in which to run the task. Defaults to the project's basedir.
ignorewhitespace	If true, white space will be ignored (equivalent to the -l flag). Defaults to false.
originalfile	The file to which to apply the patch. If originalfile is not supplied, an attempt to guess the value from the diff file is made.
quiet	If true, <patch> works silently (equivalent to the -s flag). Defaults to false.
reverse	If true, assume that the patch was created with the old and new files swapped (equivalent to the -R flag). Defaults to false.
strip	If specified, the smallest prefix containing the number value given of leading slashes will be stripped from each filename in the patch file (equivalent to -p <value>). Defaults to 0.

Example

The following example will apply the diff mydiff.dif file to the SomeClass.java file and overwrite the original file with the patched version:

```
<patch patchfile="mydiff.dif"
  originalfile="SomeClass.java"/>
```

<pathconvert>

The <pathconvert> task produces a single path value from a nested path, path reference, or fileset reference. The format of the path output can be specified, which is useful when you need paths formatted for a particular target machine that is not necessarily the same platform as the host running the script. The list of `<pathconvert>` attributes is provided in Table 4.65.

Table 4.65   *Table of <pathconvert> Attributes*

Attributes (Required)	Description
dirsep (required if pathsep and targetos are not specified)	The character(s) to use as the directory separator in the converted paths. Defaults to current JVM File.separator.
pathsep (required if dirsep and targetos are not specified)	The character(s) to use as the path separator in the converted paths. Defaults to current JVM File.separator.
property	The name of the property to be given the result of this path conversion.
refid (required if a nested path element is not specified)	The reference ID of the <dirset>, <filelist>, <fileset>, or <path> to be converted.
targetos (required if dirsep and pathsep are not specified)	A shortcut that sets the pathsep and dirsep by operating system. Can be unix, windows, netware, or os/2. By specifying a dirsep or pathsep, you override the value set by this attribute.

Nested Elements

The `<pathconvert>` task enables you to nest `<path>` elements to specify the path to be converted, and `<map>` elements to specify a prefix mapping. A prefix mapping requires a `to` and a `from` attribute to be specified. By doing this, a path with the prefix supplied in the `from` attribute will be converted to the value supplied in the `to` attribute.

Mappings are case sensitive when running the script on UNIX, but are not case sensitive on Windows. However, in both cases, care should be taken when specifying multiple mappings because ordering matters. For example, assume that you want to make the following mappings:

```
<map from="c:\javadev\images" to="/lib/images"/>
<map from="c:\javadev" to="/work/java"/>
<map from="c:\" to="/home"/>
```

They must be specified in that order because only the first applicable mapping is applied.

Examples

The following example will convert the path with the ID `mypath` to a UNIX-style formatting, replacing the prefixes of `c:\` and `d:\web` with `/` and `/html`, respectively:

```
<pathconvert targetos="unix" property="unixpath" refid="mypath">
  <map from="c:\" to="/"/>
  <map from="d:\web" to="/html"/>
</pathconvert>
```

The following example can prove quite useful. It will result in the `allclasses` property containing a comma-separated list of class files:

```
<fileset id="classfiles" dir="classes">
  <include name="**\*.class"/>
</fileset>
<pathconvert targetos="unix" pathsep=","
  property="allclasses" refid="classfiles"/>
```

<property>

As well as the predefined properties that are available for your use, you can also define your own properties using the `<property>` task. There are many ways to give a property a value using this task, the simplest is to use the `value` attribute (see Table 4.66 for a full list of attributes). Further examples that show other ways of setting a property are given later in this section.

A property is overridden if set by a parent project (started with the Ant task `<REF>`) or if set by the user.

Table 4.66   *Table of <property> Attributes*

Attributes	Description
Required	
If name is given, one of the following:	
location	Sets the property to an absolute file path, allowing for platform conventions. If an absolute path is not specified, it is calculated relative to the basedir.
refid	A reference to another object from which the value is to be sourced.
value	The value to set the property to.
If name is omitted, one of the following:	
environment	Specifies a prefix, giving access to OS-specific environment variables. This is not supported on all platforms.
file	The name of the property file specifying properties to set.
resource	The resource name of the property file specifying properties to set.

Table 4.66   *(continued)*

Attributes	Description
Optional	
classpath	If specifying a value for the resource attribute, the classpath to use to look up the resource.
classpathref	If specifying a value for the resource attribute, a reference to the classpath to use to look up the resource.
name	The name of the property to set.
prefix	Specifies a prefix to be prepended to the properties when the resource or file attributes are specified.

Nested Elements

This task supports nested `<classpath>` elements as an alternative to specifying the classpath attribute (if required).

Examples

This simple example gives the `log` property the value `error.log`:

```
<property name="log" value="error.log"/>
```

The following case illustrates the use of the `location` attribute; the `logfullpath` property will be set to the absolute path of the `error.log` file. So, for example, if the base directory is `c:\javadevelopment` (Windows), the value of the `logfullpath` property would be `c:\javadevelopment\error.log`.

```
<property name="logfullpath" location="error.log"/>
```

The following example demonstrates how to set properties in your project using a properties file. This can be of use if, for example, you want to make a set of variables modifiable by a developer who is unfamiliar with the workings of the build file. It's also of use for setting per-developer variables (in other words, variables that vary depending on the developer using the build file).

```
<property file="myproj.properties"/>
```

Finally, the following example illustrates how to use the `environment` attribute. Remember that this works only on selected operating systems.

```
<property environment="env"/>
<echo>
```

```
Number of Processors = ${env.NUMBER_OF_PROCESSORS}
ANT_HOME is set to = ${env.ANT_HOME}
JAVA_HOME is set to = ${env.JAVA_HOME}
OS is ${env.OS}
</echo>
```

<record>

The <record> task is for creating and maintaining build listeners that send their output to file. The first use of <record> for a given filename will create the file if it doesn't already exist. Subsequent calls to <record> with the same filename enable you to start and stop the logging and to change the logging level. You can simply create a recorder to log all the build messages throughout a build, or perhaps just for a particular task, by starting and stopping the recorder appropriately.

Table 4.67 lists the task attributes.

Table 4.67   *Table of <record> Attributes*

Attributes	Description
Required	
name	The name of the log file.
Optional	
action	start or stop. Defaults to the current state; start if this is the first call for this log file.
append	Used the first time this file is referenced in the build. If true and the log file already exists, the log file will be appended to; otherwise, it will be overwritten. Defaults to false.
emacsmode	If true, [task] banners will be removed, similar to Ant's -emacs command-line switch. Defaults to false.
loglevel	Sets the level of logging for this build listener. Valid values are debug, error, info, verbose, and warn. Defaults to the current level for this file. In the first instance, this is info.

Examples

The following example will create the file verbose.log if it does not already exist. In a case in which the verbose.log file does exist, its current content will be overwritten.

```
<record name="verbose.log" action="start" loglevel="verbose"/>
```

Assuming that the following example follows the execution of the previous example, it will change the logging level to debug:

```
<record name="verbose.log" loglevel="debug"/>
```

This final example will stop the logging set up in earlier examples:

```
<record name="verbose.log" action="stop"/>
```

<rename>

The <rename> task is deprecated. Use the <move> task to rename files.

<replace>

The <replace> task enables you to replace a given string with a new value within a set of files.

For example, this task is useful to toggle the value of DEBUG in source code for test-level and production-level distributions.

The full list of <replace> attributes is given in Table 4.68.

Table 4.68   *Table of <replace> Attributes*

Attributes	Description
Required	
dir (if file is not specified)	The directory containing the files to be searched or replaced.
file (if dir is not specified)	The file to be searched or replaced.
propertyfile (if nested <replacefilter> is used)	The property file to use when <replacefilter> elements specify properties.
token (unless nested <replacetoken> is used)	The string to be replaced.

Table 4.68   *(continued)*

Attributes	Description
Optional	
defaultexcludes	If false, default excludes will not be used. Defaults to true.
excludes	A comma-separated list of patterns of files to be excluded. The default is not to exclude any files (except default excludes).
excludesfile	The name of a file that specifies a list of file patterns to exclude—one per line.
includes	A comma-separated list of patterns of files to be included. The default is to include all files.
includesfile	The name of a file that specifies a list of file patterns to include—one per line.
Replacefilterfile	The name of a properties file to use as a set of replace filters, where the property represents a token and the property value is used as the new value for the token.
summary	If true, a summary will be produced detailing the number of occurrences replaced and the number of files searched. Defaults to false.
value	The string to replace each token occurrence with. Defaults to "" (empty string).

Nested Elements

As an implicit fileset, the `<replace>` task supports nested `<include>`, `<exclude>`, and `<patternset>` elements.

In addition to those elements, nested `<replacetoken>`, `<replacevalue>`, and `<replace-filter>` elements are supported. The `<replacetoken>` and `<replacevalue>` elements do not have any attributes. They are useful for specifying multiline tokens and values, respectively.

You cannot specify multiple `<replacetoken>` or `<replacevalue>` elements within the same `<replace>` task, but you can do so with `<replacefilter>`. `<replacefilter>` enables you to specify multiple tokens to be replaced, where each token specified can be given one of four values:

- The value given by the value attribute in the <replacefilter> element.

- The value specified by the property within the property file (as specified by the propertyfile attribute).

- If both of the preceding values are omitted, the value given in the enclosing <replace> task is used.

- Finally, if none of the above is used, the token will be replaced with an empty string "".

The attributes of the <replacefilter> element are given in Table 4.69.

Table 4.69　*Table of <replacefilter> Attributes*

Attributes	Description
Required	
token	The string to be searched for.
Optional	
value	The string that will replace the first string.
property	The name of the property in the property file (as specified in the propertyfile attribute of the enclosing <replace> task) that contains the value to be used as the replacement string.

Example

The following three sections, which demonstrate the nested elements at the simplest level, are equivalent. Each will replace all occurrences of the string @DEBUG@ with the string true in all files in the directory ${src}.

```
<replace dir="${src}" token="@DEBUG@" value="true"/>

<replace dir="${src}">
  <replacetoken>@DEBUG@</replacetoken>
  <replacevalue>@true@</replacevalue>
</replace>

<replace dir="${src}">
  <replacefilter token="@DEBUG@" value="true"/>
</replace>
```

<rmic>

The <rmic> task runs the rmic compiler to generate stubs and skeletons. A full listing of the <rmic> attributes is provided in Table 4.70.

Table 4.70 · *Table of <rmic> Attributes*

Attributes	Description
Required	
base	The directory in which to store the compiled files.
Optional	
classname	The name of the class to be compiled.
classpath	The location of the class files.
classpathref	A reference to a PATH defined elsewhere that is to be used as the class path.
compiler	The compiler to use. Valid values are sun, kaffe, and weblogic. Defaults to the value of the build.rmic property. If not set, the default compiler for the current JVM is used.
debug	If true, debugging info is generated. Defaults to false.
defaultexcludes	If false, default excludes will not be used. Defaults to true.
excludes	A comma-separated list of patterns of files to be excluded. The default is not to exclude any files (except default excludes).
excludesfile	The name of a file that specifies a list of file patterns to exclude—one per line.
extdirs	Specifies the location of installed extensions.
filtering	If true, token filtering will be enabled. Defaults to false.
idl	If true, IDL files will be generated. Defaults to false.
idlopts	Specifies additional options to use when IDL is true.
iiop	If true, stubs will be created for IIOP. Defaults to false.
iiopopts	Specifies additional options to use when iiop is true.
includeantruntime	Indicates whether to include the Ant runtime libraries. Defaults to true.
includejavaruntime	Indicates whether to include the default runtime libraries from the executing JVM. Defaults to false.
includes	A comma-separated list of patterns of files to be included. The default is to include all files.
includesfile	The name of a file that specifies a list of file patterns to include—one per line.
sourcebase	If true, intermediate generated source files will not be deleted. They will be placed in the base directory. Defaults to false.
stubversion	The stub protocol version to use; for example, 1.1. Defaults to the rmic compiler default (that is, compatible with both 1.1 and 1.2).
verify	If enabled, classes that do not implement Remote will be filtered out of the compilation. Disabled by default.

Nested Elements

The `classpath` and `extdirs` attributes can be set using nested `<classpath>` and `<extdirs>` elements, whereas `<exclude>`, `<include>`, and `<patternset>` elements can be nested in specifying the fileset.

Also, nested `<compilerarg>` elements can be used to specify command-line arguments to pass to the compiler. Refer to the "`<javac>`" section earlier in this chapter for attribute details.

Examples

The following example illustrates how to use the task to compile a single class:

```
<rmic base="classes" classname="MyRemoteObject.class"/>
```

One special case to take note of is when you want to specify an inner class as the `classname`. You should specify it in the format `outerclass$$innerclass` instead of `outerclass.innerclass`; for instance, in the following example, `ObjOne` is the inner class of `RemObject`:

```
<rmic base="${build}" classname="RemObjects$$ObjOne"/>
```

<sequential>

Refer to the "<Parallel> and <sequential>" section, earlier in this chapter.

<signjar>

The `<signjar>` task gives you the ability to sign JARs. The attributes of the task (see Table 4.71) correspond to the attributes associated with the `jarsigner` tool. (See `http://java.sun.com/docs/books/tutorial/jar/sign/signing.html` for more details.)

Table 4.71 *Table of <signjar> Attributes*

Attributes	Description
Required	
alias	The alias to sign under.
jar	The name of the JAR file to be signed.

Table 4.71   *(continued)*

Attributes	Description
storepass	The password for keystore integrity.
Optional	
internalsf	If true, the .SF file will be included inside the signature block. Defaults to false.
keypass	The password for the private key (if different).
keystore	The keystore location.
lazy	If true, the presence of a signature file means a JAR is assumed to be signed. Defaults to false.
sectionsonly	If true, the hash of the entire manifest will not be computed. Defaults to false.
sigfile	The name of the .SF/.DSA file
signedjar	The name to give the signed JAR file.
storetype	The keystore type.
verbose	If true, the output will be verbose. Defaults to false.

Example

```
<signjar jar="${dist}/clientApp.jar" alias="andy"
  storepass="secret" keypass="anothersecret"/>
```

This example signs the `clientApp.jar` in the `${dist}` directory with the alias `andy`, accessing the keystore via the `secret` password and the private key via the `anothersecret` password. The `.SF` and `.DSA` files created would be named `andy.sf` and `andy.dsa`, respectively.

<sleep>

The `<sleep>` task enables you to pause the build process for a given length of time. The time can be specified in hours, minutes, seconds, and milliseconds. It's possible to specify negative values for the attributes as long as the total time to pause is positive.

Note that due to operating system behavior, the sleep time is not completely accurate.

Table 4.72 describes the `<sleep>` task attributes.

Table 4.72   *Table of <sleep> Attributes*

Attributes (Optional)	Description
hours	Number of hours to sleep.
minutes	Number of minutes to sleep.
seconds	Number of seconds to sleep.
milliseconds	Number of milliseconds to sleep.
failonerror	If true, the build will stop if an error occurs. Defaults to true.

Example

This example will cause the build to pause for 30 seconds:

```
<sleep seconds = "30" />
```

The following example illustrates how you can specify negative values; in this case, you're causing the build to pause for 2 minutes and 45 seconds:

```
<sleep minutes = "3" seconds = "-15" />
```

<sql>

The `<sql>` task enables you to execute SQL statements on a database via JDBC. You can either provide the SQL statement(s) within the tag, or via an external source file. The SQL statements may optionally contain comments using `//` or REM at the start of the lines.

Table 4.73 provides a full list of the task's attributes.

Table 4.73   *Table of <sql> Attributes*

Attributes	Description
Required	
driver	The class name of the JDBC driver to be used.
password	Database password.
src (unless statement(s) enclosed within tags)	The name of a file containing the SQL statement(s) to execute.
url	Database connection URL.
userid	Database username.

Table 4.73   *(continued)*

Attributes	Description
Optional	
append	If true, output will be appended to an existing file rather than the file being overwritten. Defaults to false.
autocommit	If true, the statements are executed and committed separately. If false, the statements are executed as one transaction (defaults to false).
classpath	Specifies the class path to use for loading the driver if without the system class path.
classpathref	A reference to a PATH defined elsewhere that is to be used as the class path.
delimiter	The string that separates SQL statements. If not given, the default ";" is used.
encoding	Specifies the encoding of the files containing SQL statements. Defaults to the JVM default encoding.
onerror	The action to perform in the result of an error: continue—Show the error stop—Stop execution and commit transaction abort—Abort the execution and transaction and stop
output	Specifies the name of a file to output the results to rather than the default System.out.
print	If true, the result sets from the statements will be printed. Defaults to false.
rdbms	If true, this task will execute only if it is connecting to an RDBMS.
showheaders	Specifies whether to display the headers from the result sets. Defaults to true.
version	Specify an RDBMS version under which this task will run exclusively.

Nested Elements

The `<transaction>` element enables you to run multiple transactions within the same `<sql>` task. It works similarly to its parent tag in that it requires an `src` attribute or SQL statements embedded within the tag.

```
<transaction>
Insert ...

</transaction>

<transaction src="transaction1.txt"/>
```

You can also nest `<fileset>` and `<classpath>` elements for specifying a set of source files and the value for the `classpath` attribute, respectively. In the case of using a fileset, each of the files will be executed as an individual transaction, but the order of execution of each transaction is undefined.

Examples

This simple example executes the specified select statement if the database is a MySQL database, and displays the results to the console:

```
<sql driver="org.gjt.mm.mysql.Driver"
  url="jdbc:mysql://mysql.book.ant/ANTBOOK"
  userid="author"
  password="sams"
  classpath="C:\jars\mysql.jar"
  autocommit="true"
  rdbms="mysql"
  print="true">
select name, email from AUTHORS
</sql>
```

The following example illustrates the use of transactions. In this case, each of the SQL statements within the update.txt and secondupdate.txt files is executed as a separate transaction:

```
<sql driver="org.gjt.mm.mysql.Driver"
  url="jdbc:mysql://mysql.book.ant/ANTBOOK"
  userid="author"
  password="sams"
  classpath="C:\jars\mysql.jar"
  autocommit="true"
  rdbms="mysql"
  print="true">

  <transaction src="update.txt"/>
  <transaction src="secondupdate.txt"/>
</sql>
```

Note that to avoid having to escape special characters (such as < and >) that might occur in your statements, enclose your statements in <![CDATA[...]]>. For example, <![CDATA[select * from records where ID > 100]]>.

<style>

The <style> task enables you to automate the application of a stylesheet on an XML document using a specified XSLT processor. It can be used with an individual XML document (using the in and out attributes) or with multiple files (using the fileset attributes).

The <style> task requires external libraries to be installed, depending on which processor is chosen. For example, Apache's XML Xalan processor requires the Xalan JAR (http://xml.apache.org/xalan-j/index.html) as well as the Ant optional JAR. Note that when using Xalan 2, the processor attribute should be set to trax (Xalan 2 has a trax interface).

A full listing of supported attributes is provided in Table 4.74.

Table 4.74   *Table of <style> Attributes*

Attributes	Description
Required	
destdir (required unless in and out specified)	The destination directory for the output files.
style	The name of the stylesheet to use. If specified as a relative path, it should be specified relative to the project basedir (not the task basedir). Although supported, this is a deprecated feature).
Optional	
basedir	The base directory from which to find the source XML file(s). Defaults to the project's base directory.
classpath	The class path to use to locate the XSLT processor classes.
classpathref	A reference to a PATH defined elsewhere that is to be used as the class path.
defaultexcludes	If false, default excludes will not be used. Defaults to true.
excludes	A comma-separated list of patterns of files to be excluded. The default is not to exclude any files.
excludesfile	The name of a file that specifies a list of file patterns to exclude—one per line.
extension	The file extension to give the target files. Defaults to .html.
force	If true, new target files will be produced even if the current source files and stylesheet are older than the current target files. Defaults to false.
in	The name of a single XML document to be processed.

Table 4.74   *(continued)*

Attributes	Description
includes	A comma-separated list of patterns of files to be included. The default is to include all files.
includesfile	The name of a file that specifies a list of file patterns to include—one per line.
out	The name of the output file for the processed file.
outputtype	Specifies the output method to be used (only "xml" is guaranteed to be supported).
processor	The processor to use: trax, xalan, xslp (deprecated), or the name of a class that implements the XSLTLiason interface. Defaults to the first processor found when the search is done in this order: trax, xslp, and then xalan.
scanincludeddirectories	If true, the style will also be applied to all the files within directories matched by the includes pattern. Defaults to true.

Nested Elements

Being an implicit fileset, the `<style>` task supports nested `<include>`, `<exclude>`, and `<patternset>` elements. Nested `<classpath>` elements are also supported in order to specify the class path to use in locating the XSLT processor classes.

To specify parameters to pass to the stylesheet, nested `<param>` elements can be used (see Table 4.75).

Table 4.75   *Table of <param> Attributes*

Attributes (Required)	Description
expression	The value to give the param, expressed as an XSL expression.
name	The name of the parameter.

Example

The following example results in the production of the `winelist.html` file as a result of the application of the `presentation.xsl` stylesheet to the XML document `winelist.xml`.

```
<style in="winelist.xml" out="winelist.html" style="presentation.xsl"/>
```

<tar>

The <tar> task enables you to create tar archives.

Some care should be taken when using the <tar> task. First, be careful not to specify the same file more than once because it will be included in the archive twice. Second, you should be aware of the slight complication when dealing with files that have path lengths of greater than 100 characters. This is due to the fact that earlier versions of tar did not support paths of this length. To manage this, you have five options, as specified by the longfile attribute:

- Truncate—Paths of greater than 100 characters will be truncated to a 100-character limit. However, this means a loss of path information, which is usually, if not always, undesirable.

- Fail—The task will fail if a file with such a path exists.

- Omit—The file will be omitted from the tar.

- Gnu—The tar file produced will be a GNU tar, which means that all files will retain the full path, but the tar can only be untarred using GNU tar.

- Warn—This behaves as the Gnu option, but a warning is produced for each file that breaks the limit.

Table 4.76 lists the <tar> task attributes.

Table 4.76   *Table of <tar> Attributes*

Attributes	Description
Required	
destfile	The name to give to the created tar file.
Optional	
basedir	The base directory the task will work from.
compression	Specifies the compression to use. Valid values are none, gzip, and bzip2. Defaults to none.
defaultexcludes	If false, default excludes will not be used. Defaults to true.
excludes	A comma-separated list of patterns of files to be excluded. The default is not to exclude any files (except default excludes).
excludesfile	The name of a file that specifies a list of file patterns to exclude—one per line.
includes	A comma-separated list of patterns of files to be included. The default is to include all files.

Table 4.76   *(continued)*

Attributes	Description
includesfile	The name of a file that specifies a list of file patterns to include—one per line.
longfile	Specifies what to do with long files (those of greater than 100 characters): truncate, fail, warn, omit, or gnu. Defaults to warn.

Nested Elements

As an implicit fileset, this task supports nested `<include>`, `<exclude>`, and `<patternset>` elements as well as nested `<fileset>` elements. Another element, `<tarfileset>`, is also supported. `<tarfileset>` is basically an extended fileset that has three additional (optional) attributes (see Table 4.77), which enables you to specify additional properties for the files in the fileset.

Table 4.77   *Table of Additional <tarfileset> Attributes*

Attributes	Description
Optional	
fullpath	If specified, the file in the fileset is written with that path in the archive. The fileset should consist of only one file.
group	The group name for the tar entry (not the same as the GID).
mode	A three-digit octal string that corresponds to the mode to be used. Specified in the standard UNIX style; for example, 755.
prefix	If specified, all files in the fileset are prefixed with that path in the archive.
preserveleadingslashes	If true, leading slashes (/) will be preserved in the filenames. The default is false.
username	The username for the tar entry (not the same as the UID).

Example

This example will create the tar file `source.tar` containing all the files within the `src` directory:

```
<tar tarfile="source.tar" basedir="src"/>
```

<taskdef>

The <taskdef> task is used to make custom tasks available for use within the build file. Basically, you provide the name of the class that will implement this particular custom task and the name that you want to give the custom task. Note that you must give the task a name that is not already the name of an existing task, or the taskdef will not work.

Rather than using multiple taskdefs to set up a number of custom tasks, you can define multiple custom tasks at once by using the file and resource attributes. This is illustrated in the examples that follow. Chapter 6 provides a full custom task example that also demonstrates the use of <taskdef>. Table 4.78 lists the <taskdef> attributes.

Table 4.78   *Table of <taskdef> Attributes*

Attributes	Description
Required	
name (required unless file or resource has been specified)	The name for the task.
classname (required unless file or resource has been specified)	The name of the class that implements this task.
Optional	
classpath	The class path to use to locate the class given in classname or the resource.
file	The name of the property file from which to load name/classname pairs.
loaderref	Specifies a name of a loader to be used to load the class. This can be used to allow multiple tasks to be loaded with the same loader, allowing them to call each other.
resource	The name of the property resource from which to load name/classname pairs.

Examples

```
<taskdef name="mytask" classname="com.test.myCustomTask"/>
```

The preceding example will load the com.test.myCustomTask class and make it accessible using a task named mytask.

```
<taskdef file="taskdefs.txt"/>
```

The preceding example loads the set of tasks defined in the properties file `taskdefs.txt`, where each property is specified as *<name>=<classname>*. For example, the line `mytask=com.test.myCustomTask` is equivalent to the first example.

<touch>

Using the `<touch>` task, you can update the modification time of one or more files. The modification time can be changed to the current time (by default), or you can specify an exact time to be used. You can also use the `<touch>` task to create a file that doesn't already exist simply by specifying a nonexistent file. With that in mind, it is important that you specify the files correctly because no error is reported if a specified file doesn't exist, obviously.

One example in which `<touch>` is useful is to force Ant to recompile an entire source tree by making it believe that the files have been modified.

Table 4.79 describes the attributes of the task.

Table 4.79   *Table of <touch> Attributes*

Attributes	Description
Required	
file (required if a fileset is not specified)	The name of the file to be touched.
Optional	
datetime	The new modification time for the file(s); specified in the format MM/DD/YYYY HH:MM (A/P)M.
millis	The new modification time for the file(s); specified as the number of milliseconds since January 1, 1970, 00:00:00.

Nested Elements

The `<touch>` task supports nested `<fileset>` elements in specifying the files to be touched.

Examples

The simplest example is to update the modification time of a single file to the current time:

```
<touch file="MyClass.java"/>
```

For example, assume that you have freshly pulled out source files from CVS. By touching them, you can bring them into line with the host machine, so there aren't any files that were modified in the future.

```
<touch>
  <fileset dir="src"/>
</touch>
```

<tstamp>

Normally used within an `init` target, the `<tstamp>` task is used to make a set of timestamp properties available within the build file. By using `<tstamp>`, the dstamp, tstamp, and today properties will be set. dstamp is in the format `yyyymmdd`, tstamp is in the format `hhmm`, and today is in the format `month day year`.

The `<tstamp>` task also can be used in the naming of files, or for reporting the time and date of an event.

`<tstamp>` supports one optional attribute, as listed in Table 4.80.

Table 4.80   *Table of <tstamp> Attributes*

Attributes (Optional)	Description
Prefix	Specifies a prefix for the properties set.

Nested Elements

`<format>` elements that allow you to set a property to a particular date and time in a specified format can be nested within a `<tstamp>` task. Details of the element attributes are provided in Table 4.81.

Table 4.81   *Table of <format> Attributes*

Attributes	Description
Required	
property	The property to set.
pattern	The pattern to use with the date/time. This should follow the syntax defined by java.text.SimpleDateFormat.

Table 4.81   *(continued)*

Attributes	Description
Optional	
locale	The locale used to create the date/time, in the form language, country, variant where country and variant are optional. See java.util.Locale for more information.
offset	The offset to the current time.
timezone	Specifies the time zone to use for displaying time. Valid values are as defined by the Java TimeZone class.
unit	Specifies the unit of the offset. Valid values are millisecond, second, minute, hour, day, week, month, or year.

Examples

This example illustrates a simple use of `<tstamp>`, which displays of the property values you set using `<tstamp>`:

```
<tstamp/>
<echo message="DSTAMP : ${DSTAMP} TSTAMP : ${TSTAMP} TODAY : ${TODAY}"/>
```

The following examples show how you can refine the format of the result returned by `<tstamp>`:

```
<tstamp>
  <format property="FULL_DATE" pattern="d MMMM yyyy, hh:mm:ss:SS a, z"
    locale="en"/>
</tstamp>
<tstamp>
  <format property="US_DATE" pattern="M/d/yyyy, hh:mm:ss:SS a, z" locale="en"/>
</tstamp>

<tstamp>
  <format property="SPANISH_DATE" pattern="d MMMM yyyy, hh:mm:ss:SS a, z"
    locale="es"/>
</tstamp>
<tstamp>
  <format property="YESTERDAY" pattern="d MMMM yyyy" offset="-1" unit="day"/>
</tstamp>

<echo message="FULL_DATE : ${FULL_DATE}"/>
<echo message="US_DATE : ${US_DATE}"/>
<echo message="SPANISH_DATE : ${SPANISH_DATE}"/>
<echo message="YESTERDAY : ${YESTERDAY}"/>
```

<typedef>

The <typedef> task enables you define your own data types to be used within a project (usually within your own custom tasks). Typedefs can be used without targets.

Table 4.82 lists the <typedef> attributes.

Table 4.82   *Table of <typedef> Attributes*

Attributes	Description
Required	
name (required unless file or resource has been specified)	The name to give the data type.
classname (required unless file or resource has been specified)	The name of the class that implements this data type.
Optional	
classpath	The class path to use when loading the class specified by classname.
File	Specifies the name of a properties file that contains name/classname pairs to load.
loaderref	Specifies a name of a loader to be used to load the class. This can be used to allow multiple types to be loaded with the same loader, allowing them to call each other.
Resource	Specifies a property resource to load name/classname pairs from.

Nested Elements

A nested <classpath> element can be used to specify the class path to use.

Example

```
<typedef name="mytype" classname="org.aw.data.myCustomClass"/>
```

The preceding example will define a new data type called mytype, whose implementation is retrieved from the class org.aw.data.myCustomClass.

<Unjar>, <Untar>, <Unwar>, <Unzip>

These four tasks enable you to extract files from a JAR, tar, WAR, and Zip file, respectively. They share the same attributes as described in Table 4.83.

In all cases, file permission are not restored on extracted files.

Note that the <untar> task recognizes the long pathname entries used by GNU tar.

Table 4.83   *Table of <unjar>/<untar>/<unwar>/<unzip> Attributes*

Attributes	Description
Required	
src	The name of the archive to be expanded.
dest	The name of the directory to which to extract the archive.
Optional	
compression (<untar> only)	Specifies the compression to use. Valid values are none, gzip, and bzip2. Defaults to none.
overwrite	If true, files in the destination directory will be overwritten even if they are newer than the corresponding file in the archive. Defaults to true.

Nested Elements

Nested <fileset> and <patternset> elements are supported to specify the files to extract and the specific files to extract from them, respectively.

Examples

The following examples extract the JAR, tar, WAR, and Zip files, respectively, into the classes directory:

```
<unjar src="build.jar" dest="classes"/>
<untar src="build.tar" dest="classes"/>
<unwar src="build.war" dest="classes"/>
<unzip src="build.zip" dest="classes"/>
```

<uptodate>

The <uptodate> task will set a property if a target file (or set of files) is more recent than a set of source files.

In general, `<uptodate>` is a good task to use to avoid target execution when the files involved are not directly dependent. One such example is to check whether the set of files in an archive has changed since the archive was last compiled.

See Table 4.84 for a full listing of the `<uptodate>` attributes.

Table 4.84   *Table of `<uptodate>` Attributes*

Attributes	Description
Required	
property	The property to set.
srcfile (required unless a nested `<srcfiles>` element is used)	The name of the source file.
targetfile (required unless a nested `<mapper>` element is used)	The name of the target file.
Optional	
value	The value to give the property. Defaults to true.

Nested Elements

Nested `<srcfiles>` elements (a fileset with a different name) can be used to specify the source files involved, and for specifying multiple target files, a nested `<mapper>` element can be used.

Example

The following example will set the `doJar` property if the `backup.jar` file has been modified more recently than all the class files specified in the `<srcfiles>` element.

```
<uptodate property="doJar" targetfile="backup.jar">
  <srcfiles dir="classes" includes="**/*.class"/>
</uptodate>
```

`<waitfor>`

As a companion to the `<parallel>` task, `<waitfor>` will block a thread's execution until the specified conditions have been met. Its attributes are provided in Table 4.85.

Table 4.85 *Table of <waitfor> Attributes*

Attributes (Optional)	Description
checkevery	Sets the time of the period between checks of whether the condition holds. Defaults to 500.
checkeveryunit	Valid values are millisecond, second, minute, hour, day, or week, this attribute specifies the unit of time that the checkevery attribute refers to.
maxwait	Sets the maximum amount of time to wait for the condition to hold. Defaults to 180000.
maxwaitunit	Valid values are millisecond, second, minute, hour, day, or week. This attribute specifies the unit of time that the maxwait attribute refers to. Defaults to milliseconds.
timeoutproperty	The name of a property to set if the condition did not become true before the maximum wait time was exceeded.

Nested Elements

The <waitfor> task supports the same nested elements as the <condition> task.

Example

The following example will wait for the property userok to be set. The condition is checked every 500 milliseconds, and the timedout property is set to true if the userok property does not exist after one minute has elapsed. This could be used, for example, in parallel with a task that waits for user input, although the maxwait time would have to be adjusted accordingly.

```
<waitfor maxwait="1" maxwaitunit="minute"
  timeoutproperty="timedout">
  <isset property="userok"/>
</waitfor>
```

> **Tip**
> A good example of when the <waitfor> task is useful is in waiting for a server to start up.

<war>

The <war> task enables you to assemble a Web Archive (WAR) file, which is a file format used for deploying Web applications. The <war> task, which is effectively a shortcut to what can be produced with the `<zip>` and `<jar>` tasks using `zipfilesets`, assists in building up the set of files needed to complete the Web application in the required directory structure.

The list of `<war>` attributes is provided in Table 4.86.

Table 4.86   *Table of <war> Attributes*

Attributes	Description
Required	
destfile	The name to be given to the WAR file.
webxml	The file to be used for the deployment descriptor (that is, the source file for WEB-INF/web.xml).
Optional	
basedir	The name of the directory from which the files to jar are located.
compress	If true, files will also be compressed. Defaults to true.
defaultexcludes	If false, default excludes will not be used. Defaults to true.
encoding	The character encoding to use for filenames inside the archive. Defaults to UTF8. It is recommended that this attribute value be left as the default to avoid creating an archive unreadable for Java.
excludes	A comma-separated list of patterns of files to be excluded. The default is not to exclude any files (except default excludes).
excludesfile	The name of a file that specifies a list of file patterns to exclude—one per line.
filesonly	If true, only file entries will be stored. Defaults to false.
includes	A comma-separated list of patterns of files to be included. The default is to include all files.
includesfile	The name of a file that specifies a list of file patterns to include—one per line.
manifest	The name of the file to use as the manifest.
update	Indicates what to do if the file already exists. If true, the WAR file will be updated; otherwise, it will be overwritten.

Nested Elements

The `<war>` task supports the nested elements `<lib>`, `<classes>`, `<webinf>`, and `<metainf>`. These are filesets that specify the files to be included in the directories contained within the WAR file—WEB-INF/lib, WEB-INF/classes, WEB-INF, and META-INF, respectively. The following example demonstrates how to use them. It should be noted that you cannot use the `webinf` and `metainf` filesets to specify the `web.xml` nor `manifest.mf` to be used.

Other filesets are supported, the contents of which are placed in the root directory of the created WAR file.

Example

Inspect the following example:

```
<war warfile="petstore.war" webxml="depdesc.xml">
  <fileset dir="${classes}">
    <include name="com\sams\ant\client\**"/>
  </fileset>
  <fileset dir="${websrc}"/>
  <classes dir="${classes}">
    <include name="com\sams\ant\server\**"/>
  </classes>
  <lib dir="${jars}">
    <include name="mysql.jar"/>
  </lib>
</war>
```

The preceding listing will result in a WAR file named `petstore.war`, with the following directory structure:

WEB-INF/classes—Contains all the files in the ${classes}\com\sams\ant\server directory

WEB-INF/lib—Contains the mysql.jar file from the ${jars} directory

WEB-INF—Contains web.xml (which is a renamed copy of depdesc.xml)

The root directory in the created WAR file will contain all the files from the directories `${websrc}` and `${classes}\com\sams\ant\client`.

<xmlproperty>

The `<xmlproperty>` task gives you the ability to load properties from an XML file. Conversion is simple. The element `<project><build>src</build></project>` is equivalent to `project.build=src`. With element attributes, the translation is dependent on the `collapseattributes` attribute. If true, element attributes are treated as nested elements. Hence, `<project build="src">` is equivalent to the previous examples. If false, the same example would result in the `project(build)` property being set to `src`.

Table 4.87 displays the list of `<xmlproperty>` attributes.

Table 4.87   *Table of `<xmlproperty>` Attributes*

Attributes	Description
Required	
file	The XML formatted file.
Optional	
collapseattributes	If true, element attributes are treated as nested elements. Defaults to false.
keeproot	If true, the XML root tag is included as a first value in the property name. Defaults to true.
prefix	If specified, this will be prepended to each property.
validate	Enable validation. Defaults to false.

Examples

The following is a sample XML file that contains the properties `project.build`, `project.distrib`, and `project.src`:

```
<project>
  <build>classes</build>
  <distrib>lib</distrib>
  <src>src</src>
</project>
```

The preceding set of properties could be loaded, assuming that it was stored in the file `myproperties.xml`, using the following example:

```
<xmlproperty file="myproperties.xml"/>
```

<xslt>

Refer to the "`<style>`" section earlier in the chapter. `<xslt>` is the same task as `<style>`, but with a different name.

<zip>

The <zip> task, as its name suggests, gives you the ability to create Zip files.

Table 4.88 provides a list of the <zip> attributes. Among those attributes it's important to note the significance of the encoding attribute. As with regular Zip tools, the <zip> task uses the platform's default character encoding for filenames. This is problematic if the resultant Zip file is to be accessed via Java, and the filenames contain non-US-ASCII characters. The solution is to set the encoding to UTF8.

It should be noted that file permissions will not be transferred to resulting zipped files.

Table 4.88   *Table of <zip> Attributes*

Attributes	Description
Required	
destfile	The name to be given to the created Zip file.
basedir (if fileset not specified)	The name of the directory containing the files to be zipped.
Optional	
compress	Specifies whether the files will be compressed in the Zip file. Defaults to true.
defaultexcludes	If false, default excludes will not be used. Defaults to true.
duplicate	Specifies the behavior when a duplicate file is found. Valid values are create, fail, and skip.
encoding	The character encoding to use for filenames inside the archive. The default is platform dependent.
excludes	A comma-separated list of patterns of files to be excluded. The default is not to exclude any files (except default excludes).
excludesfile	The name of a file that specifies a list of file patterns to exclude—one per line.
filesOnly	If true, only file entries will be stored. Defaults to false.
includes	A comma-separated list of patterns of files to be included. The default is to include all files.
includesfile	The name of a file that specifies a list of file patterns to include—one per line.
update	Indicates the choice of action if the file already exists. If true, the Zip file will be updated; otherwise, it will be overwritten.
whenempty	Specifies the behavior if no files match. Valid values are skip, create, and fail. Defaults to skip.

Nested Elements

The fileset element is supported to specify files to be included in the Zip file. Additionally, the `zipfileset` element enables you to specify a fileset with a few extra attributes: `prefix`, `fullpath`, and `src`.

By specifying a value for the `prefix` attribute, the files contained within the `zipfileset` will be given a path prefix of the value specified. For example, if the `zipfileset` contains the file `com\sams\ant\MyClass.java` with the prefix value `backup`, the corresponding file will be stored in the resultant Zip file with the path `src\com\sams\ant`.

The `fullpath` attribute is used to give the file a different name (and path) in the destination Zip file. Of course, this means that the `zipfileset` can contain only one file.

The other attribute, `src`, enables you to specify a Zip file (as opposed to a directory) as the source of files for the `zipfileset`. In fact, you cannot specify both `src` and `dir`.

Nested `<zipgroupfileset>` elements can also be used. This is just a fileset that enables you to specify multiple Zip files to be merged into the archive.

Examples

In the following example, the Zip file `backup.zip` is created, containing all the files within the `${src}` directory:

```
<zip zipfile="backup.zip" basedir="${src}"/>
```

The following example illustrates how `zipfileset` elements can be used to specify the contents of the Zip file. The resultant Zip file will consist of all the `.gif` files from the working directory with path of `images/`, all the `.mpg` files within the `video.zip` with a path of `mpeg/`, and the file `main.html` (a renamed version of `index.html`).

```
<zip zipfile="distrib.zip">
  <zipfileset dir="." includes="*.gif" prefix="images"/>
  <zipfileset dir="." includes="index.html" fullpath="main.html"/>
  <zipfileset src="video.zip" includes="*.mpg" prefix="mpeg"/>
</zip>
```

Summary

This chapter has shown the depth of core tasks available to you, the Ant user. With these tasks at hand, you have a wealth of riches to take you from compilation to deployment, as well as to deal with some of the more mundane tasks. In addition to the tasks covered in this chapter, the chapters that follow will further enhance your understanding of the breadth of Ant's scope.

CHAPTER 5

Optional Tasks

Just as you are probably beginning to get a good feel for how powerful this Ant framework is, allow us to introduce you to a whole new suite of tasks commonly referred to as optional tasks. So called because, although they are not fundamental to the actual build logic of a system, they do compliment the overall management by providing useful utilities such as accessing a Telnet server or uploading a file to an FTP site. This chapter will take an exploratory look at some of the more common optional tasks that are available to you.

Additional Resources for Ant

As of version 1.5, the default distribution of Ant comes with the necessary JAR file to enable the majority of the optional tasks. However, some tasks do require the download of an additional JAR file to enable the functionally. Table 5.1 lists the tasks that require extra JAR files. To install the JAR file, simply copy it into the `/lib/` directory of the Ant installation.

Table 5.1 *Optional JAR File Locations*

Optional Task	URI `LocationJarFile`
JUnit junit.jar	http://www.junit.org/
JunitReport xalan.jar	http://xml.apache.org/
Stylebook stylebook-1.0-b2.jar	http://cvs.apache.org/viewcvs.cgi/xml-xerces/java/tools/
Ftp/Telnet netcomponents.jar	http://www.savarese.org/oro/downloads

ANTLR

Don't confuse ANTLR with Ant, the name is merely coincidence and, in this instance, stands for ANother Tool for Language Recognition. This is a tool for building compilers and lexical analyzers. You describe your language using what is known as a grammar file, which describes the make up of the language you are attempting to support. This is described using a form of BNF (Backus Naur Form), which is a language for describing languages! You can find out more about ANTLR from its Web site `http://www.antlr.org/`.

The interface to the ANTLR task is relatively straightforward as shown in Table 5.2. One thing you'll need to do before running this task is obtain the JAR file from the ANTLR Web site and place it into your Ant `/lib/` directory. Beware though; the JAR file that comes with the default distribution isn't of much use to you. You will have to modify the batch files and build the ANTLR JAR file yourself (ironically, ANTLR doesn't provide any Ant scripts for this purpose!).

Table 5.2 *Table of <antlr> Attributes*

Attributes	Description
target	The location of the grammar file to process. (Required)
outputdirectory	The directory that will receive the generated files.
glib	Optional super grammar file the target grammar overrides.
debug	If yes, this flag adds code to the generated parser that will launch the ParseView debugger on invocation. ParseView is a separate component that must be installed or your grammar will have compilation errors.
html	Emits an HTML version of the grammar with hyperlinked actions.

Table 5.2 *(continued)*

Attributes	Description
diagnostic	Generates a text file with debugging information based on the target grammar.
trace	Forces all rules to call traceIn/traceOut if set to yes. The default is no.
traceParser	Forces parser rules to call traceIn/traceOut only if set to yes.
traceLexer	Forces lexer rules to call traceIn/traceOut only if set to yes.
traceTreeWalker	Forces tree walker rules to call traceIn/traceOut only if set to yes.
dir	The directory in which to invoke the Virtual Machine.

To use the ANTLR task, simply type:

```
<antlr target="src/html.g" outputdirectory="antlr"/>
```

<cab>

This task enables you to easily create a CAB file, the archive format used by Microsoft. The concept of a CAB file format is very similar to a JAR or ZIP file in the sense that it is a collection of resource files, which can include any type of file.

This task is merely a front-end to the Microsoft utility, `cabarc` executable. Therefore, to use this task you must have the `cabarc` located in your system path. If you don't have the `cabarc` utility, you can download the Java SDK from Microsoft, which has this file as part of its distribution.

Table 5.3 details the attributes for this task, which are very similar to the ZIP and JAR utilities.

Table 5.3 *Table of <cab> Attributes*

Attributes	Description
cabfile	The name of the CAB file that will be created. (Required)
basedir	The directory from where the archive will be built. (Required)
verbose	If set to yes, the output of the utility will be displayed.
compress	Controls whether the contents of the file will be compressed. Defaults to yes.
options	Enables you to specify additional command-line options for cabarc. See the cabarc documentation for more information.

Table 5.3   *(continued)*

Attributes	Description
includes	Enables you to specify a comma-separated list of file patterns of files that should be included in the archive.
includesfile	Instead of using the includes attribute, you can specify all the patterns, line-by-line in a flat-text file. This attribute enables you to load in this file.
excludes	Similar in nature to the includes attribute except this is the patterns of files that will be excluded from the archive.
excludesfile	Similar in nature to the includesfile attribute except for excluding files.
defaultexcludes	Flags whether the default excludes should be included.

The following example illustrates a typical use for the `<cab>` task, which is to package up the class files for an applet designed to be distributed via Microsoft's Internet Explorer.

```
<cab cabfile="${lib}/ie_applet.cab"
  basedir="${build}"
  includes="**/*.class"/>
```

<depend>

The `<depend>` task is a preprocessor to the compilation stage. In a normal call to compile, the `<javac>` process works out which classes to compile by determining which class files are missing or which source files have changed since the last time the build was made. Although this is sufficient for the majority of projects, it does become a problem for some large projects.

Assume that you make a change to a base class `animal.java`, which will affect the super classes, `dog.java` and `cat.java`, from functioning correctly; maybe an interface change or a method signature change. Using the standard compilation procedures, only `animal.java` would be compiled, and the other two classes would be left untouched. This might result in run-time errors because the two classes would be making calls to methods that may or may not exist. The `<depend>` task ensures that these sort of dependencies are spotted and fixed before compilation begins.

Let's examine Listing 5.1 in action to illustrate the benefit and power of the `<depend>` task.

Listing 5.1   *Three Java Files That Relate to One Another*

```
public class animal extends Object {
  public String getType(){
    return null;
  }
}

public class cat extends animal {
  public String getType(){
    return "cat";
  }
}

public class dog extends animal {
  public String getType(){
    return "dog";
  }
}
```

We can compile these three files using a very simple `<javac>` task, which will produce three class files accordingly.

```
<target name="animal">
  <javac srcdir="${src}" destdir="${build}"/>
</target>
```

So far so good, everything is finding its natural place in the order of things. Now let's make a subtle change to the `animal.java` java file. Let's change the return type of `getType()` to an `Object` instead of a `String`, and then recompile. By calling the same target again, only one file will be recompiled, the `animal.java` class. This is because the timestamps on the other two files have not changed since the last compilation.

The problem exists that we need to force the compilation of the classes that share a dependency, without resorting to a complete rebuild in each instance. Admittedly in this somewhat contrived example a rebuild isn't really a major issue because there are only three files.

This is where the `<depend>` task comes into play. This task looks at the class files and builds up a tree of dependencies, and should one file change it will look at the other files and delete the class files accordingly. Listing 5.2 shows a simple `<depend>` task in action on our three files.

Listing 5.2   *Sample <depend> Task*

```
<target name="depend">
  <depend srcdir="${src}"
  destdir="${build}"
  cache="depcache"
  closure="yes"/>
</target>

<target name="animal" depends="depend">
  <javac srcdir="${src}" destdir="${build}"/>
</target>
```

This time if we make a call to the animal target, a call to the <depend> task will ensue, which will determine that the files dog.java and cat.java will require recompiling at the same time.

Before we take a look at some of the attributes of this task it is worth noting that the <depend> can get it wrong on occasion. Because the class depends on obtaining object dependency information from the .class file, if you compile with optimizations or debug information off, this will render the <depend> task useless. In addition to this, there are some class design considerations that will render the <depend> and misdiagnose some dependencies. For example, classes that hold static constants, where the constant changes, might not be picked up.

Table 5.4 details the attributes associated with the <depend> task.

Table 5.4   *Table of <depend> Attributes*

Attributes	Description
srcDir	This is the directory where the source files exist. If you have multiple source locations, you can use the standard <include>, <exclude>, and <patternset> inner elements. (Required)
destDir	This is the top-level directory of the class files.
cache	If this attribute is specified, the task will cache the dependency information to decrease the look up time.
closure	This controls whether the depend task should look for all classes that might be affected, directly or indirectly. The default is false, which means all classes that are indirectly dependent will be removed.
dump	This controls whether the dependency information is written to the debug log.
classpath	This is the list of JAR files and classes that this task should check dependencies against.

The <depend> task should be used with care and, although it will catch your class depend-encies for the majority of builds, it should not be relied on. For large projects, the extra time that is used determining the dependency tree might be longer than the actual time to do a complete rebuild, thus voiding the reason to use the <depend> in the first place.

<echoproperties>

One of the more useful tasks, specifically when developing your build file, is the <echoproperties> optional task. This enables you to dump all the properties that are presently available to you to the screen or file at the point you make a call to the task. Using a simple call:

```
<echoproperties prefix="ant"/>
```

will produce the following output:

```
C:\antbook\antbook_chapter5>ant echo-examples
Buildfile: build.xml

echo-examples:
[echoproperties] #Ant properties
[echoproperties] #Mon May 20 23:27:34 BST 2002
[echoproperties] ant.file=C\:\\antbook\\antbook_chapter5\\build.xml
[echoproperties] ant.project.name=antbook
[echoproperties] ant.java.version=1.3
[echoproperties] ant.home=c\:\\alanwilliamson\\ant1_5
[echoproperties] ant.version=Apache Ant version 1.5

BUILD SUCCESSFUL
Total time: 1 second
```

Did you notice the use of the prefix attribute? The reason for this was to limit all the returned properties to just the ones beginning with ant. Try it without, and you'll discover a whole host of properties, including all the standard Java properties. Table 5.5 details the attributes associated with this task.

Table 5.5   *Table of <echoproperties> Attributes*

Attributes	Description
prefix	A filter for the properties echoed.
destfile	The name of the file that will receive the list of properties. This file is formatted in the same style supported by java.utils.Property.
failonerror	If something goes wrong with the output to file, this parameter determines if the build as a whole will fail.

This task is particularly useful when developing the Ant build file. You can easily take snapshots of your build at various stages to analyze later. For this reason, it is always a good idea to prefix all your own variables with a known string to easily distinguish them from the system-defined properties.

<ftp>

As with any development project there always comes a time to ship code. Either this is a JAR file that has to be updated on a remote server, or, if the project is an open-source initiative, you are about to make the latest source code available on the Web. You can easily integrate this functionality into your build file using the optional <ftp> task, which makes interfacing to any FTP server a trivial exercise. This task is basically a wrapper to the FTP class available in the Netcomponents suite. The basic FTP commands available are get, put, del, list, chmod, and mkdir.

Table 5.6 shows the attributes available to the <ftp> task.

Table 5.6   *Table of <ftp> Attributes*

Attributes	Description
userid	The username for the FTP server.
password	The password for the username.
server	The remote address of the server you are connecting to. (Required)
port	The port number of the server you are connecting to. Defaults to 21.
remotedir	The remote directory on the FTP server.
binary	The mode in which files are transmitted. If no, they are sent as ASCII files. Default is yes.
action	The FTP command to perform put, get, list, del, chmod, mkdir. Defaults to put.

Table 5.6   *(continued)*

Attributes	Description
passive	This is the mode of the FTP session. Passive mode is generally used for tunneling through firewalls where the FTP server is not allowed to connect back to the client. Defaults to no.
verbose	Displays progress information. Set to "no", although very handy when debugging an FTP task.
depends	If this is set to yes, only the newer or changed file is sent.
newer	Synonym for depends.
separator	The separator that is used for files and directories. Defaults to the Unix style /.
umask	When a file is created on the remote server, this is the permission to which the file will be set.
chmod	This is the permission flags for existing or newly put files.
listing	This is the name of the file that will receive the file listings.
ignoreNoncriticalErrors	A flag to determine whether to continue if a noncritical error code is returned. The default is no.
skipFailedTransfers	When transferring a list of files, this controls whether a failed flag will stop the processing of the remaining files to be transferred. Defaults to false.

list

The easiest of all the tasks is the one that retrieves the list of files from a remote server, as shown in Listing 5.3. This task opens a connection to the remote server "antbook", using a passive connection.

Listing 5.3   *Retrieving the List of Files from an FTP Server*

```
<ftp server="antbook" passive="yes" userid="webadmin" password="sams"
    action="list" listing="ftp.txt">
  <fileset>
    <include name="**"/>
  </fileset>
</ftp>
```

The `<fileset>` nested element controls the files you want to list. In this example, using the standard Ant rules, we are listing all the files in the current directory. The file listing is then written out to the file "ftp.txt" in the current directory, using the format from the server, which might differ from server to server. In other words, do not rely on it; merely use it for informational purposes only.

```
-rw-r--r--   1 500 500    1298826 Jan 17  2002 openldap-stable-20020115.tgz
-rw-r--r--   1 500 500    6003 Jan 18  2002 popa3d_custom_auth.diff
-rw-r--r--   1 500 500    231 Jan 16  2002 ppp_mppe_compressed_data_fix.diff.gz
```

Do not despair if at first you can't get a listing to work. It does not take too much effort to crash this particular task, with null pointers being reported during execution. This is largely because of the disparity in the different outputs generated by individual FTP servers running on different operating systems.

mkdir

Let's assume you are going to be uploading the latest build of your project to a remote FTP server. You might want to ensure a directory exists for you to upload your files into. mkdir is an action you can use to create a directory, as shown in Listing 5.4.

Listing 5.4 *Creating a Directory on an FTP Server*

```
<ftp server="antbook" passive="yes" userid="webadmin" password="sams"
    action="mkdir" remotedir="lib" ignoreNoncriticalErrors="yes"/>
```

Note the use of the attribute ignoreNoncriticalErrors. If the task is run, and the directory already exists, the build process will fail. This might cause problems if this task is part of a bigger project. Therefore, this attribute will happily ignore the error and continue on as if nothing had gone wrong.

put

Having now created the directory, the next step is to upload the file to the server. This is performed using the code shown in Listing 5.5, which uploads all the files that have the .jar extension in the local directory lib.

Listing 5.5 *Uploading a File to an FTP Server*

```
<ftp server="antbook" passive="yes" userid="webadmin" password="sams"
    action="put" remotedir="lib" ignoreNoncriticalErrors="yes" chmod="666">
  <fileset dir="./lib/">
    <include name="*.jar"/>
  </fileset>
</ftp>
```

The common `<fileset>` nested element controls which files are sent to the server. This can include all the normal Ant rules for locating files.

In this example, we used the `chmod` attribute with a value of `666`, which makes the file read-and-write accessible for everyone. Information on what `666` actually stands for will be explained later in the section that covers the FTP command `chmod`.

get

Retrieving files from an FTP server is just as easy as sending, except we specify the action to be `get`. Listing 5.6 shows an example in which we log on to the server, and from the default directory, download all the text files into the local directory, `text`.

Listing 5.6   *Downloading a File from an FTP Server*

```
<ftp server="antbook" passive="yes" userid="webadmin" password="sams"
  action="get" ignoreNoncriticalErrors="yes">
  <fileset dir="text">
    <include name="*.txt"/>
  </fileset>
</ftp>
```

del

The `del` action enables you to delete a remote file, using the same techniques as shown in the previous action types. Listing 5.7 shows us connecting to the server to which we uploaded our JAR files, and deleting the text files.

Listing 5.7   *Deleting Files from an FTP Server*

```
<ftp server="antbook" passive="yes" userid="webadmin" password="sams"
  action="del" ignoreNoncriticalErrors="yes">
  <fileset>
    <include name="*.txt"/>
  </fileset>
</ftp>
```

chmod

The action `chmod`, is used to change the file permissions of a file on a remote server. This is for use on Unix-type systems and enables you to set the RWX-RWX-RWX flags for a particular file or directory. If you are already familiar with this structure, please feel free to skip this section and go straight to the example listing.

In Unix there are three levels of security: owner, group, and public. For each of these, you can control if owner, group, or public user have Read, Write, or eXecute rights on that file. This is controlled by setting bits for RWXRWXRWX to on or off accordingly.

You work with each group of security individually; assigning a number to each that represents the bits that have been set.

Consider the following examples:

```
[r w -] [r w -] [r w -] = [1 1 0] [1 1 0] [1 1 0] = 6 6 6
[r w -] [- - -] [- - -] = [1 1 0] [0 0 0] [0 0 0] = 6 0 0
[r w x] [r w x] [r w x] = [1 1 1] [1 1 1] [1 1 1] = 7 7 7
```

The first example gives all types of users read/write access. The second example, however, only allows the owner of the file read/write access, whereas the last example allows access to all the features from all types of user. You then take this number and place it in the attribute for chmod.

Listing 5.8 illustrates this by changing all the text files on the remote server, so only the owner of the file can use them.

Listing 5.8   *Changing the Permissions on an FTP Server*

```
<ftp server="antbook" passive="yes" userid="webadmin" password="sams"
    action="chmod" ignoreNoncriticalErrors="yes" chmod="700">
  <fileset>
    <include name="*.txt"/>
  </fileset>
</ftp>
```

\<icontract\>

This task facilitates an interface to the iContract preprocessor system that implements the Design By Contract principal. More information on iContract can be found at http://www.reliable-systems.com/tools/.

Design by Contract (DBC) is a methodology first developed by Bertrand Meyer, the original designer of the Eiffel language (one of the languages Java was based on). DBC is characterized by the notion of assertions; the capability to check the state of a class execution at specific points; and preconditions, postconditions, and invariants. A precondition is a set of rules that must be true before a given method can be allowed to execute. Conversely, a postcondition is a set of rules that must be true after a given method has run, whereas an invariant rule must remain throughout the life cycle of the object.

The iContract implementation of DBC is performed as a Java preprocessor. You describe the various conditions and rules within the comments of a given source file in much the same way you layout the documentation for JavaDoc compliance. This allows you to keep the original source code untouched because all the intelligence is buried within comment blocks.

To run your system under the watchful eye of iContract, you simply do a precompile using the `<icontract>` task, which produces a series of Java source files that can be compiled and run as normal. If one of the conditions in your file becomes untrue, an exception is thrown. Let's look at Listing 5.9 for an example Java file that has iContract directives embedded inside of it. This file is part of the sample files available on the iContract Web site. Who better to illustrate the system than the author himself, Aslak Hellesøy?

Listing 5.9   *A Sample iContract File*

```
/**
 * This interface describes a flight
 *
 * @author   <a href="mailto:aslak.hellesoy@bekk.no">Aslak Hellesøy</a>
 * @invariant getPassengers() >= 0 // never a negative number of passengers
 */
public interface Flight {

  public static final int MAX_HAND_LUGGAGE_WEIGHT = 5;
  public static final int MAX_PASSENGERS = 100;

  /**
   * Accepts a passenger and brings the passenger to its final destination
   *
   * @param passenger the passenger to bring
   * @return the name of the destination
   *
   * @pre passenger != null
   * @pre passenger.getDestination() != null
   * @pre passenger.getHandLuggageWeight() <= MAX_HAND_LUGGAGE_WEIGHT
   * @pre passenger.getHandLuggageWeight() >= 0
   * @pre passenger.hasTicket()
   * @pre getPassengers() < MAX_PASSENGERS
   *
   * @post return != null
   * @post getPassengers() == getPassengers()@pre + 1
```

Listing 5.9   *(continued)*

```
  */
  public abstract String accept( Passenger passenger );

  /**
   * Returns the name of the flight
   *
   * @return the name of the airline
   * @post return != null
   */
  public abstract String getName();

  /**
   * Returns the number of passengers checked in for this flight
   *
   * @return the number of passengers
   */
  public abstract int getPassengers();
}
```

As you can see from this file, the iContract rules aren't that hard to spot, with the @pre/@post/@invariant prefixes on the comment lines. Each rule has to be described to return a true or false condition. Without further ado let's look at the features the <icontract> task yields to aid this whole process. Table 5.7 lists all the attributes for this task.

Table 5.7   *Table of <icontract> Attributes*

Attributes	Description
srcdir	Details the location of the source files. (Required)
instrumentdir	Details the location where the source files will be placed after processing. (Required)
repositorydir	The directory where the repository files should be placed. (Required)
builddir	The directory where the compiled and the instrumented classes should go.
repositorybuilddir	The directory where the compiled repository classes should go.
pre	Should the @pre conditions be included or not. Defaults to True.
post	Should the @post conditions be included or not. Defaults to True.
invariant	Should the @invariant conditions be included or not. Defaults to True.
failthrowable	This is the full class name of the Exception that is thrown when an assertion is violated.

Table 5.7   *(continued)*

Attributes	Description
verbosity	A comma-separated list of level controls for iContract. Values can be any combination of: error*, warning*, note*, info*, progress*, debug*.
quiet	If you don't want to be warned about classes that you extend which aren't instrumented.
updateicontrol	If set to True, the properties file for iControl, as specified in the controlfile attribute, is updated.
controlfile	See previous.
classdir	This is only for the properties file update; indicates where the class files live for uninstrumented classes.
targets	The name of the file that will be used to list all the classes that iContract will instrument.

The code in Listing 5.10 is a snippet from the sample build file that is shipped with iContract. As you can see, the source code is first compiled as normal, with the `<icontract>` task taking over, and then producing the necessary additions for the necessary conditions to become active.

Listing 5.10   *A Sample iContract Build*

```
<target name="compile" depends="prepare-src" description="Compiles code">
  <javac srcdir="${build.src}" destdir="${build.classes}">
    <classpath refid="compile-classpath"/>
  </javac>
</target>

<target name="instrument" depends="compile" >
  <icontract
    srcdir="${build.src}"
    instrumentdir="${build.instrument}"
    repositorydir="${build.repository}"
    builddir="${build.instrclasses}"
    updateicontrol="true"
    classdir="${build.classes}"
    controlfile="control"
    targets="targets"
    verbosity="error*,warning*"
    quiet="true">
      <classpath refid="compile-classpath"/>
```

Listing 5.10   *(continued)*

```
    </icontract>
</target>

<target name="run-light" depends="instrument">
  <java classname="com.bekk.dbcdemo.Client" fork="yes">
    <arg value="5"/>
    <classpath>
      <pathelement location="${build.instrclasses}"/>
      <fileset dir="./lib">
        <include name="*.jar"/>
      </fileset>
    </classpath>
  </java>
</target>
```

Finally, the target `run-light` simply runs up the code using the class files that were built as a result from running the `<icontract>` task, and not the class files from the original build.

Design by Contract can be a very useful discipline to use in your development cycle. The beauty of the DBC is its capability to not interfere with the original source code and, therefore, be completely absent from any final production code. It is a very useful technique for those developers responsible for keeping the integrity of interfaces true to their original design.

<propertyfile>

This task is very useful for those developers that have to maintain property files that can be used in applications outside of the build process. Although basically a wrapper to the standard `java.util.Properties` class, there are some additional features that make this task very useful and powerful. Table 5.8 shows the attributes for the top-level tag for `<propertyfile>`.

Table 5.8   *Table of <propertyfile> Attributes*

Attributes	Description
file	The location of the file to be edited/created. (Required)
header	A header for the file.

Within this task, any number of nested <entry> elements might exist. Each <entry> element represents a key/pair value in the property file. Table 5.9 shows the attributes available for this element.

Table 5.9   *Table of <entry> Attributes*

Attributes	Description
key	The name of the key for this entry. (Required)
value	This is the value for the entry. If the operation is an addition/subtraction, this is the value that will be added/subtracted.
default	If the value is not already present in the file, this is the default value.
type	This is the type of the data field. Valid values are int, date, or string.
operation	This is the operation that will occur on the value. Valid values are +, -, or =. - is the only value for date and int fields.
pattern	This is the mask that the data appears in if type is int or date.
unit	For operations involving dates, this is the unit of the addition or subtraction. Valid values are millisecond, second, minute, hour, day, week, month, and year. Day is the default unit.

Let's have a look at this task in action, with a very simple example that creates a property with a number of attributes, shown in Listing 5.11.

Listing 5.11   *Creating a Simple Property File*

```
<propertyfile file="antbook.property" comment="An Antbook example">
  <entry key="author1" value="Kirk"/>
  <entry key="author2" value="Andy"/>
  <entry key="author3" value="Alan"/>
  <entry key="author4" value="Joey"/>
</propertyfile>
```

This creates the antbook.property file with the following contents:

```
#An Antbook example
#Mon May 27 21:10:39 BST 2002
author1=Kirk
author2=Andy
author3=Alan
author4=Joey
```

You will notice the order of the file isn't the same order you had your `<entry>` elements. Don't be concerned with this because it is a side effect of using the `java.util.Properties` class. Another side effect of this class is that if you are using an existing properties file with lots of embedded comments, these will be lost on a subsequent read and write. So be careful when throwing property files that you have lovingly crafted by hand to the mercy of this task.

Before we leave this task, it is worth noting the arithmetic operations that can be performed on the data for a given key. Let's look at a working example.

Imagine we want to keep track, for curiosity's sake, the number of times we built a particular project and the date of the last build. We would want to create the file initially and for each time the task was called, read in the number of compiles, and increment the value by 1. The example in Listing 5.12 produces the file:

```
#Number of times
#Mon May 27 21:23:29 BST 2002
stats.lastbuild=2002/05/27 21\:23
stats.compile=2
```

The first thing the target does is to look for the key "`stats.compile`", if it doesn't exist, it defaults to the value 1. If it does exist, it sets the type to "`int`", and then performs the + operation on it, adding the number specified in the value attribute.

Listing 5.12   *Keeping Track of Builds*

```
<target name="propertyfile-stats">
  <propertyfile file="antbook.stats" comment="Number of times">
    <entry key="stats.compile" default="1" value="1" operation="+" type="int"/>
    <entry key="stats.lastbuild" value="now" type="date"/>
  </propertyfile>
</target>
```

The "`stats.lastbuild`" merely plugs in the current date using the special keyword "`now`". This keyword will only work if the attribute type is equal to "`date`".

The `<propertyfile>` task is very useful for storing the runtime values of a particular Ant build or, if used with the `<input>` task, for providing a convenient interface to automatically update important configuration files.

<javacc>

The JavaCC (Java Compiler Compiler) is another popular tool, similar in nature to ANTLR, for building language compilers. It is one of the more popular tools for Parser Generator applications. You can download it from `http://www.webgain.com/products/java_cc/`.

Ant provides the `<javacc>` task for controlling the build process of JavaCC, assuming you have already installed JavaCC onto your system from the previous URL. This task requires knowing the location of this installation, so it can find the necessary class files to complete the operation. Table 5.10 details the attributes for this task, with the majority being flags that are set on or off depending on the JavaCC feature you want enabled.

Table 5.10   *Table of <javacc> Attributes*

Attributes	Description
target	The JavaCC grammar file to compile. (Required)
javacchome	The location of the JavaCC installation. (Required)
outputdirectory	The directory where the resulting files will be written. The default is the directory where the grammar file is located.
buildparser	Sets the JavaCC BUILD_PARSER flag.
buildtokenmanager	Sets the JavaCC BUILD_TOKEN_MANAGER flag.
cachetokens	Sets the JavaCC CACHE_TOKENS flag.
choiceambiguitycheck	Sets the JavaCC CHOICE_AMBIGUITY_CHECK integer value.
commontokenaction	Sets the JavaCC COMMON_TOKEN_ACTION flag.
debuglookahead	Sets the JavaCC DEBUG_LOOKAHEAD flag.
debugparser	Sets the JavaCC DEBUG_PARSER flag.
debugtokenmanager	Sets the JavaCC DEBUG_TOKEN_MANAGER flag.
errorreporting	Sets the JavaCC ERROR_REPORTING flag.
forcelacheck	Sets the JavaCC FORCE_LA_CHECK flag.
ignorecase	Sets the JavaCC IGNORE_CASE flag.
javaunicodeescape	Sets the JavaCC JAVA_UNICODE_ESCAPE flag.
lookahead	Sets the JavaCC LOOKAHEAD integer value.
optimizetokenmanager	Sets the JavaCC OPTIMIZE_TOKEN_MANAGER flag.
otherambiguitycheck	Sets the JavaCC OTHER_AMBIGUITY_CHECK integer value.
sanitycheck	Sets the JavaCC SANITY_CHECK flag.
static	Sets the JavaCC STATIC flag.
unicodeinput	Sets the UNICODE_INPUT flag.

Table 5.10   *(continued)*

Attributes	Description
usercharstream	Sets the USER_CHAR_STREAM flag.
usertokenmanager	Sets the USER_TOKEN_MANAGER flag.

The example shown in Listing 5.13 shows using the `<javacc>` task, building the `cfParser.jj` file into the directory defined by the Ant user property `src`.

Listing 5.13   *Running JavaCC*

```
<javacc
  target="${src}cfParser.jj"
  javacchome="${javacchome}"
  outputdirectory="${src}"
  ignorecase="true"/>
```

<jjtree>

JJTree is a tool that is a preprocessor for JavaCC grammar files. See the section on the `<javacc>` task for more information on where to obtain the JavaCC suite of tools. Table 5.11 details the attributes for the `<jjtree>` task.

Table 5.11   *Table of <jjtree> Attributes*

Attributes	Description
target	The JavaCC grammar file to compile. (Required)
javacchome	The location of the JavaCC installation. (Required)
outputdirectory	The directory where the generated file will be written. The default is the directory where the grammar file is located.
buildnodefiles	Sets the JJTree BUILD_PARSER flag.
multi	Sets the JJTree MULTI flag.
nodedefaultvoid	Sets the JJTree NODE_DEFAULT_VOID flag.
nodefactory	Sets the JJTree NODE_FACTORY flag.
nodepackage	Sets the JJTree NODE_PACKAGE string.
nodeprefix	Sets the JJTree NODE_PREFIX string.
nodescopehook	Sets the JJTree NODE_SCOPE_HOOK flag.
nodeuserparser	Sets the JJTree NODE_USES_PARSER flag.

Table 5.11 *(continued)*

Attributes	Description
static	Sets the JJTree STATIC flag.
visitor	Sets the JJTree VISITOR flag.
visitorexception	Sets the JJTree VISTOR_EXECPTION string.

A sample usage of this task can be seen in Listing 5.14 which preprocesses our files before sending them for compilation.

Listing 5.14 *Running JJTree Before JavaCC*

```
<jjtree
  target="${src}cfParser.jjt"
  javacchome="${javacchome}"
  outputdirectory="${src}"/>

<javacc
  target="${src}cfParser.jj"
  javacchome="${javacchome}"
  outputdirectory="${src}"
  ignorecase="true"/>
```

<javah>

The <javah> task is a wrapper to the javah utility shipped with the JDK. This utility is used for generating the header and stub files for the Java Native Interface (JNI). As you can see from Table 5.12 the attributes to this task are the same as the command-line options.

Table 5.12 *Table of <javah> Attributes*

Attributes	Description
class	A comma-separated list of fully qualified classes that will be processed. (Required)
outputfile	The name of the file for the resulting headers. (Required, if no destdir specified)
destdir	The directory where JavaH will save the header/stub files. (Required, if no outputfile specified)
force	The JavaH flag to make sure all the output files are written.
old	This is to allow the old JDK1.0 header files to be generated.

Table 5.12   *(continued)*

Attributes	Description
stubs	When old is set, this flag tells JavaH to generate the C code from the Java object file.
verbose	Flag for JavaH to generate output as it processes each file.
classpath	The classpath to use.
bootclasspath	The location of the bootstrap class files.
extdirs	The location of the extensions directory.

Using the `<javah>` task is very easy, specifying the necessary parameters where necessary.

```
<javah destdir="${src}/c" class="antbook.javahexample"/>
```

If you have a lot of class files to process, you can use the inner element tag, `<class>`, to specify the class names.

```
<javah destdir="${src}/c">
  <class="antbook.javahexample"/>
</javah>
```

`<jspc>`

For JSP developers this task can be a very useful one to have within your build process. The `<jspc>` task takes JSP pages and compiles them into Java source files for possible future compilation with `<javac>`. This enables you to quickly validate your JSP page without invoking it via a Web browser or for deployment to systems that do not have the necessary infrastructure installed, for example, systems that lack the full JDK for compiling.

The task utilizes the JSP compiler from Tomcat 4, which you will need to download and extract the `jasper-compiler.jar` and `jasper-runtime.jar` files. Simply place these in your `classpath` or the `/lib/` directory of your Ant installation. Table 5.13 shows the attributes for this task.

Table 5.13   *Table of <jspc> Attributes*

Attributes	Description
destdir	The directory where the Java source files will be placed. (Required)
srcdir	The directory where the JSP pages reside. (Required)
verbose	The verbosity level that will be used for output.

Table 5.13 *(continued)*

Attributes	Description
compiler	The class name of the JSP compiler.
package	The name of the package for the generated Java source files.
ieplugin	If you are using the <jsp:plugin> tag within your JSP page, and the Java COM class ID changes, you can specify it using this attribute.
mapped	Flag to generate individual write() calls for each line of HTML text in the JSP page.
classpath	The classpath for the JSP compiler.
classpathref	The reference to the classpath information.
failonerror	A flag to stop the task if an error is encountered. The default action is to stop.
uribase	The location of the extensions directory.
uriroot	This is the root directory from where URI files should be resolved.

Using the sample JSP page shown in Listing 5.15, we'll use the `<jspc>` task to compile this page to a Java source file. Note that this JSP page makes explicit calls to interfaces within the Servlet API and therefore, we'll need to either specify the `servlet.jar` file in the `classpath` attribute, or place the JAR file in the `/lib/` directory of the Ant installation.

Listing 5.15 *A Simple JSP Sample Page*

```
<html>
  <head>
    <title>JSP Test Page</title>
  </head>
<body bgcolor=#ffffff>
  <h4>JSP Test Page</h4>
  <p>
  request.getRequestURI() = <%=request.getRequestURI()%><br>
  request.getServletPath() = <%=request.getServletPath()%><br>
  request.getRealPath("/") = <%=request.getRealPath("/")%><br>
</body>
</html>
```

Using the following task, we can compile our JSP page into a Java source file.

```
<jspc srcdir="." destdir=".">
  <include name="**/*.jsp" />
</jspc>
```

This task uses the standard directory features of Ant to retrieve the list of files it must process. All normal rules apply. The `<jspc>` task operates like the `<javac>` compiler in the way it determines which files to compile by using the timestamps of each file.

After successful execution, the resulting `.java` files will be available in the directory specified in the `destdir` attribute. These files can then be processed through the standard `<javac>` task for ultimate compilation to class files.

`<junit>`

As the complexity of software increases, so does the possible number of different execution paths through the system. For this reason, gone are the days where you could simply assume it's all going to work seamlessly without any hiccups. Although the notion of unit testing isn't new, what is relatively new is the introduction of this practice into mainstream programming.

One of the biggest problems with asking a developer to test her code is more of a social problem as opposed to a technical one. No developer likes to admit she is developing bad or buggy code. Most take the moral high ground, claiming that their code is above testing. So, to make sure code can be tested, the framework has to be very easy and nonintrusive. Enter in JUnit (`http://www.junit.org/`), an open-source initiative that makes creating tests a very trivial task, but adds in a whole a new level for conformance testing that should bring a smile to any project manager.

For those of you not familiar with any unit testing methodologies, JUnit is a great place to start and the integration into Ant makes the whole process completely painless. An in-depth review of JUnit is outside the scope of this book, but Listing 5.16 shows a quick example of how you might use JUnit, and then how you would use it to test a completely contrived example. This class will simply maintain an integer, but badly because when we ask it to add 1 to the value it will add 2 instead.

Listing 5.16   A Bad Class That We'll Use in Our Unit Testing

```
public class corruptClass extends Object {
  int X;

  public corruptClass( int X ){
    this.X = X;
  }

  public int getX(){
    return X;
```

Listing 5.16   *(continued)*

```
  }

  public void addOne(){
    X += 2;
  }
}
```

Granted this is the sort of thing that you can easily spot when the code is laid out like this, but such a fundamental error could be missed if this class had many methods inside it. Compiling this class will not throw any errors because, syntax wise, it is correct. What we must do now is create a separate class that will test this class in a runtime scenario.

> **Note**
> To use this task successfully you need to download the junit.jar from the main JUnit Web site (http://www.junit.org/) and insert it into the /lib/ directory of your Ant installation.

Using the JUnit framework we would simply create a class, as shown in Listing 5.17. Simply extend the `junit.framework.TestCase` class and create a constructor that will pass the given string down to the base class.

Listing 5.17   *The JUnit Class to Test the corruptClass*

```
import junit.framework.*;

public class corruptClassTest extends TestCase {
  public corruptClassTest( String _string ){
    super( _string );
  }

  public void testAddition(){
    corruptClass cC = new corruptClass( 4 );
    cC.addOne();
    assertEquals( cC.getX(), 5 );
  }
}
```

The JUnit framework uses Java Reflection to determine the tests that have to run. You define a series of tests by declaring a separate method, with the signature

```
public void testXXX()
```

where *XXX* is any valid method you want to give it. Inside these methods you place your test cases. So, how do you signal when something isn't right? You use the underlying `assertXXX(...)` methods to perform tests on various conditions. In our example here, we want the test to fail if the return value isn't equal to 5.

Now that we have our testing class, we need to integrate this into Ant using the `<junit>` task, as shown in Listing 5.18. The first thing we do is to set up a simple target that will manage the compilation of our tests. Because we don't want to compile everything, we limit the compilation to just the classes that begin with the pattern "`corruptClass`".

Listing 5.18   *Using the <junit> Task*

```
<target name="compiletests">
  <javac srcdir="${src}"
         destdir="${build}"
         includes="corruptClass*.java"
         optimize="off"
         debug="on"/>
</target>

<target name="junit1" depends="compiletests">
  <junit printsummary="on" showoutput="yes">
    <classpath>
      <pathelement path="${build}" />
    </classpath>
    <test name="corruptClassTest"/>
  </junit>
</target>
```

We then define the `<junit>` task inside a target we've named `junit1`. This will run the JUnit framework against the class we've specified in the `<test>`-nested element. We'll take a more detailed look at the specifics of this task in a moment. But first, let's run the target and observe the following output.

```
c:\antbook\antbook_chapter5>ant junit1
Buildfile: build.xml

compiletests:
    [javac] Compiling 1 source file to c:\antbook\antbook_chapter5\classes

junit1:
    [junit] Running corruptClassTest
```

```
[junit] Tests run: 1, Failures: 1, Errors: 0, Time elapsed: 0.01 sec
[junit] TEST corruptClassTest FAILED
```

```
BUILD SUCCESSFUL
Total time: 5 seconds
```

As expected one of the tests did indeed fail.

With an example under our belt, let's take a detailed look at some of the configurations we can adjust with this task. Table 5.14 details the top-level options available to the `<junit>` task.

Table 5.14 *Table of <junit> Attributes*

Attributes	Description
printsummary	This flag controls whether a one-line summary is outputted to the console per test. Valid values: on—a summary is printed off—no summary is printed withOutAndErr—same as on, but also includes the output from System.out and System.err.
fork	Controls whether the tests are run in a separate JVM. Defaults to no.
haltonerror	If an error is encountered in the tests, this flag controls whether the build process is halted. Defaults to no.
errorproperty	If an error occurs, this is the name of the property that will be set to illustrate this.
haltonfailure	If an error or failure is encountered in the tests, this flag controls whether the build process is halted. Defaults to no.
failureproperty	If an error or failure occurs, this is the name of the property that will be set to illustrate this.
filtertrace	This flag filters out all the stack traces that belong to Ant and JUnit for a cleaner output. Default is on.
timeout	If a test doesn't complete in a given amount of milliseconds, it will be cancelled.
maxmemory	If another JVM is to be forked, this controls the maximum amount of memory that can be allocated.
jvm	The command that is used to invoke the JVM if fork is set. The default is java.
dir	If another JVM is to be forked, this is the directory to fork the JVM from.
newenvironment	Do not propagate the old environment when new environment variables are specified.

Table 5.14   *(continued)*

Attributes	Description
includeantruntime	Implicitly add the Ant classes required to run the tests and JUnit to the classpath in forked mode.
showoutput	Send any output generated by tests to Ant's logging system as well as to the formatters. By default only the formatters receive the output.

Forking Your Process

One of features of the `<junit>` task is the capability to have your test run in a separate JVM from the one controlling Ant. This has a number of advantages, namely the capability to run tests in a clean environment with a controlled `classpath`. Also, if something should go completely wrong with your test classes, it holds the major benefit that it won't crash the Ant build process.

To support this feature a number of nested tags can be deployed within the `<junit>` task to pass various parameters through to the new JVM instance. Table 5.15 shows the attributes for the `<jvmarg>` nested element. This enables you to pass in attributes to the JVM.

Table 5.15   *Table of <jvmarg> Attributes*

Attributes	Description
value	A single command-line argument.
line	A space-delimited list of command-line arguments.
file	The name of a file as a single command-line argument; will be replaced with the absolute filename of the file.
path	A string that will be treated as a pathlike string as a single command-line argument. You can use either ; or : as path separators and Ant will convert it to the platform's local conventions.

In addition to passing values to the JVM, you can also set up environment variables that will be available to the runtime, via the `<sysproperty>`-nested element as detailed in Table 5.16.

Table 5.16   *Table of <sysproperty> Attributes*

Attributes	Description
key	The name of the environment variable.
value	The value of the key.

Table 5.16 *(continued)*

Attributes	Description
path	The value for a PATH-like environment variable. You can use either ; or : as path separators and Ant will convert it to the platform's local conventions.
file	The value for the environment variable, which will be replaced by the absolute filename of the file by Ant.

Formatting the Output

One of the great features of the `<junit>` task is its capability to collate information pertaining to the tests that its just run. One of the features is to format this data in an XML format for later use with the `<junitreport>` task, which is detailed later in the chapter. Table 5.17 lists the attributes for the `formatter` nested element.

Table 5.17 *Table of <formatter> Attributes*

Attributes	Description
type	The type of format that will be generated: xml, plain, or brief.
classname	The name of the class if a custom formatter is to be used.
extension	This is the extension that will be appended to the output filename.
usefile	Boolean that determines whether output should be sent to a file.

Specifying the Test Cases

The `<junit>` task has a number of ways you can specify the class files to be included in the test. The first, and easiest, way is to specify an individual class to be tested, using the nested `<test>` element, as detailed in Table 5.18. The attributes are the same as that of the `<junit>` task, so the table only lists the additional attributes.

Table 5.18 *Table of <test>/<batchtest> Attributes*

Attributes	Description
name	The name of the class to test.
todir	Directory to write the reports to.
outfile	Base name of the test result. The full filename is determined by this attribute and the extension of formatter.
if	Only run this test if the named property is set.
unless	Only run this test if the named property is not set.

An example of this nested element was shown in our earlier listing. A broader version of this, which enables you to pull in a list of classes at once is the `<batchtest>` nested element. This takes in the same attributes as the `<test>` attributes, except it enables you to nest `<fileset>` elements to pattern match the files.

For example, using the `<batchtest>` element, we could rewrite our earlier example as

```
<batchtest todir="${report}">
  <fileset dir="${src}">
    <include name="**Test.java" />
  </fileset>
</batchtest>
```

This will load up all the classes that end with `Test` in the current source directory.

`<junitreport>`

This task is very useful for consolidating the entire XML file set, generated by the `<junit>` task, into viewable HTML files for easy dissemination. If you feel wadding through reams of log files looking at the results of your testing is a little tedious, you will thoroughly enjoy the output from this task. Nothing like a beautifully formatted report to tell you that all your tests passed (or failed!).

The task relies on a number of additional libraries to function correctly; namely Xalan2.x or higher. This is readily available from the main Apache Web site at `http://xml.apache.org/xalan-j/`.

Download the latest distribution and extract the JAR files `xalan.jar` and `bsf.jar` placing them in the Ant library directory. The main `<junitreport>` attributes are shown in Table 5.19.

Table 5.19   *Table of `<junitreport>` Attributes*

Attributes	Description
tofile	This is the name of the main XML file that was produced by the <junit> task. Defaults to TESTS-TestSuites.xml.
todir	This is the directory where all the individual XML files from the <junit> were written. Defaults to the current directory.

One of the first roles of this task is to collate all the files from the output of the `<junit>` task. This is performed using a standard `<fileset>`-nested element. For example, the following code snippet will look inside the directory marked by the property `report` and prepare a list of files with the pattern `"TEST-*.xml"`.

```
<fileset dir="${report}">
  <include name="TEST-*.xml"/>
</fileset>
```

Having collated all the files, we need to define how we want the report to be formatted. The only control over this is whether to specify frames and the location of the output files. You can also specify an alternative stylesheet to be used to transform the data. Table 5.20 details the attributes for the `<report>`-nested element.

Table 5.20   *Table of <junitreport:report> Attributes*

Attributes	Description
format	This defines whether frames will be used. It is either frames or noframes. Default: frames
styledir	This parameter enables you to change the directory of an alternative stylesheet to use. If you specify this and format="frames", you must name the stylesheet junit-frames.xsl, and alternatively for format="noframes", the stylesheet must be named junit-noframes.xsl.
todir	This is the directory where the HTML/CSS files will be written. Defaults to the current directory.

Listing 5.19 shows a common use for this task. As you can see, there is very little complication associated with it. The majority of the problems stemming from the use of this task originate from not having the correct JAR files in place. It is very important that you make sure the correct JAR files are installed in the Ant library directory, otherwise the translation will fail.

Listing 5.19   *A Typical Usage for the junitreport Task*

```
<junitreport todir="${report}">
  <fileset dir="${report}">
    <include name="TEST-*.xml"/>
  </fileset>
  <report format="frames" todir="${report}/html"/>
</junitreport>
```

Upon termination, the output directory `${report}/html` will contain a suite of HTML files addressed from `index.html` that will summarize the complete test suite as ran by the `<junit>` task.

<replaceregexp>

Regular expressions (sometimes referred to as *RegEx*), although not a new phenomenon, are a relatively new concept for a lot of developers. Regular expressions are designed to find and match patterns within in blocks of text. Crispin Roven, from *Wired*, once wrote in an article a number of years ago that regular expressions "look like #!?#@!!# comic book expletives," and if you're familiar with regex, you'll know exactly what Crispin means!

Regular expressions are like any power tool, if used correctly and responsibly, they can be a wonderful addition to any developer's arsenal. If used incorrectly, you can find yourself spending more time on these "comic book expletives" than you care to imagine.

> **Note**
> For a great quick-help guide refer to the documentation at
> http://jakarta.apache.org/regexp/apidocs/org/apache/regexp/RE.html.

Ant comes with a task that enables you to easily apply regex expressions to a single or series of files. This enables you to quickly add the capability to search and replace for specific text patterns within your development files into your build process. For example, you could easily setup a task that would look through your source files looking for a particular string that could be replaced by the time the last build was performed. This is similar to the information from CVS, except it would enable you to introduce the build date as oppose to the date when the source was last checked in.

Table 5.21 shows the list of attributes that are associated with this task.

Table 5.21   *Table of <replaceregexp> Attributes*

Attributes	Description
file	The file in which the task will run. You can optionally specify the list of files using a nested fileset element.
match	This is the regular expression that will be run on the file. You can optionally specify the regular expression using the nested element regex.
replace	The pattern that will be used upon a successful find. You can optionally specify this substituted text using the substitution element.
flags	You can use these flags to control the processing of the task: g = Replace all occurrences found; globally. i = Ignore the case of the string when performing the match. m = Multiline. Treat the string as multiple lines of input, using ^ and $ as the start or end of any line, respectively, rather than start or end of string. s = Singleline. Treat the string as a single line of input, using . to match any character, including a newline, which it would not normally match.

Table 5.21 *(continued)*

Attributes	Description
byline	This controls how the file is processed. If set to true, each line is processed at a time. The default state is to process the whole file as a single string.

Let's look at the example discussed previously. Assume you have the following line in one of your Java files

```
public String BUILD_DATE = "@BUILDDATE: @";
```

This will be the date the last compilation was made. We can create a new task that will look for this and replace it with the latest date. For example:

```
public String BUILD_DATE = "@BUILDDATE: 2237 July 3 2000@";
```

Listing 5.20 shows the task for this functionality. As you can see first we make a call to the `<tstamp>` task to initialize all the date/time variables, resulting in TSTAMP and TODAY being set for us to use. Next, we specify the `<replaceregexp>` task, explicitly stating that we are going to be looking at one file, the version.java within the {src} directory.

Then, we build our regular expression, "@BuildDate:(.)+@". Pay particular note to the "(.)+". This states that there could be any number of characters after the colon.

Listing 5.20 *A Sample Regular Expression Task*

```
<target name="regex">
  <tstamp/>
  <replaceregexp file="${src}/version.java"
    match="@BuildDate:(.)+@"
    replace="@BuildDate: ${TSTAMP} ${TODAY}@"
    byline="true"/>
</target>
```

When we run this task the following output is generated, resulting the string being found and replaced with the correct string.

```
C:\antbook\antbook_chapter5>ant regex
Buildfile: build.xml
regex:
[replaceregexp] Replacing pattern '@BuildDate:(.)+@' with
                '@BuildDate: 2237 July 3 2002@' in
                'C:\antbook\antbook_chapter5\src\version.java' by line.
BUILD SUCCESSFUL
Total time: 2 seconds
```

\<setproxy\>

This is a very useful task to run before any tasks that require access to a resource that can sit outside a firewall. The \<setproxy\> task enables you to set the proxy settings for the JVM in which the Ant task is running within. Table 5.22 shows the attributes associated with this task.

Table 5.22   *Table of \<setproxy\> Attributes*

Attributes	Description
proxyHost	The name of the proxy to use for HTTP/FTP requests. The proxy is disabled if this is blank.
proxyPort	Defaults to port 80 if the port of the proxyHost is not specified.
socksProxyHost	The name of the SOCKS proxy server.
socksProxyPort	Defaults to port 1080 if the port of the socksProxyHost is not specified.
nonProxyHosts	A comma-separated list of hosts where the proxy will be bypassed.

Assuming you had a proxy server running at `proxy.yourdoman.com` on the port `8080`, you would use this task:

```
<setproxy proxyHost="proxy.yourdomain.com" proxyPort="8080"/>
```

\<sound\>

If the Java you are running is greater than 1.3, you might want to consider adding a little sound to your builds. This is a particularly good idea for ones that might take a little longer than normal, so an audible signal to let you know it's finished could be useful. You can do this using the \<sound\> task, which has the capability to trigger a sound on either a success or failure of a build file, as shown in the example in Listing 5.21.

Listing 5.21   *Integrating a Sound File into the Build Process*

```
<target name="splash-example">
  <splash showduration="1000"/>
  <property name="sound" value="true"/>
</target>

<target name="sound-example" if="sound" depends="splash-example">
  <sound>
```

Listing 5.21   *(continued)*

```
    <success source="c:\\sounds\\complete.wav"/>
    <fail source="c:\\sounds\\redalert.wav" loops="1"/>
  </sound>
</target>
```

The target, `sound-example` sets up the `<sound>` task to listen for the success or failure signals. Then, we make a call to the `splash-example` target, which is merely a testing target for the purpose of the example. The `<sound>` utilizes two nested elements: `<success>` and `<fail>`, which are described in Table 5.23.

Table 5.23   *Table of <success>/<fail> Attributes*

Attributes	Description
source	The path to the sound file that is to be played. (Required)
loops	The number of times you want this file to be played. No times played = loops + 1.
Duration	Time in milliseconds for how long the sound is to play for.

These elements determine which sound file to play depending on the build success. One of the nice features of this optional task is the capability to randomly pick a file from a directory of sound files. A wee surprise to the sound when you successfully build!

\<splash\>

As you've probably realized by now, the majority of the Ant framework evolves around the command line. Apart from the odd feedback line that comes back, there is no real progress indicator. Enter in the `<splash>` task. This is a special task that when invoked will remain active until the build process is complete, showing a progress bar. To use this task, simply insert the `<splash>` element before a call to a lengthy target, as demonstrated in Listing 5.22.

Listing 5.22   *Inserting a Splash and Progress Bar*

```
<target name="splash-example">
  <splash showduration="100"/>
</target>
```

This will display a small pop-up window of the Ant logo, with a progress bar running underneath it. The majority of developers probably won't use this task, but it is very handy when your shipping build scripts for projects where the audience might not be as technically proficient. The task even has attributes, shown in Table 5.24, to allow you to optionally use images pulled from the Web.

Table 5.24 *Table of <splash> Attributes*

Attributes	Description
imageurl	A complete URL to an image. Defaults to antlogo.gif from the Ant directory.
showduration	The initial period in which the splash screen will be displayed before moving on. Measured in milliseconds.

<telnet>

The telnet optional task is designed to interact primarily with remote Telnet servers, but can be easily used for any ASCII-based TCP server. You could use this task after you perform an upload using the FTP task, to log on to a system to restart a process. Another application would be to use this task to test a given a SOAP request or basic HTTP server. Table 5.25 gives a rundown of the attributes for this task.

Table 5.25 *Table of <telnet> Attributes*

Attributes	Description
userid	The username for the Telnet server.
password	The password for the username.
server	The remote address of the server you are connecting to. (Required)
port	The port number of the server you are connecting to. Defaults to 23.
initialCR	After connection made, send a Carriage Return to the server. Defaults to no.
timeout	The time to wait for a response from the server; expressed in seconds.

Interacting with a Telnet Server

The core usage for the `<telnet>` task is to interact with a Telnet server. For example, you might want to log on and restart the Web server or trigger some other script. Take a look at Listing 5.23 that shows a very basic logging sequence to a Redhat machine, and then triggers the `apachectl restart` script to restart Apache.

Listing 5.23   *Triggering the Apache Restart*

```
<target name="apache-restart">
  <telnet userid="webadmin" password="mypassword"
          server="myserver.mydomain.com">
    <read timeout="5" string="$"/>
    <write echo="false">/usr/local/apache/bin/apachectl restart</write>
    <read timeout="5" string="$"/>
  </telnet>
</target>
```

The nested elements, `<read>` and `<write>`, control the interaction with the remote server. The `<read>` element will sit and listen for a return string, waiting for the given amount of time before aborting. Conversely, the `<write>` element sends a line of text to the server.

Both of these elements operate on lines of text at a time, reading and writing new line and carriage returns automatically.

Interacting with an HTTP Server

It's fair to say that there isn't really anything special going on here with the `<telnet>` task that ties it to the Telnet protocol. For example, the login procedure will fail if your Telnet server doesn't send back the correct strings for it to recognize (`ogin:` and `word:`). You might think this to be a bit of a cheat, but as you will discover it is this power that enables you to use the `<telnet>` task for interacting with other services other than just Telnet, for example a Web server.

The example in Listing 5.24 shows a simple HEAD request to a Web server.

Listing 5.24   *Making a HEAD Request to a Web Server*

```
<telnet server="www.n-ary.com" port="80">
  <read/>
  <write echo="false">HEAD / HTTP/1.1</write>
  <write echo="false">host: www.n-ary.com</write>
  <write echo="false"></write>
  <read string="text/html"/>
</telnet>
```

When run, the HTTP HEAD request will be made to the Web server with the following information returned.

```
telnet-example2:
  [telnet] HTTP/1.1 200 OK
```

```
[telnet] Date: Sun, 19 May 2002 17:09:07 GMT
[telnet] Server: Apache/1.3.22 (Darwin) mod_jk
[telnet] Cache-Control: max-age=60
[telnet] Expires: Sun, 19 May 2002 17:10:07 GMT
[telnet] Connection: close
[telnet] Content-Type: text/html
```

This enables you to trigger URLs that might have an action associated with them. For example, updating a Web page after a build has just completed.

Another use of this technology is testing SOAP services. You can easily setup a `<telnet>` job that will package up a SOAP request and send it to a SOAP server. An example `<telnet>` job for this purpose is shown in Listing 5.25.

Listing 5.25   *Making a SOAP Request to a Web Service*

```
<telnet server="www.public.com" port="8080">
  <read/>
  <write echo="false">POST /public.wsdl HTTP/1.1</write>
  <write echo="false">host: www.public.com</write>
  <write echo="false">Content-type: text/xml;</write>
  <write echo="false">Content-length: 496</write>
  <write echo="false">SOAPAction: "getServiceResponsePublic"</write>
  <write/>
  <write echo="false"><![CDATA[<your SOAP request>]]></write>
  <read string="/definitions&gt;"/>
</telnet>
```

As you can see we are basically formatting the standard HTTP POST method, formatting the header accordingly. Notice the line for the actual SOAP request and use of the CDATA. This is a special XML directive that enables you to embed arbitrary text without having to replacing the characters that might conflict with the XML parsing. Because a SOAP request is a pure XML request, you need to place your request inside the `<![CDATA[ ... ]]>` directive.

`<xmlvalidate>`

With Ant's reliance on XML for its build files, it probably doesn't come as a big surprise to learn of a task that will take an XML file and check it for errors. The `<xmlvalidate>` task will use the SAX parser that ships with Ant to validate a given file or list of XML files. You can of course use another implementation of a SAX processor if you want, by simply specifying the class name of the alternative.

Table 5.26 shows the list of attributes that are associated with this task.

Table 5.26   *Table of <xmlvalidate> Attributes*

Attributes	Description
file	The file in which the task will run. You can optionally specify the list of files using a nested fileset element.
lenient	If set to true, the file is only checked to see it is well formed.
classname	The class name of the parser to use.
classpathref	You can specify the classpath information of the alternative parser or use the classpath-nested element to define it.
failonerror	If an error is found, this task reports and error.
warn	Displays the parser warnings.

The easiest way to call this task is to simply specify the XML file you want to check:

```
<xmlvalidate file="build.xml"/>
```

This runs the validator on the standard Ant build file, which you would think, is valid XML!

```
C:\antbook\antbook_chapter5>ant xml
Buildfile: build.xml

xml:
[xmlvalidate] C:/antbook/antbook_chapter5/build.xml:1:37:
              Document root element "project", must match DOCTYPE root "null".
[xmlvalidate] C:/antbook/antbook_chapter5/build.xml:1:37:
              Document is invalid: no grammar found.
BUILD FAILED
C:\antbook\antbook_chapter5\build.xml:150:
    C:\antbook\antbook_chapter5\build.xml is not a valid XML document.

Total time: 2 seconds
```

As you can see, the Ant file is not a strict XML file, but you can see the power this task can have.

Summary

This chapter took you through some of the most useful optional tasks available with the core distribution of Ant. As you've discovered, they compliment the core tasks very nicely and enable you to enrich your development environment, with such facilities as even uploading a file to your FTP server. With Ant being a very popular open source project, new optional tasks are being added all the time, so be sure to keep an eye on the official Ant site for updates.

CHAPTER 6

Extending Ant with Custom Tasks, Data Types, and Listeners

The previous two chapters introduced the rich array of built-in and optional tasks. As large as this set of tasks is, there always seems to be some task that's needed but that Ant doesn't support. As you might have guessed by the number of optional tasks, an API exists that allows a third party to extend Ant. An examination of Ant's built-in tasks reveals that they also use this API. Because this API is central to how Ant functions, let's take some time to enhance our understanding of it. After exploring that API, we'll finish the chapter discussing how to build a custom build listener. Before we start, let's identify a task to help us better understand the interactions between it and the API.

Matching Class to Source

It's generally accepted that before you deploy a Java application, all the source code should be recompiled in an environment devoid of all project-related class files. If we're working with a project that contains hundreds or thousands of classes, this can be a time-consuming step that's often skipped by developers. When you neglect to perform a clean build, you risk the possibility that unwanted or rogue classes remain in the distribution tree and, consequently, in the `classpath`. More often than not, these rogue classes lie dormant, just waiting for an inopportune time to cause trouble. If the developer is lucky, the rogue class results in a phantom bug that leads to its discovery and removal. The other scenario is that the rogue class hides bugs from the developer. These bugs might appear only after the application has been deployed into either a clean test or (even worse) a production environment. By that time, the presence of the rogue class will most likely result in a delay in the schedule.

It's safe to assume that we can trace every class file back to its corresponding source file. If we had a tool that could perform this type of audit, we could rebuild a subset of the source with the confidence that it's free of rouge classes. Such a tool would iterate through a list of all the classes found in the `classpath`, and then use the Java source and class naming conventions to locate the corresponding source file in the source path. The tool would then report each class for which it cannot find the corresponding source. All the classes listed in the report can be investigated to determine whether they should be deleted. Let's build this audit tool and call it `ClassToSource`. But first, let's spend some time discovering how Ant configures and then executes a task.

Life Cycle of a Task

Every Ant task passes through four distinct phases: creation, initialization, execution, and destruction. To gain an understanding of how Ant moves a task through these phases, let's begin by examining a typical build process.

The main entry point into Ant is the class `org.apache.tools.ant.Main`. It's responsible for the initial configuration of the class `org.apache.tools.ant.Project`. First, it uses information found on the command line to preset any properties before it moves on to create a `Project`. Once created, the `Project` under goes a standard initialization process that, among other things, defines Ant data types and tasks. A `ProjectHelper` is used to fill out the project with the configurations found in the build file. This step involves parsing the XML file into targets, tasks, and properties. After it's created, the `init()` method is called on each task.

The target specified on the command line is placed on a stack. If no target is specified, the default target is placed on the stack. As Ant evaluates each target, it adds its dependencies to the stack. Ant then takes off a target from the stack and looks at the `unless` and `depends` clauses. If the `unless` clause evaluates to true, the target is skipped. If the `depends` clause contains targets, they're executed prior to execution of the current target. After the thread of control returns to `Main`, it deals with any exceptions and then fires an event indicating that the build has completed. The diagram in Figure 6.1 shows the overall sequence of events.

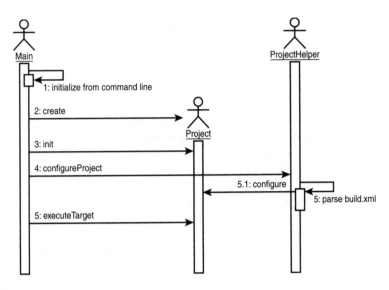

Figure 6.1
Sequence diagram showing a build.

Following the flow in the sequence diagram will help you to visualize the interactions between each supporting class. The sequence diagram shows that the build script specifies properties to be defined. It also specifies a set of build targets and their enclosed tasks. As a target is constructed and initialized, any enclosed tasks are also constructed and initialized. Main is responsible for adding either the default target or the target specified on the command line in a list. The list is then inspected for dependent targets, which are in turn added to the list. The process is repeated until all dependencies are rooted out. The Project.executeTargets() method is responsible for this behavior. From this description, we can see that although a target is initialized only once, it can be executed several times.

> **Note**
> Although Ant attempts to detect cycles in target dependencies, there are a small number
> of conditions under which they can occur.

If you examine the list of tasks found in Listing 6.1, you'll see names such as javac, java, and even ant (as described in Chapter 4, "Built-in Tasks"). Furthermore, you'll also find that these tasks contain a common set of attributes, such as failonerror, documentation, and so on. Ant provides a concrete implementation for all the standard tasks. Various individuals and organizations have given the implementation for optional tasks to the Jakarta project. All tasks carry a name that can be defined either implicitly or explicitly. The `typedef` task provides the means for an explicit mapping (refer to Chapter 4). An implicit mapping can be made by altering the resource bundle `org.apache.tools.ant.taskdefs.defaults.properties`. The references found in this file are resolved when the project is initialized.

The Documentation Attribute

The document attribute is designed to carry help information for an Ant target. This information is displayed if you execute Ant using the projecthelp flag. This functionality enables you to provide online documentation on how someone should use your custom task.

To add a custom task to Ant, we must consider the following points. First, we must provide an implementation that offers the desired functionality. From there, we must supply a mapping from the concrete implementation to the task name. Finally, Ant must be able to construct, configure, and then execute the custom task. Let's spend some time discussing each of the points in this list.

The `ProjectHelper` class helps coordinate the activities of an XML SAX (Simple APIs for XML) parser. `ProjectHelper` asks the project for an instance of a task for a given name. Upon finding the class, the `Project` uses the `newInstance()` method to create an instance of the class that supports the task. After undergoing a minimal amount of configuration, the newly created task object is returned to `ProjectHelper`. Each of the task's attributes is set to the value found in the Ant build script. JavaBean conventions are used to determine the correct set method. Following this step, the `init()` method is called. It's only during the execution of a target that the `execute()` method is called—it's during this call that the task carries out its function. At this point, it might be useful to work out an informal contract to help define the interactions that must take place between Ant and our custom task.

An Informal Contract for a Custom Task

One very useful design feature found in Ant is the decoupling that exists between Ant and its tasks. The code makes direct references only to the abstract class `org.apache.tools.ant.Task`. In doing so, Ant provides us with a plug point that we can use to add in our custom task. If we extend `org.apache.tools.ant.Task`, we'll have created our first custom task. Now, to get it to do something, we must provide an implementation for the method `public void execute() throws BuildException`. As previously mentioned, for Ant to be able to see the new class, a mapping between the class and the task's name (as it appears in the build script) must be provided.

If it's decided that the mapping will be specified in the `default.properties` file, you must distribute a modified `ant.jar` along with the custom task. On the other hand, using the `taskdef` task appears to provide a much less intrusive solution to the problem. Recall from Chapter 4 that a `taskdef` enables us to define the mapping without requiring us to modify the properties file.

The next point to consider is the task's attributes. In this regard, Ant make use of the JavaBean specification. So, as you define the attributes for the task, you must be sure to include the appropriately named `set` methods. In addition, there are certain conditions (which will be specified later) under which Ant may make use of an `add` method. If any specialized initializations are needed, they can be implemented in the `public void init() throws BuildException` method. This method is called after the attributes are set but before the task is executed.

If a task throws a `BuildException`, the build fails. Consequently, its recommended that all tasks implement the common attribute `failonerror`. If this attribute is set to false, `execute` should not throw a `BuildException`. The default value for `failonerror` should be true.

Finally, we must consider the XML that is used to describe the custom task. In defining the element needed to support the task, we need to consider the name of the task, the names of the attributes, and the possibility that we might need to use nested elements (as will be described later).

Let's start with the name of the task. By now, we've all seen the more popular tasks, such as `javac` and so on. And we now have enough information to deduce that the `javac` tag is used by Ant to find the class that supports the `javac` task. Because a custom task is no different from a regular task, we must define and use the tag just as the built-in tasks do.

The attributes come in name/value pairs. The name is translated into the name of the appropriate set method. Reflection is then employed to figure out a reference to the method. That method is invoked with the proper parameter, which in turn causes a field in the task object to be set. Consequently, the name of the attribute must match that of the corresponding set method (minus the set portion of the name). As you can see, you must take care in how instance variables derive their name.

The last point to consider is the question of nested elements. The element of the contract is complex enough that we'll defer its discussion until after we covered some of the more basic material. Now, let's put all this newly acquired information to use and start the process of building our custom task, `ClassToSource`.

Requirements for ClassToSource

In identifying a need for a custom task, we must identify the requirements that are the biases for our use cases or user stories. Three stories—one each for user activity (UA1), reporting (UR1), and configuration (UC1)—can be extracted from the previous description. These requirements are listed in Table 6.1.

Table 6.1   *User Stories*

Use Case	Description
UA1:	For each class on the classpath, find the matching source file using the source path.
UA2:	Ignore inner classes.
UA3:	Ignore JAR files.
UR1:	Generate a report listing each class for which there is no corresponding source.
UC1:	Let the user decide whether to fail the build if no source files are found.

In addition to these user stories, we need a few technical stories to complete the description of the contract between the custom task and Ant. These are described in Table 6.2.

Table 6.2   *Technical Stories*

Technical Use Cases	Description
TC1:	A task should extend the class org.apache.tools.Task.
TC2:	A task must supply a public default constructor.
TC3:	A task must supply a get and set accessor method for each attribute.
TC4:	A task must override public void execute() throws BuildException.
TC5:	A task may override public void init().

A JavaBean as a Task

It isn't a requirement that your task must extend org.apache.tools.Task because Ant will wrap a JavaBean, and through that wrapper it can configure and execute the bean. However, this mechanism is more expensive computationally. Therefore, it's recommended for a custom task to extend org.apache.tools.Task.

Before the task can be used, we must complete the configuration stories (CS) as shown in Table 6.3.

Table 6.3 *Configuration Stories*

Configuration Use Cases	Description
CS1:	Ant's classpath must contain the source for all classes.
CS2:	The task must be defined by a taskdef task.

An Implementation for ClassToSource

From UA1, we know that the user must supply both a source path and a class path. Each of these paths may be a composite of several path elements. These path elements are used to search for either class or source files. This description provides a compelling enough reason to justify representing each with its own separate class. Let's introduce the SourcePathElement and ClassPathElement classes.

A SourcePathElement is a single component in the source path. You can query it for all its source files. After it's created, a SourcePathElement should exist and be immutable. The same requirements are true for a ClassPathElement.

We'll construct two test projects: The first contains class files with matching source, and the second is missing a source file. We'll also write a jUnit test class for SourcePathElement and ClassPathElement. After all the test cases have been run, we'll move on to the next step.

Because the requirements for SourcePathElement and ClassPathElement are identical, it shouldn't be surprising that the code is almost identical. Because of this, we can extract the super class PathElement. The UML diagram in Figure 6.2 provides a visualization of the class hierarchy.

Having completed the groundwork, we're now ready to complete the remaining stories.

To satisfy TC1, we'll introduce the class ClassToSource. As expected, ClassToSource extends Task. It provides a default constructor and the methods setSourcePath(String path), setClassPath(String path), setFailonerror(String value), and public void execute() throws BuildException. Because there's no need to perform any initializations, public void init() is not overridden. The setSourcePath() and setClassPath() methods cause the parameter to be parsed into the collections sourcePath and classPath, respectively. The method of real interest is execute(). Let's take a closer look at it in Listing 6.1.

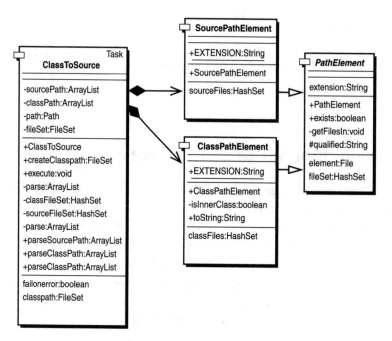

Figure 6.2
UML for ClassToSource and supporting classes.

Listing 6.1   *execute() and execute0()*

```
public void execute() throws BuildException {
    log("Reconciling class and source files");
    try {
        execute0();
    } catch (BuildException be) {
        if (failonerror)
            throw be;
        else
            log(be.getMessage());
    }
    log("Reconciliation completed");
}

public void execute0() throws BuildException {
    HashSet classFiles = this.classFileSet();
    Iterator iterator = this.sourceFileSet().iterator();
    while (iterator.hasNext())
```

Listing 6.1   *(continued)*

```
        classFiles.remove(iterator.next());

    if ( classFiles.size() != 0) {
        Iterator i = classFiles.iterator();
        while (i.hasNext())
            log("No source found for " +
                (String)i.next());
        throw new BuildException(
                    "class with no source found"
                    );
    } else
        log("No class files found");
}
```

The algorithm isn't all that elegant. It takes a list of all class files and removes from the list any class file for which there's a matching source file. If any class files are left at the end of the process, they're reported and a BuildException is thrown if the failonerror flag is true. As you can see, I use a log instead of writing directly to System.out or System.err. Okay, now that the code has been written, let's move on to run the jUnit test.

The first time I ran a jUnit test, execute threw a null pointer exception. After a quick investigation, I determined that the log methods depend on the task being defined within the scope of a project. Although creating an empty project object (as shown in Listing 6.2) in setUp() solved the problem, it also illustrated that jUnit testing required a more complex configuration than what I anticipated.

Listing 6.2   *A Sample jUnit Test for Ant*

```
public void setUp() {
    reconcile = new ClassToSource();
    reconcile.setProject(new Project());
}

public void testExecuteGood() {
    reconcile.setSourcePath("../anttask-test/good/src");
    reconcile.setClassPath("../anttask-test/good/classes");

    try {
        reconcile.execute();
    } catch (BuildException be) {
        fail(be.getMessage());
```

Listing 6.2   *(continued)*

```
    }
    assertTrue(true);
}
```

After the jUnit tests ran, it was time to include the new task in a build file. To complete this step, Listing 6.3 demonstrates how to configure the taskdef task.

Listing 6.3   *A build.xml File*

```
<project name="ant_simple" default="compile" basedir=".">

    <!--
         Before running this build script, check the settings
         in the environment.properties file.
      -->

    <!-- Local Settings for:
             - ant_home
             - ant_custom
      -->
    <property file="environment.properties" />


    <target name="init">
        <tstamp/>

        <!-- Project Directories -->
        <property name="src" value="src" />
        <property name="classes" value="classes" />


        <taskdef name="cts"
                 classname="com.sams.ant.taskdef.ClassToSource"
                 classpath="${ant_custom}" />

    </target>


    <target name="compile" depends="init">
        <mkdir dir="${classes}" />
```

Listing 6.3   *(continued)*

```
        <cts sourcePath="${src}"
             classpath="${classes}" />

        <javac srcdir="${src}" destdir="${classes}" />
    </target>
```

```
</project>
```

In using the Ant logging facilities, we completely satisfied the UR1 story. Although there's more to be said about Ant's reporting facilities, they meet the majority of a user's needs. Listing 6.4 is the output produced by Ant.

Listing 6.4   *Sample Output from ClassToSource*

```
C:\ant\extending-ant >ant
Buildfile: build.xml

init:

compile:
      [cts] Reconciling class and source files
      [cts] Reconciliation completed

BUILD SUCCESSFUL
Total time: 1 second
C:\ant\extending-ant>
```

Adding Nested Elements to a Custom Task

In previous chapters, you've seen that nested elements are used by many Ant tasks. Nested elements help simplify the definition of complex attributes. For example, the javac task requires both sourcepath and classpath attributes. In providing us with a simpler means to express a complex attributes, Ant enables us to improve the readability of the build script. As we all know, improving readability goes a long way toward improving maintainability.

As is the case with the javac task, the ClassToSource task requires us to specify both a sourcepath and a classpath. We've already seen how javac has benefited from the use of nested elements. It seems only sensible that ClassToSource would also benefit from the addition of this feature. Let's move on to discover how nested elements can be added to a custom task.

Ant Data Types

An underlying data type supports each nested element. Each data type must extend the class org.apache.tools.ant.typedef.DataType. One of the best sources of information about Ant is the source code itself. If we look into Ant's source, we see that ProjectHelper defines the inner class NestedElementHandler. NestedElementHandler employs an IntrospectionHelper to help sort through the details creating a data type. The mechanics of how the IntrospectionHelper carries out its role are complex and won't be discussed here. If you're truly interested, I recommend that you run through the source for IntrospectionHelper with a good debugger.

The salient point in this story is that an IntrospectionHelper invokes either the create() or add() method implemented by the task. The method must create and then return a new instance of the data type. For example, the code fragment in Listing 6.5 supports the creation of a fileset for an attribute x.

Listing 6.5   *Nested Element Support for Attribute x*

```
public FileSet createX() {
    x = new FileSet();
    return x;
}

public void addX(FileSet set) {
    x = set;
}
```

In the case of the create() method, Ant configures the newly created fileset object. In the case of the add() method, Ant passes in the data type fully configured.

> **Tip**
> On the surface, there's little difference between the create() and add() methods.
> However, under the covers, the create() method requires Ant to perform much less work.

Because Ant provides several different data types, we can find a data type that meets our needs. A quick look through the documentation reveals three candidate data types: FileList, FileSet, and Path. Let's devote some time to reviewing the features offered by each data type, and then discuss their differences and nuances.

The FileSet Data Type

A *fileset* is a group of files that are found under a directory tree root. The root of the directory tree is specified by the required parameter `dir`. From there, files can be included or excluded using the parameters described in Table 6.4. Let's explore how the `FileSet` data type might be used to replace the simple source and class path attributes of `ClassToSource`.

Table 6.4   *Attributes of the FileSet Data Type*

Attribute	Description
dir	The root directory of the fileset.
includes	Excludes a default set of files; yes/true is the default value.
includesfile	A comma-separated list of files to include. This list may include patterns.
excludes	A comma-separated list of files to exclude. This list may include patterns.
excludesfile	The name of the file containing excludes patterns.

Tip
Any file that appears in the excludes list is excluded even if it also appears in the includes list.

Adding FileSet to ClassToSource

As you'll recall, for Ant to recognize that a task has nested elements, the task must implement an appropriate `create()` method. For the custom task `ClassToSource`, we need a `create()` method for each of the `classpath` and `sourcepath` attributes. The implementation is shown in Listing 6.6.

Listing 6.6   *Methods for the Nested Elements sourcepath and classpath*

```
public FileSet createSourcePath() {
    sourcepath = new FileSet();
    return sourcepath;
}

public FileSet createClassPath() {
    classpath = new FileSet();
    return classpath;
}
```

The next step is to modify the existing methods in `ClassToSource` to use the `FileSet` data type instead of the simple strings. The first method we consider is `execute0()` (see Listing 6.7). As before, we get a list of class files and source files. For each source file, we remove the corresponding class file. If, by the end of the process, we haven't removed all the class files, we must report the offending class and throw a `BuildException`. This part of the logic hasn't changed, so there's no need to make any changes here. We're off to a good start.

Listing 6.7   *ClassToSource.execute0()*

```
public void execute0() throws BuildException {
    HashSet classFiles = this.classFiles();
    Iterator iterator = this.sourceFiles().iterator();
    while (iterator.hasNext())
        classFiles.remove(iterator.next());

    if ( ! classFiles.isEmpty()) {
        Iterator i = classFiles.iterator();
        while (i.hasNext())
            log("No source found for " +
                (String)i.next());
    throw new BuildException(
    "source cannot be found for all classes");
    }
}
```

Now let's decide how the class and source file lists are to be constructed. It's at this point that we start to deviate from the original implementation.

Because the `FileSet` somehow contains the list of files that we're interested in, all we need to do is figure out how to extract them. For this information, we can turn to the API in the Javadoc for Ant. From the Javadoc, we can see that `FileSet` uses `DirectoryScanner` to find the files. If you look at the Javadoc for `DirectoryScanner`, you find a number of methods that list excluded and included files and directories. The method we're interested in is `public String[] getIncludedFiles()`. With this information, we can refactor `private Hash Set classFiles()` and `private ArrayList sourceFiles()`. The refactored methods are shown in Listing 6.8.

Listing 6.8   *The Refactored classFiles() and sourceFiles() Methods*

```
private HashSet classFiles() {
    String[] filelist = this.classpath.
        getDirectoryScanner(super.getProject()).
                        getIncludedFiles();
    HashSet set = new HashSet();

    String className;
    for (int i = 0; i < filelist.length; i++) {
        if ( filelist[i].endsWith(".class"))
            if (filelist[i].indexOf('$') < 0) {
                className = filelist[i].substring(
                    0, filelist[i].length() - 6);
                set.add(className);
            }
    }
    return set;
}

private ArrayList sourceFiles() {
String[] filelist = this.sourcepath.
        getDirectoryScanner(super.getProject()).
                        getIncludedFiles();
    ArrayList list = new ArrayList();
    String className;
    for (int i = 0; i < filelist.length; i++) {
        if ( filelist[i].endsWith(".java")) {
            list.add(filelist[i].substring(
                0, filelist[i].length() - 5));
        }
    }
    return list;
}
```

In the previous version of `ClassToSource`, the source and class paths were passed as single
attributes. It was up to `ClassToSource` to parse and interpret these attributes. Also, we
found that using strings to represent a path element presented some problems. This was
resolved by introducing the classes `PathElement`, `SourcePathElement`, and
`ClassPathElement`, which all contain the desired behaviors. In this version of
`ClassToSource`, a `FileSet` and the supporting class `DirectoryScanner` become

responsible for all this behavior. Consequently, all the methods used to support that functionality have been factored out of ClassToSource, and the two concrete classes and one abstract class designed to model elements of the source and class paths have been eliminated.

If you review the effects of this refactoring, you'll find that code base has been both reduced and simplified. Let's move on to see how this affects the build.xml file.

Modifying the build.xml File

To complete the transformation, we must modify the build.xml file so that it's in alignment with our new version of ClassToSource. It's during this process that cracks begin to appear our decision to use the FileSet data type. But before continuing with that discussion, let's finish the final piece of development and then test this new version of ClassToSource.

Recall from the previous section that the cts task was defined and then executed in the compile target. You can see in Listing 6.9 that this has remained the same. What's changed is that the simple attributes classpath and sourcepath have been replaced with a nested element.

Listing 6.9   *The compile Target for ClassToSource*

```
<target name="init">
    <taskdef name="cts"
        classname="com.sams.ant.taskdef.ClassToSource"
        classpath="${ant_custom}" />

    <patternset id="cts.classset" >
        <include name="**/*.class"/>
    </patternset>

    <patternset id="cts.sourceset" >
        <include name="**/*.java"/>
    </patternset>
</target>

    <target name="compile" depends="init">
        <mkdir dir="${classes}" />

        <cts>
            <classpath dir="${classes}" id="cts.classset"/>
            <sourcepath dir="${src}" id="cts.sourceset" />
```

Listing 6.9 *(continued)*

```
    </cts>

    <javac srcdir="${src}" destdir="${classes}" />
  </target>
```

As before, executing the script results in a `BuildException` being thrown (see Listing 6.10).

Listing 6.10 *Running ClassToSource*

```
C:\ant\extending-ant >ant
Buildfile: build.xml

init:
Overriding previous definition of reference to cts.classset
Overriding previous definition of reference to cts.sourceset

compile:
Overriding previous definition of reference to cts.classset
Overriding previous definition of reference to cts.sourceset
     [cts] Reconciling class and source files
     [cts] No source found for
           com\sams\ant\sample\TestComponentInterface

BUILD FAILED
file: C:\ant\extending-ant/test_scenarios/bad/build.xml:41:
classpath contains artifacts not found in sourcepath

Total time: 1 second
C:\ant\extending-ant >
```

In the change to the `FileSet` data type, we lost some flexibility. In the previous version, we were able to test for source and classes that weren't located under the same root directory. `FileSet` requires that we specify a single root directory using the `dir` attribute. Consequently, the test we could complete in a single task now requires us to execute two separate tasks. Because projects may have many elements in their paths, the build file in this version could be more difficult to build and maintain than in the previous version. This is significant enough to warrant looking for an option other than `FileSet`.

The Path Data Type

At first glance, `Path` looks like a good replacement for `FileSet`. It's certainly flexible enough to enable us to declare many source and class trees. In fact, `Path` is flexible enough that it enables a user to specify just about anything that is required. The `FileSet` data type came with a very useful helper class, `DirectoryScanner`. A quick scan through the Javadoc for `Path` does not turn up an equivalent class. Instead, it provides an array of `String` (as you can see in the following Javadoc snippet).

Javadoc for org.apache.tools.ant.typedefs.Path.list()

java.lang.String[] list()	Returns all path elements defined by this and nested path objects.

What the Javadoc doesn't tell us is what an element in the `String` array looks like. The `FileSet` data type returned an array of strings that represent the directory paths relative to a base directory. For example, the path to the source file for `ClassToSource` was returned as `com/sams/ant/taskdef/ClassToSource.java`.

Replacing FileSet with Path

The changes required to replace `FileSet` with `Path` are very minor. The first change is to alter the `create` methods to work with `Path`. The corresponding fields must be retyped. The next step is to modify the line in the methods that lists the source and class files. The last step is to refactor the `build.xml` file. The results of the refactoring are shown in Listing 6.11.

Listing 6.11   *The compile Target for ClassToSource*

```
<project name="ant_path" default="all" basedir=".">

    <!--
        Before running this build script, check the settings
        in the environment.properties file.
    -->

    <!-- Local Settings for:
            - ant_home
            - ant_custom
    -->
    <property file="environment.properties" />
```

Listing 6.11   *(continued)*

```
<target name="init">
    <tstamp/>

    <!-- Project Directories -->
    <property name="src" value="src" />
    <property name="classes" value="classes" />


    <taskdef name="cts"
            classname="com.sams.ant.taskdef.ClassToSource"
            classpath="${ant_custom}" />

</target>


<target name="compile" depends="init">
    <mkdir dir="${classes}" />

    <cts>
        <classpath >
            <fileset dir="${classes}" />
        </classpath>
        <sourcepath>
            <fileset dir="${src}" />
        </sourcepath>
    </cts>

    <javac srcdir="${src}" destdir="${classes}" />
</target>


<target name="all" depends="compile"/>


</project>
```

The `cts` target now enables the user to specify multiple root directories. It's also much easier to read than the first version. Let's see how it works. First, let's add a line to log each file that is found in the class and source paths. Listing 6.12 displays the output of running the `ClassToSource` task defined in Listing 6.11.

Listing 6.12   *Output from Paths Using FileSet*

```
C:\ant\extending-ant >ant
Buildfile: build.xml

init:

compile:
      [cts] Reconciling class and source files
      [cts] No source found for C:\ant\extending-ant\
ant-project-path\test_scenarios\good\classes\com\sams\
ant\sample\TestComponentInterface
      [cts] No source found for C:\ant\extending-ant\
ant-project-path\test_scenarios\good\classes\com\sams\
ant\sample\TestComponent

BUILD FAILED
file: C:\ant\extending-ant/ant-project-path/test_scenarios/
      good/build.xml:33:
      classpath contains artifacts not found in sourcepath

Total time: 1 second
C:\ant\extending-ant\ant-project-path\tes
t_scenarios\good>

Total time: 1 second
Process terminated with exit code 1
C:\ant\extending-ant >
```

It turns out that list() returns the full path for each entry. This presents a bit of a problem because the extraneous bits of path information will cause ClassToSource, as it is currently implemented, to fail. The problem becomes how we can filter out this extra path information. The only real solution appears to be to parse the source and class files to determine the proper fully qualified name. But it was stated earlier that this parsing should be avoided. Further, Path is extremely flexible in what it enables you to specify. In fact, Path is so flexible that it would be somewhat difficult for ClassToSource to deal with it properly. Taking everything into consideration, it seems that we would be better served by developing our own custom DataType that is specifically designed to match ClassToSource's precise needs.

Custom DataTypes

Just as the purpose of a `Task` is to provide functionality, the purpose of a `DataType` is to provide state. The result of this separation is increased ability to configure tasks and an increased ability for reuse. Let's see how we can put this to work to solve the problem of how to specify class and source paths for `ClassToSource`.

Both the `Task` class and `DataType` class share the same abstract super class, `ProjectComponent`. Subclasses of these two types receive equal treatment by Ant during the configuration pass. The big difference comes in how Ant employs them. As we've seen, a `Task` is designed to carry out a specified unit of work. On the other hand, a `DataType` is designed to define a configuration parameter to be used by a `Task`. The parameter might need to be constrained (as in an enumerated type) or it could be too complex to express in a simple attribute. In either case, the `DataType` is constructed but never executed.

A `DataType` may be defined at the root level or within the target or task level. A `Task` may be defined only at the target level. Therefore, an instance of a `DataType` (via the `id` attribute) may be reused. Armed with this information, let's move forward to discuss the construction of our custom `DataType`.

A Custom DataType for ClassToSource

As we've just witnessed, the `Path` and `FileSet` `DataTypes` offer a tremendous amount of flexibility. So much flexibility, in fact, that they become difficult to use and debug. Using these `DataTypes`, users can specify things that can inhibit `ClassToSource`'s ability to deal with the information provided. It would be better if we had a `DataType` that was a little more restrictive.

One way to think of a class or source path is to view it as a set of directories. Let's introduce a class called `DirectorySet` and state some requirements for it. The `DirectorySet` class should

- Accept a set of directories that contain Java packages holding either source or class files

- Provide a listing of all source of the class files found in that set of directories

Let's use these requirements to construct the class.

Constructing DirectorySet

As previously stated, the mechanisms used by Ant to configure a `DataType` follow the same pattern as those used to configure a `Task`. You're required to supply methods whose names follow the same conventions as those used to define methods for a custom `Task`. This requires the `DataType` to include a `set()` method for each attribute and `add()` or `create()` methods for each nested element. Let's start building our custom data type by defining some attributes for `DirectorySet`.

The first question is how should we specify each directory in a `DirectorySet`. If we use an attribute to specify a class or source path, we'll be required to specify the entire path in that attribute. But that leaves us in the same position we were in when we started the original implementation. What we really want is to be able to specify a `cts` target as demonstrated in Listing 6.13. In this XML snippet, each directory is specified as a nested element. As is the case with any nested element, the directory must be supported with an underlying `DataType`. Thus, let's introduce a new custom `DataType` called `Directory`. As we'll see, factoring `Directory` out of `DirectorySet` results in a useful simplification of both the design and support code.

Listing 6.13   *A Build File for a DirectorySet*

```
<taskdef name="cts"
    classname="com.sams.ant.taskdef.ClassToSource"
    classpath="${ant_custom}" />

<cts>
    <classpath>
        <dir name="${classes}" />
    </classpath>
    <sourcepath>
        <dir name="${src}"/>
    </sourcepath>
</cts>
```

As before, the first line in Listing 6.13 defines our custom task. The `classpath` and `sourcepath` nested elements still exist, although their representation has changed to that of a `DirectorySet`. The task's `create()` method returns an instance of that `DataType`. From this point forward, Ant treats our custom `DataType` in the same manner that it treats all others.

Our newest custom `DataType`, Directory, is specified by the nested element `dir`. As before, Ant makes a call to the `DirectorySet.createDir()` method. This method is responsible for creating a `Directory` and returning it to Ant. Ant then uses the `name` attribute to invoke `Directory.setName()`. To summarize what is happening, as Ant parses the build file, it uses the tag to determine which method should be called on the enclosing object or XML element. It then recursively continues to initialize the inner object until it hits an end-of-element delimiter. At that time, it changes its focus back to the enclosing object or XML element.

Finally, there's no protocol to describe how `ClassToSource` is to interact with `DirectorySet`. Let's specify this protocol in the next section.

Why Isn't a typedef Task Used?

The manner in which Ant treats typedefs renders them less useful than they first appear to be. The interesting feature of data types is that they can be configured outside of a target. These predefined typedefs should be available to be used repeatedly by different tasks. Although this isn't the crux of the problem, a typedef task must be contained within a target. The real problem is that a typedef isn't resolved until the task is executed. But, as you've seen, tasks aren't executed until the entire build script has been parsed. Consequently, any outer-level definition of a custom data type results in a build exception being thrown while the build file is being parsed because Ant will not have completed the definition for the custom type.

The reason we can use a custom data type in our custom task is because the create() method knows which type to work with. Consequently, it doesn't rely on Ant to resolve the nonexistent reference. The same rules apply for custom tasks. The reason why they don't throw a build exception is that they are wrapped as an UnknownElement. The UnknownElement is then resolved and configured at the time the task is executed.

The workaround for this problem is to add a definition for the custom task in the defaults.properties file found in the org.apache.tool.ant.typedefs package.

An Implementation for DirectorySet

We could use the existing implementation of `ClassToSource` if `DirectorySet` could provide a list of files in an array of strings. Because this can be achieved fairly easily, let's follow that route. Listing 6.14 is a listing of the source for `DirectorySet`.

Listing 6.14   *Source for DirectorySet*

```
public class DirectorySet extends DataType {

    public final static String CLASS = "class";
    public final static String SOURCE = "java";

    private String type;
    private HashSet set;
```

Listing 6.14   *(continued)*

```
    public DirectorySet() {
        super();
        set = new HashSet();
    }

    public void setType(String type) {
        this.type = type;
    }

    public Directory createDir() {
        Directory dir = new Directory();
        dir.setType(this.type);
        set.add(dir);
        return dir;
    }

    public String[] getFileList() {
        HashSet allFiles = new HashSet();
        Iterator iter = set.iterator();
        while (iter.hasNext()) {
            Directory dir = (Directory)iter.next();
            String[] files = dir.getFileList();
            for ( int i = 0; i < files.length; i++)
                allFiles.add(files[i]);
        }

        String[] list = new String[1];
        list = (String[])allFiles.toArray(list);

        return list;
    }
}
```

If you inspect the implementation for the getFileList() method, you see an acknowledgement that the operation is expensive. After a result set has been calculated, it's retained. Second, the gathering of files is deferred to Directory. Only one detail has not been explained: the type field. The reasoning for this field will become apparent fairly shortly.

An Implementation for Directory

If you examine the source for Directory (Listing 6.15), you'll find that the DirectoryScanner class has been utilized. The base directory is set to that specified by the dir attribute. Initially, the filter is set to **/*. The only problem is that this filter will include every file found under the root directory. Because sourcepath and classpath are different entities, they should be treated separately. In other words, it isn't desirable to have class files in the list of source files, nor is it desirable to have source files in the class file list.

Listing 6.15   *Source for Directory*

```
public class Directory extends DataType {

    private String dir;
    private String[] dirList;
    private String type;

    public Directory() {
        super();
    }

    public void setType(String type) {
        this.type = type;
    }

    public void setName(String directory) {
        this.dir = directory;
    }

    private String[] fileList() {
        DirectoryScanner scanner = new DirectoryScanner();
        scanner.setBasedir(this.dir);
        String[] args = {"**/*"};
        if (type != null)
            args[0] = args[0].concat("." + type);

        scanner.setIncludes(args);
        scanner.scan();
        return scanner.getIncludedFiles();
    }
```

Listing 6.15   *(continued)*

```
    public String[] getFileList() {
        if (dirList == null)
            dirList = fileList();
        return fileList();
    }
}
```

To prevent the filter from finding these and other unwanted artifacts, the user of `Directory` must specify the type of files to be considered. The types are specified by the two constants: CLASS and SOURCE. Because the user is a `DirectorySet`, it's expected to set this field. Ultimately, this responsibility has been passed along to `ClassToSource`. The `create()` methods in `ClassToSource` have the correct context to properly set this field. Therefore, a `DirectorySet` sees either class files or source files, not both. Finally, `DirectorySet` is responsible for combining all the result sets calculated by each of its contained directories.

As you saw in Listing 6.13, `ClassToSource` defines two nested elements: `classpath` and `sourcepath`. If you examine the source (the code fragment in Listing 6.16), each of these nested elements is supported by a `create()` method. The `create()` method has the added task of configuring the type of `DirectorySet`. Ant initializes all the other public attributes.

Listing 6.16   *Code Fragment for ClassToSource*

```
public class ClassToSource extends Task {

    private DirectorySet sourcepath;
    private DirectorySet classpath;
    private boolean failonerror = true;

    public ClassToSource() {}

    public void setFailonerror(boolean value) { failonerror=value; }

    public DirectorySet createClasspath() {
        this.classpath = new DirectorySet();
```

```java
        classpath.setType(DirectorySet.CLASS);
        return classpath;
}

public DirectorySet createSourcepath() {
    this.sourcepath = new DirectorySet();
    sourcepath.setType(DirectorySet.SOURCE);
    return this.sourcepath;
}

public void execute() throws BuildException {
    log("Reconciling class and source files");
    try {
        execute0();
    } catch (BuildException be) {
        if (failonerror)
            throw be;
        else
            log(be.getMessage());
    }
    log("Reconciliation completed");
}

public void execute0() throws BuildException {
    HashSet classFiles = this.classFiles();
    Iterator iterator = this.sourceFiles().iterator();
    while (iterator.hasNext())
        classFiles.remove(iterator.next());

    if ( ! classFiles.isEmpty()) {
        Iterator i = classFiles.iterator();
        while (i.hasNext())
            log("No source found for " + (String)i.next());
        throw new
          BuildException(
```

Listing 6.16   *(continued)*

```
                    "classpath contains artifacts not found in sourcepath"
                );
        }
    }

    private HashSet classFiles() {
        String[] filelist = this.classpath.getFileList();
        HashSet set = new HashSet();

        for (int i = 0; i < filelist.length; i++)
            if (filelist[i].indexOf('$') < 0)
                set.add(filelist[i].substring(
                        0, filelist[i].length() - 6));

        return set;

    }

    private ArrayList sourceFiles() {
        String[] filelist = this.sourcepath.getFileList();
        ArrayList list = new ArrayList();
        String className;
        for (int i = 0; i < filelist.length; i++)
            list.add(filelist[i].substring(
                    0, filelist[i].length() - 5));

        return list;
    }
}
```

As you can see, the source for ClassToSource remains pretty much the same. One last note is that HashSet is used to collect class files. This helps to sort out cardinality issues that might have occurred in the source file space.

Using a Predefined Data Type

You might recall from Chapter 4 that each element carries with it the common attribute id. The project uses this ID as a key to store the reference it defines. These references are visible to all objects that have access to the project. On the other hand, for a task to use a predefined data type, it must do some work—this useful feature does not come for free.

> **Tip**
> Unlike tasks, data type definitions don't have to be contained within a target.

Again, you might recall from the data type definitions that they support a field known as a *refid*. This attribute, inherited from DataType, serves two purposes. First, it tells the task that the values for this field have been defined elsewhere. Second, its value allows the task to retrieve those values from the project. The functionality required to support this feature has been added into DirectorySet as shown in Listing 6.17. Let's spend the rest of this section understanding the role of each feature.

Listing 6.17   Fragments of DirectorySet That Add Support for a Refid

```
public void setRefid(Reference r) throws BuildException {
    if (! set.isEmpty())
        throw tooManyAttributes();
    super.setRefid(r);
}

public void setType(String type) {
    this.type = type;
}

public Directory createDir() {
    if (isReference())
        throw tooManyAttributes();
    Directory dir = new Directory();
    dir.setType(this.type);
    set.add(dir);
    return dir;
}

public String[] getFileList() {
    HashSet allFiles = new HashSet();
    Iterator iter = this.iterator();
    while (iter.hasNext()) {
```

Listing 6.17   *(continued)*

```
        Directory dir = (Directory)iter.next();
        String[] files = dir.getFileList();
        for ( int i = 0; i < files.length; i++)
            allFiles.add(files[i]);
    }
    String[] list = new String[1];
    list = (String[])allFiles.toArray(list);

    return list;
}

protected Iterator iterator() {
    if ( isReference())
        return this.getRef(getProject()).iterator();
    else
        return set.iterator();
}

protected DirectorySet getRef(Project p) {
    if (!checked) {
        Stack stk = new Stack();
        stk.push(this);
        dieOnCircularReference(stk, p);
    }

    Object o = ref.getReferencedObject(p);
    if (!(o instanceof DirectorySet)) {
        String msg = ref.getRefId()+" doesn\'t denote a dirset";
        throw new BuildException(msg);
    } else
        return (DirectorySet) o;
}
```

There are two areas of change: first in the configuration of DirectorySet, and second in its usage. Let's start with the latter.

Using DirectorySet

When ClassToSource's execute() method is called, it collects a list of source and class files by making a call to getFileList(). The very subtle change to this method is that instead of the integrator method being called directly against the set, it's now called against an implementation provided by DirectorySet. If this configuration is contained in a reference object, that object is retrieved using the refid key and the list of files is obtained from it. Otherwise, the iterator is obtained from the local value. The logic in getRef() ensures that we really get a DirectorySet and, because references could be circular, the logic checks to ensure that we don't drop into an infinite loop following them. Listing 6.18 is a snippet of a sample build file that demonstrates how to use a predefined DirectorySet.

Listing 6.18   *Using a Predefined DirectorySet*

```
<dirset id="settest">
    <dir name="./task-support/good/classes" />
</dirset>

<cts>
    <classpath refid="settest" />
    <sourcepath>
        <dir name="./task-support/good/src"/>
    </sourcepath>
</cts>
```

Configuring DirectorySet

Because we're configuring a DirectorySet that's external to the task, it might be confusing if we allow the user to specify values when using references. Consequently, the createdir() method checks whether this instance is a reference. If it is, the method throws an exception. Because the ClassToSource task decides whether the DirectorySet is a source or class path element, it's allowed to make that assignment. References are configurable at the time of execution. As a result, the final field set by Ant is refid. That method throws an exception if any of the other fields that it checks have been set. Again, this aligns with the thinking that all values should be obtained from the reference. Extending Directory to support refid is left as an exercise to the reader.

Custom Listeners

On startup, Ant registers all listeners that were specified on the command line with the project. During the build, the listener is notified of several build events and is sent log messages. Ant build events are listed in Table 6.5. Each Ant listener implements the org.apache.tools.ant.BuildListener interface. To build our own custom listener, all we need to do is implement that interface.

Table 6.5   *Ant Build Events*

Event	Timing
Build Started	Fired at the beginning of the build
Build Finished	Fired on completion of the build
Target Started	Fired when a target is started
Target Finished	Fired when a target is started
Task Started	Fired when a task has been started
Task Finished	Fired when a task completes
Log Message	Fired whenever a message is logged

There are two purposes for the event listener. The first purpose is for custom logging. The second is for reacting to certain build events. For example, although the AntClassLoader class registers itself as a build listener, it reacts only to the Build Finished event.

> **Tip**
> Although it's possible to specify many listeners, you may only specify one logger.

The information contained in the instance of BuildEvent that's passed as an argument varies with the type of event that fired. For instance, the target and task fields are set for target and task events, respectively. The exception field is set only for finished events and only if an exception was thrown. If a log message event is thrown, the priority and message fields contain valid information. The priorities, defined by Ant in the class Project, are listed in Table 6.6. The default value is Project.MSG_VERBOSE.

Table 6.6   *Log Message Priority Levels*

Priority	Value
0	MSG_ERR
1	MSG_WARN
2	MSG_INFO
3	MSG_VERBOSE
4	MSG_DEBUG

The three command-line flags, -quiet, -verbose, and -debug, set the message priority levels to MSG_WARN, MSG_VERBOSE, and MSG_DEBUG, respectively. The record task (described in Chapter 4) can be used to add listeners that respond to the other message levels.

Let's put this information together to build a custom listener that executes a simple command in response to receiving a buildFinished event.

Listing 6.19 contains an implementation of a custom listener. As specified, it implements the BuildListener interface. Because the requirement is to react to a buildFinished event, only the corresponding method contains actual code. The other methods are there to satisfy the BuildListener interface.

Within the body of buildFinished are two problems of interest. The first problem to solve is how to get the name of the executable. Asking the project for the value of the property named execlistener.executable easily solves this. This property can be defined either on the command line or within the build script itself.

The next problem to consider is how to report exceptions. Again, having a reference to the project proves to be helpful. We can take advantage of the fact that the project knows how to contact all the listeners. All we need to do is ask the project to log the message.

Listing 6.19   *ExecListener*

```
public class ExecListener implements BuildListener {

    public final static String EXECLISTENER_PROPERTY_NAME =
            "execlistener.executable";

    private Throwable throwable;
    public ExecListener() {}

    public void buildStarted(BuildEvent event) {}

    public void buildFinished(BuildEvent event) {

        String command = event.getProject().getProperty(
            EXECLISTENER_PROPERTY_NAME);
        if ( command == null) {
            event.getProject().log( "Exception: no command specified.",
                                Project.MSG_WARN);
            return;
        }

        try {
            Runtime runtime = Runtime.getRuntime();
            Process process = runtime.exec( command);
            process.waitFor();
```

Listing 6.19   *(continued)*

```
        } catch(Exception e) {
            event.getProject().log(
                        "Exception " +
                        e.getClass().toString() +
                        " : " + e.getMessage(),
                        Project.MSG_WARN);
        }
    }

    public void targetStarted(BuildEvent event) {}
    public void targetFinished(BuildEvent event) {}
    public void taskStarted(BuildEvent event) {}
    public void taskFinished(BuildEvent event) {}
    public void messageLogged(BuildEvent event) {}
}
```

Listing 6.20 is a build file that compiles and then tests ExecListener. By this time, the targets should be fairly familiar. Even so, the technique used to test ExecListener might be a bit confusing. Consider this: We can install the listener only when we start Ant, but we don't get the listener until Ant compiles it. The listener target breaks this chicken-and-egg problem by using the java task to call Ant. At this point, Ant has already compiled the custom listener and the listener target has coerced Ant into running some trivial task. When this task completes, buildFinished is executed. Note that we need the fork attribute to be set for this to work. If the fork attribute isn't set, Ant tries to run the specified target in the same virtual machine which, of course, does not have the listener installed.

Listing 6.20   *Build File to Compile and Test ExecListener*

```
<project name="ant_fileset" default="all" basedir=".">

    <!--
        Before running this build script,
        check the settings in the
        environment.properties file.
    -->

    <!-- Local Settings for:
            - ant_home
    -->
    <property file="environment.properties" />
```

Listing 6.20   *(continued)*

```
<target name="init">

    <!-- Project Directories -->
    <property name="src" value="src" />
    <property name="classes" value="classes" />

</target>

<target name="compile" depends="init">
    <mkdir dir="${classes}" />
    <javac srcdir="${src}" destdir="${classes}" />
</target>


<target name="clean" depends="init">
    <delete dir="${classes}" />
</target>

<target name="listener" depends="init">
    <java classname="org.apache.tools.ant.Main"
          fork="yes" >
        <arg value=
         "-Dexeclistener.executable=notepad.exe " />
        <arg line=
   "-listener com.sams.ant.listeners.ExecListener" />
        <arg value="listenertest" />
        <classpath>
            <pathelement location=
                "${classes}" />
            <pathelement location=
                "${ant_home}/lib/ant.jar" />
            <pathelement location=
                "${ant_home}/lib/optional.jar" />
        </classpath>
    </java>
</target>

<target name="listenertest" >
    <echo message="testing listener"/>
</target>
```

Listing 6.20   *(continued)*

```
<target name="all" depends="clean,compile,listener" />

</project>
```

Listing 6.21 is sample output created by running the aforementioned build script. Note that when the `listener` target is called, the resulting output is prefixed by the `[java]` tag.

Listing 6.21   *Sample Output*

```
C:\ant\extending-ant\ant-project-listener>ant
Buildfile: build.xml

init:

clean:
   [delete] Deleting directory
C:\ant\extending-ant\ant-project-listener\classes

compile:
    [mkdir] Created dir:
C:\ant\extending-ant\ant-project-listener\classes
    [javac] Compiling 1 source file to
C:\ant\extending-ant\-project-listener\classes

listener:
     [java] Buildfile: build.xml

     [java] listenertest:
     [java]       [echo] testing listener

     [java] BUILD SUCCESSFUL
     [java] Total time: 1 second

all:

BUILD SUCCESSFUL
Total time: 10 seconds
C:\ant\extending-ant\ant-project-listener>
```

Summary

This chapter demonstrated how to extend Ant by adding a custom task. The custom task was extended to include a built-in data type. When we discovered that the built-in data types didn't quite fit, we introduced a custom data type. In the process of adding a custom task, we were able to extend Ant functionally. While adding a custom `DataType`, we were able to increase Ant's usability and readability. When that was completed, we added reference support for our custom data type, `DirectorySet`. The final section of this chapter described how to build and deploy a custom listener.

- Tasks may be executed many times, but initialized only once.

- Custom tasks should extend the class org.apache.tools.ant.Task.

- Custom tasks must provide a public set() method for each attribute.

- Custom tasks must provide the default public constructor.

- Custom tasks must override public void execute() throws BuildException.

- Custom tasks may override public void init() throws BuildException.

- Custom tasks must be defined either by a taskdef task, or by modifying the default.properties file in the taskdef subdirectory.

- Custom tasks should respect the failonerror flag.

- Custom tasks should use Ant's logging facilities and not write to System.out or System.err.

- Data types can be used to express a complex attribute.

- A custom DataType may be declared by extending org.apache.tools.ant.typedef.DataType.

- Each attribute in a DataType must have a corresponding set() method.

- DataTypes may use nested DataTypes.

- A create() method must be defined for each nested element.

- Custom DataTypes share the common fields defined by DataType.

- For a custom task to use a data type, it must define a corresponding create() or add() method.

- For a task to use predefined data types, it must integrate with and implement pieces of the reference framework.

- A custom listener must implement the org.apache.tools.ant.BuildListener interface.

- The data contained with the BuildEvent object varies with the event.

- Build events are used to trigger actions as well as to log events.

- The build process fires many events.

CHAPTER 7

Troubleshooting Ant Build Scripts

An important aspect of any development process is debugging. In most cases, you'll go through a number of coding and debug cycles. It shouldn't come as a surprise that this statement also applies to the development of Ant build scripts. The good news is that it's typically easier to debug an Ant build script than it is to debug application code. The bad news is that Ant lacks a runtime debugger, but it does come with the capability to set a debug flag on the command line. Setting the debug flag triggers Ant to generate a fairly verbose log of every step it takes. In addition to this, all the techniques that you'd normally use to debug an application can be used to debug Ant build scripts. If the simple debugging techniques fail to resolve the problem, you can either resort to stronger techniques or turn to one of many support groups. This section is devoted to a full discussion of the range of options that are at your disposal when your build script does what you told it, not what you meant for it to do.

Common Debugging Techniques

The first step in fixing your Ant script is recognizing what went wrong and where it happened. In this regard, Ant is very helpful in letting you know where your errors occur, although it might still take some detective work to determine where things went wrong.

One of the techniques that you can use to help you determine where the error occurs is reading the error message until you understand it. Again, this might sound simple, but it sometimes takes me time to understand what the error message is really telling me. The next step is to read the documentation or inspect one or two working examples. Either of these steps might yield clues as to what went wrong. If at the end of this process, you're still puzzled, it might be time to consider using another technique.

Tip
Use the echo task to print the values of properties.

Read the Error Messages
Programmers sometimes get so used to irrelevant error messages that they sometimes do not take the time to understand the message being presented to them onscreen. My experience with Ant is that its error messages are typically very relevant.

Isolating the Bug

The primary reason you'd want to isolate the code containing a bug from the rest of the code base is that it's often easier to find a problem when there are fewer sources for conflict. It's part of a divide-and-conquer strategy that will help make the task more manageable. The first step is to extract as little of the offending code as is necessary to carry the bug into the debugging environment. You might even find that you discover the error in the process of isolating the code.

Isolating a bug in an Ant build script should be simple because tasks should be fairly well isolated within a target. You might need to drag along a few configuration parameters to support the target. If the task works in the new environment, it could be that a configuration that occurred earlier in the process has interfered with the configuration of the task in question. If the task doesn't work in the new build script, you still have to figure out whether, in the process of isolating the task, you're artificially introducing a new error or you're dealing with the original problem. In either case, you'll need to fix the problem. After the problem is fixed, you'll need to integrate the newly formed task back into the main build script. Listing 7.1 is an example of a typical Ant build error message.

Listing 7.1   Sample Output from Ant

```
buildfile: build.xml

init:

compile:
```

Listing 7.1   *(continued)*

```
/export/home/ant/build.xml:
23: destination directory "/export/home/ant/${task-support}/good/classes"
does not exist or is not a directory
```

In this instance, the suspicious looking `${task-support}` portion of the path looks like it's an unexpanded Ant property. An inspection of the `build.xml` file fails to turn up an element to set a value for the task-support property. What the inspection does turn up is the `property` element, `<property file="${ant.project.name}.properties" />`. We know from Chapter 3, "Global Concepts," that the attribute `ant.project.name` should expand to `antbook`. We know also that this file will be loaded into this build, so it is possible that the property is set in the file `antbook.properties`. When I looked into the file `antbook.properties`, I found that it contained the line `task_support=../task-support`. The conclusion is that the property in the `build.xml` file has been mistyped. After that problem has been corrected, the script runs as expected.

If this divide-and-conquer technique is unsuccessful, maybe it's time to walk away from the keyboard and give yourself time to think about the problem. You might also want to find a friendly ear to listen as you explain the problem. Often you'll solve the problem as you listen to your explanation. One thing is for certain: You should always assume that the bug is yours. This is especially true when you are debugging simple configurations.

Syntax Errors

As is the case with conventional languages, build scripts can suffer from basic XML syntax errors. The first thing that Ant attempts to do is build project, target, task, property, and data type objects that are described in the build file. To do so, Ant uses a Simple API for XML (SAX) parser. The build will fail immediately if the SAX parser throws an exception. Consequently, you discover syntax errors one at a time. Eliminating syntax errors can be a time-consuming, tedious process. This is where an editor can help.

Several editors support the construction of XML files by color-coding different elements. Missing a quote, angle bracket, or brace (some of the most common syntax errors) should cause the editor to display elements in an unexpected color. For example, if strings are color-coded green, missing the closing quote will turn a large portion (if not all) of the build file green. This is a great visual clue that you have a syntax error.

If you are using an XML editor, you might need a DTD. The `antstructure` task can produce a document type definition (DTD) for you. Listing 7.2 will produce a DTD file, but beware: The DTD won't be valid if you dynamically define a task using `taskdef`. The same would also be true of the `typedef` task. The workaround is to modify the generated DTD.

Listing 7.2   *Producing an Ant DTD*

```
<antstructure output="mylocal.dtd"/>
```

The Apache Web site is a good resource for finding a list of up-to-date DTD sources.

You might have noted in the previous example that although Ant picked up the typing mistake in the property name, it did so only as a result of trying to interpret a directory that didn't exist. So, although properties look like variables, they really are properties. It is important to remember that Ant is declarative. The effect of this is that once set, properties are immutable. It is also important that you decide on a naming convention that helps you manage your namespace and avoid property name collisions.

Semantic Errors

Most semantic errors are the result of misinterpreting or miscoding a problem. Configuration management of a build is typically a well-understood process. Another source of semantic errors is a result of improper flow through control structures such as `if` and `while` constructs. But Ant does not have any of these constructs. Flow control is pretty much limited to the `if`, `unless`, and `depends` attributes of the target element. These simple structures offer just enough to control the flow through most build processes and not much more. Thus, one of the beauties of Ant is that you won't run into many semantic errors unless your build script is extremely large and unwieldy. If this is the case, you should consider refactoring the build scripts. This subject will be covered in Chapter 9, "Partitioning a Build or Projects and Subprojects."

Programmatic Errors

Of all the different types of errors that can occur, programmatic errors are the most common. Most of the discussion from here on will focus on dealing with these type of errors. A good XML editor combined with a DTD can be useful in helping you find a subset of programmatic errors that might not otherwise be picked up until the time of execution. The XML editor should use the DTD to expose all the attributes supported by a particular XML element. It should also highlight the required attributes. Again, this technique does make it more difficult to include user-defined tasks and data types.

It is helpful to review the Ant documentation as you are building a target. As a rule of thumb, I avoid placing more than one major task within a single target. About the only exception to this rule is on the rare occasion when the tasks are never executed separately.

Also, I always like to review the Ant documentation for each task as I'm constructing the target. Following these guidelines should help you to introduce fewer programmatic errors into your build scripts.

There are three issues regarding properties. The first issue is determining when the properties are set. The second issue is knowing whether the value is valid. The third issue, as you have seen previously, is understanding that after an Ant property is set, its value cannot be changed. The first step is to examine the build script to see how it treats the property in question. If this looks okay, you should suspect that the property is being set externally. As you might recall from the introductory chapters, properties can be set from a number of sources that are all external to the actual build script. These include the command line, property files, and programmatic means. It might take some detective work, but you have to consider each of these sources.

If it is important for a parameter to be set, you should consider using the `condition` task. This task can be used in conjunction with a `fail` statement to form a crude assert statement. Listing 7.3 is an example of a means by which this can be accomplished.

Listing 7.3   *A Crude Assert*

```
<target name="assert" if="fail.build">
    <fail message="OS: not Unix" />
</target>

<target name="my_target_assert">
    <condition property="fail.build">
        <not>
            <os family="unix"/>
        </not>
    </condition>
    <antcall target="assert"/>
</target>

<target name="unixtarget" depends="my_target_assert">
    <echo message="OS: Unix" />
</target>
```

In this code fragment, the target `unixtarget` is not executed until after its dependent target, `my_target_assert`. If the Ant script is running on a UNIX OS, `build.failed` will not be set and the `assert` target will not be executed. If the `build.failed` target is set, the `fail` task will be called, which will end all. This is a crude assert because we can examine whether something does or does not exists, whether a parameter is set, and so on. What we cannot do is check for a specific value of the property. For this, we would need to write a custom task.

Ant Message Levels

As described earlier, Ant supports five levels of messages. The default level is designed to deliver informational messages, warnings, and errors. The `quiet` flag causes Ant to only report on errors. The `verbose` flag results in more output, but it's the `debug` flag that causes Ant to flood the screen with an abundance of information. This level of information is most helpful in debugging Ant build scripts. Let's consider the output that Ant would produce from the script shown in Listing 7.4 when run in silent, normal, verbose, and debug modes. The demonstration is designed to accent the quantity and quality of information that is displayed when the `debug` flag is set.

Listing 7.4   *Sample Ant Build Script*

```
<project name="antbook" default="compile" basedir=".">

    <property file="${ant.project.name}.properties" />

    <target name="init">

        <!-- Project Directories -->
        <property name="src" value="src/custom" />
        <property name="classes" value="classes" />

    </target>
    <target name="compile" depends="init">
        <javac srcdir="../${src}" destdir="${classes}" />
    </target>

</project>
```

First, let's consider running in quiet mode. The output is shown in Listing 7.5.

Listing 7.5   *Output from a Failed Build*

```
/export/home/sams/ ant ñquiet
BUILD FAILED

/export/home/sams/build.xml:12: srcdir "/export/home/sams/src/custom"
does not exist!
```

As you can see, only the bare minimum of information is reported. In this case, you see that the `srcdir` attribute used in the line `<javac srcdir="../${src}"`

destdir="${classes}" /> is set to a directory that does not exist. Now that we know that the problem is an improperly specified srcdir attribute, let's use that information to see how the error is reported when the verbose flag is set. The output in Listing 7.6 contains a lot more information, including a stack trace, the build sequence, the name of the build file, and the values for the other two properties: src and classes.

Listing 7.6 *Output Produced by Setting the verbose Flag*

```
Ant version 1.4 compiled on September 3 2001
Buildfile: build.xml
Detected Java version: 1.3 in: /opt/java/jdk1.3/jre
Detected OS: Solaris 2.8
parsing buildfile  /export/home/sams/build.xml with
URI = file:/export/home/sams/build.xml
Project base dir set to: /export/home/sams
Build sequence for target 'compile' is [init, compile]
Complete build sequence is [init, compile]

init:
Setting project property: src -> src/custom
Setting project property: classes -> classes

compile:

BUILD FAILED

/export/home/sams/build.xml:
12: srcdir "/export/home/sams/src/custom" does not exist!
        at org.apache.tools.ant.taskdefs.Javac.execute(Javac.java:478)
        at org.apache.tools.ant.Task.perform(Task.java:217)
        at org.apache.tools.ant.Target.execute(Target.java:164)
        at org.apache.tools.ant.Target.performTasks(Target.java:182)
        at org.apache.tools.ant.Project.executeTarget(Project.java:601)
        at org.apache.tools.ant.Project.executeTargets(Project.java:560)
        at org.apache.tools.ant.Main.runBuild(Main.java:454)
        at org.apache.tools.ant.Main.start(Main.java:153)
        at org.apache.tools.ant.Main.main(Main.java:176)

Total time: 1 second
```

Let's perform the same exercise with the debug flag set. Note that Listing 7.7 contains an extraordinary amount of information. I have shortened the output by trimming large blocks from the section that lists which tasks have been initialized and the virtual machine (VM) property settings.

Listing 7.7   Output Produced by Setting the debug Flag

%bin/ant -debug

```
Ant version 1.4 compiled on September 3 2001
Buildfile: build.xml
Setting project property: ant.java.version -> 1.3
Detected Java version: 1.3 in: /opt/java/jdk1.3/jre
Detected OS: Solaris 2.8
  +User task: tar       org.apache.tools.ant.taskdefs.Tar
  +User task: fail      org.apache.tools.ant.taskdefs.Exit
  +User task: uptodate      org.apache.tools.ant.taskdefs.UpToDate
........................
  +User task: rmic      org.apache.tools.ant.taskdefs.Rmic
  +User datatype: fileset      org.apache.tools.ant.types.FileSet
..............................
Setting project property: java.runtime.name ->
Java(TM) 2 Runtime Environment, Standard Edition
Setting project property: sun.boot.library.path -> /opt/java /jdk1.3/jre\bin
Setting project property: java.vm.version -> 1.3.0-C
..........................
Setting ro project property: ant.version ->
Ant version 1.4 compiled on September 3 2001
Setting ro project property: ant.file -> /export/home/sams/build.xml
parsing buildfile  /export/home/sams/build.xml with
URI = file:/export/home/sams/build.xml
Setting ro project property: ant.project.name -> antbook
Adding reference: antbook -> org.apache.tools.ant.Project@5e3974
Setting project property: basedir -> /export/home/sams
Project base dir set to: /export/home/sams
    +Task: property  [property] Loading /export/homes/sams/antbook.properties
Setting project property: tools_home -> /opt
Setting project property: ant_home -> /opt/apache/jakarta-ant-1.4
Setting project property: apache_home -> /opt/apache
Setting project property: task_support -> ../task-support
  +Target: init
    +Task: property
    +Task: property
  +Target: compile
```

Listing 7.7 *(continued)*

```
    +Task: javac
Build sequence for target `compile' is [init, compile]
Complete build sequence is [init, compile]

init:
Setting project property: src -> src/custom
Setting project property: classes -> classes

compile:

BUILD FAILED

/export/home/sams/build.xml:
12: srcdir "/export/home/sams/src/custom" does not exist!
        at org.apache.tools.ant.taskdefs.Javac.execute(Javac.java:478)
        at org.apache.tools.ant.Task.perform(Task.java:217)
        at org.apache.tools.ant.Target.execute(Target.java:164)
        at org.apache.tools.ant.Target.performTasks(Target.java:182)
        at org.apache.tools.ant.Project.executeTarget(Project.java:601)
        at org.apache.tools.ant.Project.executeTargets(Project.java:560)
        at org.apache.tools.ant.Main.runBuild(Main.java:454)
        at org.apache.tools.ant.Main.start(Main.java:153)
        at org.apache.tools.ant.Main.main(Main.java:176)

Total time: 1 second
```

In the final analysis, the problem with the sample build script is simple enough that we don't need all this information. But it is valuable to know that what kind of information is available should you run into a bug that is difficult to diagnose. The quantity and quality of the information are strong enough to help you verify most assumptions that you made while writing the configuring the Ant build script.

Using a Java Debugger

Occasionally, you'll run into a case in which the information provided by the debug flag is still not enough to solve the problem. In such a case, there is a powerful weapon that can be used to help track down the bug: a Java debugger. If you're not a Java developer, you'll want to enlist the assistance of a developer. If none is available, you might want to skip the rest of this section and move on to the one of the many available support channels.

Setting Up for Debugging Ant

The first step in this process (assuming that you have your favorite debugger ready to go) is to acquire the source. The instructions in Chapter 1, "Introduction to Ant," tell you how to get the latest Ant binary. That distribution does not include the source. In the process of following those instructions, you might recall seeing files with names such as `jakarta-ant-1.4.1-src.zip`. This file contains the source for Ant version 1.4.1. Find this file for the version you're currently using and download it. Note that the UNIX distribution will be contained in a tar ball. After you've downloaded the source, extract the source from the file into some location from which a debug session can be configured.

In the process of extracting the source from the compressed file, you might notice that there are more than 500 source files in the Ant distribution. Much to their credit, the developers of Ant have done a nice job of separating and containing behavior into separate classes. As a consequence, even the most complex debugging session should never touch more than a half-dozen or so classes. With most debugging sessions, you'll touch no more than two or three classes.

> **Some Software Metrics for Ant**
> Much to the credit of the Ant developers, the average class size is fewer than 90 lines of code and 90% of the classes have fewer than 140 lines of code. These size and complexity metrics are a good indication that a debugging session is feasible activity.

If you look into the `src` tree, you'll find that it contains five subdirectories. `src` is the main subdirectory that contains the source code for binary distribution `<javac srcdir="../${src}" destdir="${classes}" />`. Consequently, the other four subdirectories can be ignored. I recommend that you just remove them altogether.

Finally, it is important to set up your debugging environment. The most important aspect of this is your class path. There are a couple reasons for this that will become apparent in the next section. Let's move on to define a process for debugging Ant.

Proceeding to Debug Ant

Before starting to debug, you might find it useful to review the materials in Chapter 6, "Extending Ant with Custom Tasks, Data Types, and Listeners," that describe how Ant creates and treats custom tasks and data types. Understanding this material will help you understand what you are looking at when you finally get on with debugging.

Before you can debug Ant, you'll need to recompile the classes with the `debug` flag turned on. Instead of compiling the entire Ant project, I find it easier to compile only the two or three classes that are relevant to the bug. It is most likely that this information is contained in the output produced by the `debug` flag. In many cases, the problem will show up in a specific task. Because the class-to-task relationship is one to one, the first class to compile is the one class that maps to the offending task. All the classes that support tasks are found in the package `org.apache.tools.ant.taskdefs`.

In addition to the class supporting the task of interest, you will also want to compile `org.apache.tools.ant.ProjectHelper`. As you might recall from Chapter 6, that class supports the parsing of the supporting build file into objects. Inside that class, you'll find several inner classes. Each of the inner classes is responsible for parsing one of the elements in the build file. The inner classes are listed in Table 7.1.

Table 7.1   *Inner Classes to Parse the Build Script*

Inner Class	Role
AbstractHandler	Root class of all handlers. Handles common attributes and controls flow between concrete handlers.
RootHandler	Handles the root element in the build script. Its only child is a project element.
ProjectHandler	Defines a project. Its only children are target and property.
TargetHandler	Defines a target. Its allowable children are tasks and property.
TaskHandler	Defines a specific task. If any children are allowed, they will be a nested element.
NestedElementHandler	Handles all nested elements by resolving them and sending them to the enclosing task.
DataTypeHandler	Handles all data types declared outside of a task.

If you're having trouble with a property, you might be interested in not only the class `org.apache.tools.ant.taskdefs.Property`, but also in the method `replaceProperties`, which can be found in `ProjectHelper`. It is in this method that a property is parsed, all the macros are resolved, and the value is bound to the project using the `name` attribute as the key.

As Ant parses the `build.xml` file, it is required to initialize tasks. After the project is built, it carries out work by calling each task's `execute` method. From this information, it seems that the most sensible place to first set breakpoints is on the `init` and `execute` methods. From that point, you should be able either to determine the problem or to at least have a basic idea of what steps need to be taken. In this regard, you might also find that you need to compile `org.apache.tools.ant.IntrospectionHelper`. If Ant finds a forward reference in the initialization process, it delays resolving that reference until time of execution. The `IntrospectionHelper` is responsible for completing the resolution of properties and tasks that contained forward references or were otherwise not defined during initialization.

At this point, I'm going to recommend that you do something that I usually highly recommend against. Specifically, that is to configure your class path to contain first the output directory for the compiler, and then the Ant JAR file. On one hand, doing so eliminates the need to compile the entire Ant project. On the other hand, you're playing tricks with a class loader that might be implementation-specific, which might result in you debugging a class file that is out of sync with the source. In this case, you're not changing code, you're just trying to debug a problem. As your debugging session progresses, you might find that you need to compile a few more classes. Generally, to debug any problems, you should need to compile, at most, only three or four of the classes.

The entry point to Ant is the class `org.apache.tools.ant.Main`. It supports all the command-line options that are passed to it via the `ant.bat` or `ant` script (depending on which OS you are using). After you're at this point, you've reduced the problem to a straightforward, good old Java debugging session. One final note: Make sure that your compiled classes appear on the class path before `ant.jar`. Doing this allows the class loader to find the classes that contain the information needed to support debugging.

Support Resources and Rules of Engagement

Before embarking on an intensive debugging session (as described previously), you are well advised to go through the Ant FAQ page found on the Jakarta Apache Web site. The FAQ addresses a number of basic and currently known problems. If the FAQ does not address your needs, you can turn to one of several forums at jGuru (`http://www.jguru.com/forums/Ant`). Alternatively, the Apache Web site supports two mailing lists and a bug report system known as Bugzilla. Each of the mailing lists can also be accessed via the Web site `http://www.japache.org`. The bug listings can be found at `http://nagoya.apache.org/bugzilla`.

If you find that your problem is a result of a bug, it is advisable to download the latest build because it is likely that someone else will have already fixed the problem. If your debugging session turns up a new bug, I recommend that you report it to the developer's mailing list before submitting a full bug report.

A well-aimed question at one of the Ant mailing lists will generally yield an abundance of useful results and comments. In general, a more concise question will lead to a more helpful response. There are currently two lists. The user list is designed to answer questions concerning the use of Ant. This includes configuration and setup questions. The developer list is best for questions regarding the actual source code or handling development tasks.

In some cases, you might be faced with a question that appears to span both lists. In that case, it is recommended that you pick only one list to post to. An example of such a situation would be if you're having trouble coding a custom task. This has the potential of being either a user or developer question. The list to post to depends on the nature of the problem.

Both the user and developer lists generate a considerable amount of traffic. Because of this, you might want to access the lists using the alternative Web-based interface hosted by www.japache.org. At that site, you can read messages that have been posted in either list. The alternative is to subscribe to the lists themselves.

When posting questions, be cognizant that the monitors and participants are all volunteers and, as such, should be treated with respect. It is because of their efforts that you are able to enjoy the use of this great tool.

At the Bugzilla site, you can request a summary report or perform a specific query. If you're not familiar with how to submit bug reports or even what constitutes a bug, it is probably best for you to turn to one of the two mailing lists.

In addition to these resources, you can find information at

```
http://sourceforge.net/projects/ant-contrib
http://sourceforge.net/projects/antheap
```

Common Problems and Solutions

The following provides a list of solutions to the common problems that users have run into:

Problem: If a property were not defined, I would expect the delete task to fail because the file does not exist. However, it doesn't fail and the Ant build continues along its merry way. Am I missing something?

Solution: The <delete> task doesn't consider not finding the specified file an error when you are deleting a file that doesn't exist.

Problem: Is it possible to use . (current directory) as part of the class path?

Solution: Yes, it is possible, although it is recommended that you use ${user.dir} for the current working directory and ${basedir} if you mean the base directory of your Ant build file.

Problem: Does the scope of a global property extend to nested build files?

Solution: Until Ant 1.5, the answer was yes. Since Ant 1.5, you can set an inheritAll flag to false to change this.

Problem: Where is the default `build.properties` located on Windows 2000 machines?

Solution: `user.home` is set to `C:\Documents and Settings\username`.

Problem: How do I handle deadlock when running jUnit tests?

Solution: jUnit supports a `timeout` attribute.

Problem: I am having trouble getting the following script to JAR everything except the jUnit tests. The following script does not exclude the `junit` directory:

```
<target name="jar">
    <jar jarfile="${outputPath}/../myjar.jar"
         basedir="${outputPath}"
         excludes="${outputPath}/com/sams/ant/junit/**/*"
    />
</target>
```

Solution: Your `excludes` attribute should specify a path relative to your specified `basedir` attribute. Try setting it to `com/sams/ant/junit/**`.

Problem: I've created a new data type for use by a new task, but `typedef` does not work. Why?

Solution: This has been reported as bug 4452, which has been fixed in Ant 1.5. For 1.4.1, you must modify the properties file found in the `typedef` package to include the custom data type. For details, refer the section on `typedef` in Chapter 6.

Problem: Is it possible to specify dependencies between entries in `build.properties`? For example:

```
my.A=foo
my.B=${my.A}/bar
```

Solution: Yes, it will even resolve forward references.

Problem: What's the best way to run makefiles from Ant?

Solution: Use the `exec` task.

Problem: Is there a way to set the class path based on which operating system I'm running in?

Solution: Try the following:

```
<target name="setClasspath">
    <condition property="classpath" value="foo/helper.jar">
        <os family="unix" />
    </condition>
    <condition property="classpath" value="c:\lbar\helper.jar">
        <os family="windows" />
    </condition>
</target>
```

Alternatively, you can set the class path in separate properties file, one for each platform. You'll find techniques in Chapter 9 that address this issue.

Problem: How can I have my build continue even though there was a build failure?

Solution: Many tasks have a `failonerror` flag. For those that don't, you can obtain the `TryCatch` task from `http://sourceforge.net/projects/ant-contrib`.

Problem: I'm having trouble navigating with Ant. How does Ant treat directory paths?

Solution: All nonabsolute paths are relative to the `basedir`.

Problem: Is there any way to turn off the default `excludes`?

Solution: Yes, directory-based tasks support the `defaultexcludes` attribute. Setting it to "no" will achieve this.

Summary

What you've seen are several options that are available to help troubleshoot an Ant build script. In addition to these techniques, you've discovered several resources that are available on the Web. The combination of these resources actually helps make Ant more debuggable than most commercial software packages.

Tips

The following summarizes the main points introduced in the chapter:

- Debugging remains an important activity.
- Start by recognizing where things went wrong.
- Debugging Ant scripts is typically not overly complicated.
- You can still apply traditional debugging techniques.
- Explain the problem to someone.
- Read the documentation.
- Use the `echo` task to display values.
- Use a divide-and-conquer strategy to isolate a problem.
- Ant error messages generally aim you in the right direction.
- Ant will report on all syntax errors during the XML parsing phase.
- Use an editor that recognizes and supports XML.
- Properties are immutable, so choose a naming scheme to help avoid namespace collisions.

- Flow control in Ant is very limited.
- Ant produces messages at informational, verbose, and debug levels.
- You can use a source-level debugger to debug Ant scripts.
- jGuru hosts an Ant discussion forum at http://www.jguru.com/forums/Ant.
- Both a developer and a user mailing list are accessible from the Ant Web site.
- Questions should be posted on only one of the two mailing lists.
- Concise questions typically get concise answers.
- Ant bugs are listed at `http://nagoya.apache.org/bugzilla`.
- The Ant Web site has both a troubleshooting and FAQ section.

CHAPTER 8

Performing End to End Builds on a Nightly Basis

In this chapter, we'll discuss a topic that is becoming increasingly important to more and more development shops: unattended End to End (EtE) nightly builds. Why should you care how to do an EtE build while everyone is asleep? We'll talk about that and then show you how Ant makes it easy to do this type of build.

What Is End to End Building?

Let's see what End to End building is, and begin to construct our build file that will perform all this work. In this section, we'll cover the following topics:

- Overview of EtE builds
- Parameters for our discussion
- A skeleton build file

Overview

An End to End build is the process of taking a piece of software through the entire build/test/deploy cycle in one fell swoop. This includes fetching source from a source repository, compiling it, JAR/WAR/EAR-ing it, testing it, generating reports, sending those reports to interested parties and, finally, deploying the project. At each step, there is the potential for failure; if any step of the build fails, the entire build process will typically abort. This is generally the desired behavior because you probably don't want broken software going into production or published on your downloads page!

The concept of unattended End to End builds encompasses several technologies that need to be integrated. These include

- Source code management (SCM) tools such as the Concurrent Versions System (CVS) or SourceSafe

- A Java compiler such as javac or Jikes

- The standard jar tool for creating Java Archives (JARs), Web Archive (WARs), and Enterprise Archives (EARs)

- Testing tools such as JUnit

- A Simple Mail Transfer Protocol (SMTP) mail client for e-mailing reports

- Deployment tools such as ejbc (for app servers) and FTP for moving the project to the destination machine

Ant makes accomplishing this integration quite easy. Using an Ant build file scheduled with a system-level scheduler such as the UNIX cron tool or the Windows 2000 Task Scheduler, you can have Ant kick off a build at midnight, fetch the latest version of your code from CVS, build it, run your JUnit test suites against it, generate reports from the test, e-mail those reports to appropriate members of your staff, and then deploy it, assuming a clean build. I probably wouldn't do an automatic deploy to production, but you could certainly auto-deploy to your Quality Assurance (QA) or integration test machines. Having test reports mailed to developers and managers informs everyone what happened during the build with a minimum of effort on their parts.

Parameters for This Discussion

So, now that you have a vague idea of what EtE builds are, let's talk about what we're going to build, the systems involved, and our general plan of attack. We'll assume that we're building a simple Java Web application that includes one JavaServer Page (JSP), a servlet, two supporting Java classes and, finally, the Web application descriptor file web.xml. This is a seriously stripped-down application, but to avoid overwhelming you with the details of the project, that's the way it has to be. We'll discuss all the pieces of the build, including using both CVS and SourceSafe.

> **Note**
> The source for each of the classes, the JSPs, the web.xml file, and the completed build.xml can be found on the publisher's Web site.

We have three machines involved with this project. They are

- otto—Our development box
- bud—Our source repository
- duke—Our deployment server

We'll fetch our source from the CVS/SourceSafe repository on bud, build the code and test on otto, and deploy to a public directory on duke so that our crack QA staff can put it through its paces in the morning.

Skeleton Build File

Now we'll begin construction of our build file. Given the parameters discussed earlier and the machines that we'll be using, we can start a skeleton build file. As Listing 8.1 shows, we know that we need the basic scaffolding that all Ant build files need.

Listing 8.1   *The Starting Point for the Build File*

```xml
<?xml version="1.0"?>

<project name="etetest" basedir="." default="deploy">

</project>
```

Next, we must define the properties that will govern the build. We will, of course, need properties for

- The name of the project for creating the WAR file
- A timestamp for use in the JAR name
- The hostnames of the two remote machines involved
- The source directory
- The local directory containing supporting files
- The local destination directory
- The destination directory on the deployment machine

- The Java compiler to use

- The name of the WAR file to create

- Security credentials for logging in to the source repository

- Security credentials for deploying the finished product

Given what you learned in Chapter 3, "Global Concepts," regarding suggested directory tree layouts, we'll create our `build.properties` file as shown in Listing 8.2, and our `init` target as shown in Listing 8.3.

Listing 8.2   *Our Properties File*

```
name=etetest
src.dir=src
build.dir=build
build.dir.classes=${build.dir}/classes
war.name=${name}-${DSTAMP}.war
etc.dir=etc
servlet.jar=d:/Tomcat/common/lib/servlet.jar
junit.jar=d:/opensource/junit/junit3.7/junit.jar
reports.dir=reports
build.compiler=modern
src.repo.box=bud
src.repo.home=/home/cvspublic
vss.repo.home=/projects/etetest
repo.user=harry
repo.pass=dean
cvsroot=:pserver:${repo.user}@${src.repo.box}:${src.repo.home}
deploy.box=duke
depoloy.dir=/uploads
deploy.user=miller
deploy.pass=zander
manager.email=jsmith@mycompany.com
qa.email=qa@mycompany.com
```

Listing 8.3   *Shows Our init Target*

```
<target name="init">

    <tstamp/>
    <property file="build.properties"/>
```

Listing 8.3   *(continued)*

```
    <path id="classpath">
        <pathelement path="${servlet.jar}"/>
        <pathelement path="${junit.jar}"/>
    </path>
    <property name="classpath" refid="classpath"/>
</target>
```

Let's go over what we have here to make certain that you understand what's going on. In our init target, we first call tstamp, which creates properties pertaining to the current date that can be referenced later. These properties are DSTAMP, TSTAMP, and TODAY. These will be useful in naming our deliverables. Then we set up the bulk of our properties using a properties file, which was shown in Listing 8.2.

Taking a look at Listing 8.3, the first property in our properties file, name, will serve as the base name for the WAR file we'll create later. As noted in previous chapters, this property could have been named anything. It is convenient to call this property name because that is how it will function. The second line, tstamp,

The next three lines tell the Java compiler where to find the source files and where to place the compiled .class files. The src.dir property serves double duty as the destination for our source code repository checkout, which we'll cover in a little while.

The war.name property will be used to tell the war task what to call the generated Web archive. The etc.dir property will also be used by the war task to find the deployment descriptor, web.xml, for our Web archive.

Notice that in the war.name property we reference another property called DSTAMP. This property was created for us by our tstamp task and enables us to encode the current date into our finished archives. This is extremely useful when you want to have multiple versions of your project living happily together.

Next we have two properties that will be used in our class path. These properties point to the Servlet API classes contained in servlet.jar and the JUnit unit testing framework's classes stored in junit.jar. These will be included in the class path shortly. The reports.dir property will be used by the junit task to know where to place its output files.

Next we meet the build.compiler property, which tells Ant which compiler to use. modern is what you should generally use. classic is not a mode you want to use because it is remarkably slow (and might be phased out at some point). jikes is certainly the fastest of the compiler modes, but you must, of course, have Jikes installed for this one to work.

The next five properties all have to do with CVS. The first, `src.repo.box`, is the name of the machine on which our repository lives. `src.repo.home` is the patch to the repository on that machine. `repo.user` and `repo.pass` are the CVS username and password to use, respectively. `cvsroot` is the string that will be passed to the `cvs` task to log in to the repository.

> **Caution**
>
> Having usernames and passwords in plain text like this is indeed a security risk, but there's really no way around it. If this is a problem for you, I suggest that you create limited access accounts on each box and use those. For example, create a user on your source repository box that can perform Gets, but can't modify or delete.

We then have one property called `vss.repo.home` that we will use for our demonstration of fetching source from Visual SourceSafe. This is the full path to our project in the repository.

The next four properties are the machine, directory, username, and password for our deployment machine. We'll be moving our final project to this box at the end of our build, and we need to know where that is and how to log in.

Finally, we have the e-mail addresses of those staff members who need to get e-mail from our nightly build. These will be used by the `email` task at the completion of our build.

Back in our build file, in Listing 8.2, we'll construct the class path that the `javac` task will use for compilation. This consists of a `path` structure that contains two `pathelement` tags. These specify individual JAR files that should be included in the class path. Here we reference properties that will be evaluated to the full pathnames of `servlet.jar` and `junit.jar`. We then assign this path reference to a property with the same name, `classpath`. This way we can reference the class path from tasks that take either a reference or a property.

Now that we've gotten our skeleton build file ready, we'll begin putting in the targets that will do the heavy lifting for us.

Targets for EtE Builds

In this section, we'll create the targets to carry out our unattended end to end build. We'll create 11 targets to perform this work, and those targets will use several of the built-in and optional tasks that Ant provides. Here are the major topics for this section:

- An overview of the tasks we will create
- Setting up a recorder to get a full log of the build

- Preparing the output directory

- Fetching the source code from both CVS and SourceSafe

- Compiling the files

- Running JUnit tests on our code

- Reporting test results

- Generating a Web archive for deployment

- Deploying what we've built

- What to do with those reports

Tasks We'll Use

We'll use numerous tasks for our EtE build, running the gamut of functionality and responsibility. In the previous section, we laid out what must happen in our build file. Now we'll
describe how to make that happen with Ant. The following list contains the tasks that we'll
use:

- <property>—For setting build properties

- <record>—For logging everything that happens in the build to a file

- <cvspass>—For logging into the CVS repository

- <cvs>—For getting our source from CVS

- <vssget>—For getting our source from SourceSafe

- <mkdir>—For creating a binary output directory

- <javac>—For compiling all our source files

- <war>—For creating a Web Archive (WAR) containing the JSPs, servlets, and their
  supporting classes

- <junit>—For running unit tests on the code

- <junitreport>—For nicely formatting the results of the <junit> test run

- <ftp>—For deploying the new JAR/WAR/EAR/Sip to a remote machine

- <copy>—For copying and deploying

- <zip>—For creating archives of our reports

- <mail>—For sending the logs of the build to appropriate staff members

Recording the Details of the Build

When executing your builds, it's handy to be able to capture a record of everything that happened during the build, especially when it is performed unattended. There is a task, called `record`, that provides this very functionality. The gist of this task is that you start the recorder as early in your build process as possible and turn it off at the end. You then have a complete transcript, so to speak, of your build.

The `record` task works by attaching a listener to your build and intercepting any messages that any task sends to the console. These messages are then logged to the specified file. It is possible to start up multiple recorders, all writing with different options to different log files. For our purposes, we'll be using only one recorder.

To implement our recorder, we'll create a new Ant target called `startrecorder`. Our task relies on two of the properties that are set in the `init` target, so we must indicate this dependency by stating that our target depends on `init`. Listing 8.4 is the target to start the recorder.

Listing 8.4   *Starting the Recorder*

```
<target name="startrecorder" depends="init">
    <record name="${reports.dir}/${name}-${DSTAMP}-log.txt"
            action="start" append="false"/>
</target>
```

Chapter 4, "Built-in Tasks," has a full rundown on "`record`" and its attributes. For our "`startrecorder`" target, we'll make use of only three attributes: `name`, `action`, and `append`. The `name` attribute contains the name of the log file to which we want to send data. Here we're creating a filename using three properties defined in the `init` target. `reports.dir` is the directory name of where the report file should be created, `name` will be evaluated to `etetest`, and `DSTAMP` will evaluate to the current date. We then append `-log.txt` to it and our filename is set. The `action` attribute is like the power switch of the recorder. The two possible values for it are `start` and `stop`. You can probably guess what each does. We call `start` here to begin the record running. Later, we'll run the `record` task with the `stop` attribute value to turn it off. When I execute my build file, I end up with a record of the activities in a file called `etetest-20020516-log.txt`.

It's important to start the recorder running as soon in the build process as possible in order to get the most accurate record of the proceedings. It wouldn't be out of line to start the recorder as soon as possible in the `init` target after all the properties it relies on have been defined. I used a separate target in this example to set it apart from the property definitions for clarity.

Similarly, we'll create a `stoprecorder` target to turn off the recorder. This target will look just like `startrecorder` except that the `action` attribute will be set to `stop` instead of `start`. Listing 8.5 shows this target.

Listing 8.5   *Stopping the Recorder*

```
<target name="stoprecorder">
    <record name="${name}-${DSTAMP}-log.txt" action="stop"/>
</target>
```

When will we actually invoke the `startrecorder` target? That remains to be seen. We want it to start recording at the earliest possible moment, but we need to define a few more targets before we really know when that moment is. For now, we'll just sit content in the knowledge that this target is ready to go when we need it.

Preparing the Output Directory

We'll need a directory in which to place the compiled Java classes. We want to create this directory before we try to start dropping files into it (obviously). And because javac won't create this directory for us, we'll need to do it ourselves. We'll create another target called `prepare` that will depend on `init` and contain our `mkdir` task. There will likely be other tasks we must include in the `prepare` target, but for now this is all we need. Listing 8.6 shows our `prepare` target.

Listing 8.6   *Creating an Output Directory*

```
<target name="prepare" depends="init">
    <mkdir dir="${build.dir.classes}"/>
</target>
```

This task will create the specified directory (the value of the `build.dir.classes` property) in the current directory.

Now let's fetch our source to build.

Fetching the Source from a Source Repository

All serious development groups (and even most serious developers working on projects at home) use some sort of source code management (SCM) system. CVS is by far the most-used SCM system for projects hosted on the Internet. CVS is easy to use, extremely robust for multi-developer projects, supports concurrent modifications to individual files, and best of all, it's free! You can read all about CVS at `www.cvshome.org`. Although CVS is making inroads into corporate development shops, SourceSafe is probably the leader in that space. Therefore, we'll demonstrate how to fetch our source from both CVS and SourceSafe. (Incidentally, there are Ant tasks to interface to several other SCM systems, including ClearCase, Continuus, PerForce, PVCS, and StarTeam.)

Fetching from CVS

We'll begin as we always do: by creating the skeleton target that we need. Because we depend on certain properties being set, we'll declare our dependency on init. We'll combine all our CVS-related tasks into this one target, which we'll call fetchCVSSource (we'll show fetchVssSource later in the chapter). Listing 8.7 shows our basic CVS fetch target.

Listing 8.7   *Beginning the Fetch from CVS*

```
<target name="fetchCvsSource" depends="init">
</target>
```

The first thing we need to do is log in to our CVS source repository. (A login is necessary if you're using a CVS server (pserver), not a locally mounted drive.) In our init target. we set a property called src.repo.box that contains the actual machine name of the repository box. We also set properties for the username and password for this box called repo.user and repo.pass. If you've used CVS before, you know what a CVSROOT string looks like. For our example, we need a CVSROOT string that looks like Listing 8.8.

Listing 8.8   *The CVS pserver Value*

```
:pserver:harry@bud:/home/cvspublic
```

We created just such a string in our init target (via the properties file) from the other variables.

> **Note**
> It should be noted that the hostnames we're using are obviously on our local network. If you're working across the Internet, you need fully qualified domain names. An example of a CVSROOT string with an FQDN is
>
> :pserver:anoncvs@cvs.apache.org:/home/cvspublic

We can accomplish this easily using the properties we set. Here's our cvspass task invocation in Listing 8.9.

Listing 8.9 *Logging In to the Remote CVS Server*

```
<cvspass cvsroot="${cvsroot}" password="${repo.pass}"/>
```

This task will place an entry in the `.cvspass` file living in the executing user's home directory. If you don't issue a logout at the end of the build, this entry will remain, and you will effectively be "logged in," although this has no impact on you or the server.

Now that we're logged in, we need to fetch our source. Because this build file is most likely living inside the project that is under source control, we won't need to do a formal checkout of the source. In CVS terms, we'll only need to do an update. This will get the latest versions of the files from the server and intelligently try to merge them into our versions. This is generally a pretty painless event, but occasionally there are conflicts and CVS can't figure out how to merge the changes. In such a case, the build will cease and you can investigate what went wrong.

But for us, this really shouldn't be an issue right now. We need to pass a command string to CVS that tells it what we want it to do. We'll tell CVS to update our files, deleting (pruning) any directories that we have that no longer contain any files, and creating any new directories that have appeared in the repository. This is accomplished by passing the command string `update -P -d` to CVS. Listing 8.10 shows how we do it.

Listing 8.10 *Causing CVS to Perform an Update*

```
<cvs cvsRoot="${cvsroot}" command="update -P -d" failonerror="true"/>
```

Here we're using the same `cvsroot` property that we used for the `cvspass` task. The command string we created in Listing 8.10 is passed in as the command to execute, and finally the `failonerror` attribute, when set to true (the default is false), causes the entire build process to abort if there is an error in the CVS command. CVS connects to the server and performs this update on all the files in the project, downloading new files and merging changes for existing files. And that's all we need to do.

Now let's see to do this with SourceSafe.

Fetching from SourceSafe

In the optional set of Ant tasks are several tasks for working with SourceSafe. These include `vssget`, which is the only task we'll use here. This task performs the same jobs as `cvspass` and `cvs` did in our last target. We must specify the server and remote project name, plus username and password. Listing 8.11 shows our SourceSafe target.

Listing 8.11   *How to Get Our Code from SourceSafe*

```
<target name="fetchVssSource" depends="init">
    <vssget recursive="true"
        login="${repo.user},${repo.pass}"
        vsspath="${vss.repo.home}"
        writable="false"/>
</target>
```

As we did with the CVS-related target, we'll give this target a meaningful name, such as fetchVssSource. This task will get the latest version of everything, recursively, from the VSS project identified in ${vss.repo.home} (for example, $/projects/etetest) and dump those files in the current directory.

> **Note**
>
> Two assumptions are made about using this task. First, you must have SS.EXE located somewhere in your path. SS.EXE is the command-line version of Visual SourceSafe. It is provided with the standard install of VSS. If you don't include it in your path, Ant can't execute it and any SourceSafe tasks will fail. (If you get a nasty IOException with the text of CreateProcess from Ant when trying to run any VSS task, that's your clue that it can't find SS.EXE.) The second assumption is that you have a valid ss.ini file that points to the repository machine. Consult your SourceSafe documentation for details.

Compiling the Files

Now we need to compile our Java source files for use in our application. We do this using the javac task.

> **Note**
>
> It's interesting to note that setting the property build.compiler to jikes will cause the javac task to use Jikes instead of the javac compiler.

As you saw in Chapter 4, there are many attributes that can be used with javac, almost all of which are totally optional. We'll use just a few.

In our sample application, we have three Java source files that need to be compiled: a servlet and two supporting classes. Because a servlet is involved, we need to include those J2EE classes that support servlets. I'm using the servlet.jar that comes with version 4.0.3 of the Tomcat server. Recall that we set a property for it in our build.properties file that looks like Listing 8.12.

Listing 8.12   *The Property Pointing to servlet.jar*

```
servlet.jar=d:/Jakarta-tomcat-4.0.3/common/lib/servlet.jar
```

We'll also add this JAR file to our class path definition in `init`.

Because we must make sure that our destination directory has been created before we try to execute our build, we should make our `compile` target dependent on our `prepare` target. We don't need to specify that we also depend on the `init` target because `prepare` already does that, so `init` will be executed for us. The `compile` target looks like Listing 8.13.

Listing 8.13 *Compiling the Source Files*

```
<target name="compile" depends="prepare">
    <javac srcdir="${src.dir}"
        destdir="${build.dir}/classes"
        classpath="${classpath}"
        debug="on"/>
</target>
```

Listing 8.13 compiles any `.java` file that we find under our `${src.dir}` directory and puts the compiled class files into `${build.dir}/classes`, keeping line number debug information in the compiled classes. The class path will include the standard Java classes (like the JDK) as well as our `servlets.jar` file, which shipped with Tomcat 4.0.3.

Assuming that the compile worked, we can proceed.

Executing Unit Tests Against Our Code

Now that we've compiled all (both) of our classes and our WAR file is built, we need to test them. We'll perform a bit of unit testing on these classes using the extremely popular tool called JUnit. You can read more about JUnit at `www.junit.org`. Chapter 5, "Optional Tasks," of this book covers all the ins and outs of using JUnit, so I refer you to that chapter for more information. We'll use only a few of the options of the `junit` task, but you should get an idea of how it is generally used in practice.

> **Caution**
> Because both the junit and junitreport tasks are optional, you must have the optional.jar file in the class path that Ant is using. If you installed Ant from source, this has already been taken care of. If you installed a binary and didn't specifically download and install optional.jar, you should go back to the download site and get it. Refer to Chapter 2, "Preliminaries," for information about downloading and installing Ant.

What we'll be testing has nothing to do with the visual aspects of the application. Unit testing deals with only the functionality of the classes involved from a logic perspective. Testing the graphical user interface is a science unto itself, and that is not what we're doing. We'll simply verify that our two support classes, `Class0` and `Class1`, behave properly.

Because we have two classes to test, we'll have two classes that extend
`junit.framework.TestCase`, and one class that extends `junit.framework.TestSuite`.
Our first test class, `TestClass0`, is shown in Listing 8.14. These classes should be placed in
a subpackage of our `antbook` package called `test`. We'll be able to easily filter out these
classes from our WAR file.

Listing 8.14   *The Test Case for Class0*

```
package chapter8.test;

import junit.framework.*;
import chapter8.*;

public class TestClass0
    extends TestCase
{
    private Class0 class0;

    public TestClass0(String name)
    {
        super(name);
    }

    public void setUp()
    {
        class0 = new Class0("Otto");
    }

    public void testGetName()
    {
        assertEquals("Otto", class0.getName());
    }

    public void testSetName()
    {
        class0.setName("Dean");
        assertEquals("Frank", class0.getName());
    }
}
```

Because our classes are so simple, our test cases are simple as well. As you can see, we're
testing the `getName()` and `setName()` methods of `Class0`. `testGetName()` simply checks

that the value set in the setUp() method is what we get back from a getName(), whereas testSetName() verifies that setName() works by calling it and then calling getName() to check the results. The test class for Class1, TestClass1, is just as simple. It has only one property, id, so you only need to write test methods for setId() and getId(). If you don't want to type this in, you can download it from the publisher's Web site. The file is called TestClass0.java.

> **Note**
> There is a deliberate error in this test file to force a test failure to demonstrate some features of the junit and junitreport tasks. The final assertEquals is looking for a value of Frank even though we've just set the name to Dean. This is contrived, to be sure, but we need a test failure as an example. We'll fix it later so that the build will complete.

Because we have more than one test case, it's a good idea to put all our test case classes into a test suite that JUnit will execute. This is done by creating a class called TestAll.java, which answers with a TestSuite when prompted by the JUnit framework. Listing 8.15 is our TestAll test suite class.

Listing 8.15   *Creating a Test Suite for JUnit to Execute*

```
package chapter8.test;

import junit.framework.*;
import chapter8.*;

public class TestAll
    extends TestCase
{
    public TestAll(String name)
    {
        super(name);
    }

    public static Test suite()
    {
        TestSuite suite = new TestSuite();
        suite.addTestSuite(chapter8.test.TestClass0.class);
        suite.addTestSuite(chapter8.test.TestClass1.class);

        return suite;
    }
}
```

Now that these three test classes are created and compiled, we need to add a test target to our build file. For the moment, it'll contain only one task: the `junit` optional task. In the next section, we'll go back and add a `junitreport` task to format the output of JUnit. But for now, let's concentrate on the testing.

Like so many of the tasks we're using in this chapter, the `junit` task has lots of options that you can specify. We'll use a very few of them here. I refer you to Chapter 5 for a further discourse on `junit` and its attributes. Listing 8.16 is our `test` target.

Listing 8.16   *Testing the Java Classes*

```
<target name="test" depends="compile">
    <mkdir dir="${reports.dir}"/>
    <junit failureproperty="testsFailed">
        <classpath>
            <pathelement path="${classpath}"/>
            <pathelement path="${build.dir.classes}"/>
        </classpath>
        <formatter type="xml"/>
        <test name="chapter8.test.TestAll" todir="${reports.dir}"/>
    </junit>
</target>
```

Let's discuss what's going on in this target. First, we create a directory to hold the output of our test runs. We specify the name of this directory in our `init` target and it's referenced as `${reports.dir}`. We then call JUnit using the `junit` task. The only attribute that we need to specify is `failureproperty`. In the event of a test failure, the property specified by `failureproperty` will be set. This can be used by later targets to decide if they should execute. We'll use this property with our `war` target; we don't want to build the WAR file if all the tests aren't successful. We'll also use the `failureproperty` with our reporting and e-mailing targets.

The `junit` task needs a class path to work with in order to find and run our tests. We could use the class path that we defined in `init`, but it doesn't include the `${build.dir.classes}` directory, which is where our tests live. If we don't include that directory, we won't be able to run any tests. So, how can we solve this? `junit` wants a `Path`-like structure, which is what we defined in `init`, called `classpath`, and then assigned to a property called `classpath`. We can create a new class path here that references the old one, and add our project's `classes` directory. Two `pathelement` tags handle the job nicely.

The `formatter` tag tells Ant what sort of format the output file should be for the test run. If we don't include a `formatter` tag, no file will be created from a test run. The two other formatter options are plain and xml. The plain formatter generates a text file with the results of running a test. The xml formatter generates, as you might surmise, an XML file containing the same results. We'll use the XML formatter because we'll ultimately pass our results through the junitreport task, which needs XML to work on.

Finally, we specify which test suite to run with the test tag. The name attribute tells JUnit which class contains our tests and the todir attributes tells it where to dump the output files. We could specify multiple test tags, but because we combined both of our test cases into a single test suite, we can do it all with one test tag. If you didn't want to use a test suite, the test target would look like Listing 8.17.

Listing 8.17   *Testing the Java Classes*

```
<target name="test" depends="compile">
    <mkdir dir="${reports.dir}"/>
    <junit failureproperty="testsFailed">
        <classpath>
            <pathelement path="${classpath}"/>
            <pathelement path="${build.dir.classes}"/>
        </classpath>
        <formatter type="xml"/>
        <test name="chapter8.test.TestClass0" todir="${reports.dir}"/>
        <test name="chapter8.test.TestClass1" todir="${reports.dir}"/>
    </junit>
</target>
```

Whichever approach you choose, you should end up with report file(s) in the directory specified by ${reports.dir}. If you opted for the single test suite, as in Listing 8.16, you'll have a file called TEST-chapter8.test.TestAll.xml. If you decided to specify each test case separately, as in Listing 8.17, you'll have two files: one called TEST-chapter8.test.TestClass0.xml, and another called TEST-chapter8.test.TestClass1.xml. Because XML is rather wordy and hard to look at, you can change the formatter to plain and look at the files yourself. Be sure to change the formatter back to xml before you try the junitreport task.

If you execute the build at this point by typing **ant test** at the command line, you should see output similar to Figure 8.1.

Notice that we had a test fail—that's the deliberate error I mentioned earlier. I wanted you to be able to see what happens when a test fails and how other targets can take action depending on this condition. You can change Frank to Dean in TestClass0 to make the test pass, but for now leave it as it is.

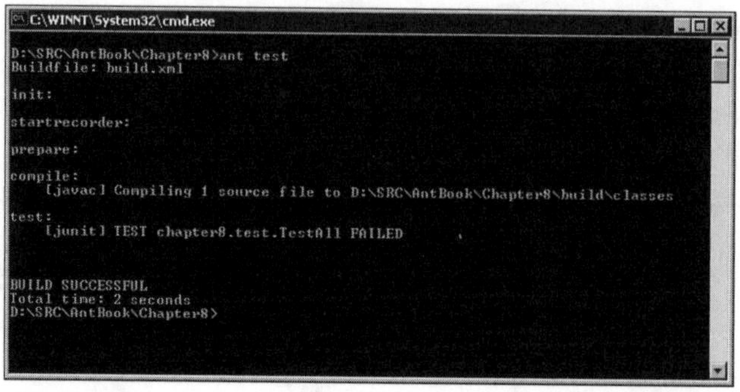

Figure 8.1
Output from building and testing our code.

Reporting Test Results

The output from the `junit` task is either too plain or to wrapped up in XML to be terribly useful. The `junitreport` task can take the XML output by the `junit` task and turn it into a frameset report (in the case of several output files) or a frameless report for simple cases.

> **Note**
> Because the junitreport task will be performing XSL transformations on the junit output files, you must have an XSL library installed. Specifically, you need to put xalan.jar, from the Apache XML Group's Xalan project, into your class path. You can either include it in the system class path or put xalan.jar in your ANT_HOME/lib directory.

Listing 8.18 shows our `test` target with a `junitreport` task added. This listing will create a single file called `junit-noframes.html` in the directory called `${reports.dir}/html`. Because our project is so simple, this is a good choice. However, if we had lots of tests in lots of packages, it would probably make more sense to use the `frames` option.

Listing 8.18 *Generating a Single JUnit Report File*

```
<target name="test" depends="compile">
    <mkdir dir="${reports.dir}/html"/>
    <junit failureproperty="testsFailed">
        <classpath>
            <pathelement path="${classpath}"/>
            <pathelement path="${build.dir.classes}"/>
        </classpath>
        <formatter type="xml"/>
        <test name="chapter8.test.TestAll" todir="${reports.dir}"/>
    </junit>
```

Listing 8.18   *(continued)*

```
<junitreport todir="${reports.dir}">
    <fileset dir="${reports.dir}">
        <include name="TEST-*.xml"/>
    </fileset>
    <report format="noframes" todir="${reports.dir}/html"/>
</junitreport>
</target>
```

The bold section is what we added to our test target for reporting. The junitreport task here takes a single argument called todir. This attribute tells the task where to create its XML file that will aggregate all the other XML files it finds. You can specify a name for this file by adding the tofile attribute, but the default is a file called TESTS-TestSuites.xml in the given directory.

We then tell the task what existing XML files it should consider as output from junit by creating a fileset consisting of all files that match the TEST-*.xml pattern. That's the format of junit output files if you didn't specify what those files should be named.

We then specify our report format and where it should go. The options for format are frames and noframes. frames creates an HTML frameset very similar to the JDK documentation. Use this option when you have many classes that span many packages. noframes produces a single file report with the report content. Use this option when your test suite is small, like ours is. The second attribute of the report tag is todir, which tells the task where to dump the resulting HTML file(s). It is unfortunate that there is no option to change the name of the output file. If you use noframes, you get a file called junit-noframes.html; if you specify frames, you get an index.html file located in the directory you specified in todir. This seems like a strange oversight on the Ant developers' part.

Figure 8.2 shows what this report format looks like.

As I mentioned earlier, Listing 8.19 shows the same test target generating a frameset JUnit report. Look closely because there is very little difference.

Listing 8.19   *Producing an HTML Frameset Report*

```
<target name="test" depends="compile">
    <mkdir dir="${reports.dir}/html"/>
    <junit failureproperty="testsFailed">
        <classpath>
            <pathelement path="${classpath}"/>
            <pathelement path="${build.dir.classes}"/>
        </classpath>
```

Listing 8.19 *(continued)*

```
        <formatter type="xml"/>
        <test name="chapter8.test.TestClass0" todir="${reports.dir}"/>
        <test name="chapter8.test.TestClass1" todir="${reports.dir}"/>
    </junit>
    <junitreport todir="${reports.dir}">
        <fileset dir="${reports.dir}">
            <include name="TEST-*.xml"/>
        </fileset>
        <report format="frames" todir="${reports.dir}/html"/>
    </junitreport>
</target>
```

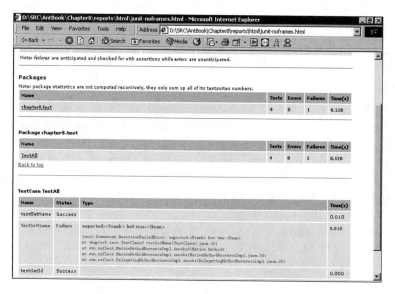

Figure 8.2
Screenshot of the noframes report.

Notice that the only thing we changed was the `format` attribute of the `report` tag. (This target also specifies each test case rather than using a suite.) Figure 8.3 shows the report generated from this invocation of `junitreport`.

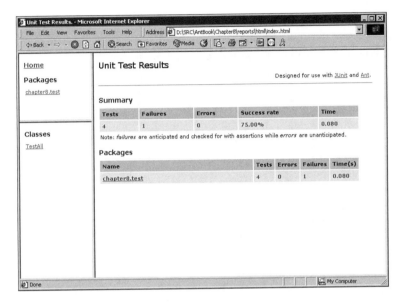

Figure 8.3
Screenshot of the frames report.

Generating a Web Archive for Deployment

Now that our class files are compiled and tested, we need to build a Web archive, or WAR file. A WAR file is nothing more than a regular JAR file, with a WEB-INF directory and certain files placed in specific locations. You could easily create a WAR file using the jar task, but Ant provides a specialized version of jar for just this purpose. The war task makes it much easier to create a WAR file than just using jar.

When creating a WAR file, we need to tell the Ant task which file to use as the Web application descriptor, or web.xml, file, which files to place in the WEB-INF/classes directory, and which JAR files to place in WEB-INF/lib. In our case, we'll use ${etc.dir}/web.xml for the Web application descriptor. We want our compiled classes to go into the WEB-INF/classes directory and nothing to go in the WEB-INF/lib directory. (We don't have any third-party classes in our project, so there is nothing that needs to go into WEB-INF/lib.)

> **Note**
> Normally, you would put third-party JARs into WEB-INF/lib. This could include frameworks such as the Jakarta Group's Struts project, or Cocoon, or custom tags for your JSPs. Generally, the classes for the project at hand aren't jarred up and put in the lib directory; they stay under the classes directory.

One set of classes that we *don't* want to end up in our WAR file is our test classes. Because we placed these classes in their own subpackage, it's a trivial matter to remove them. I'll explain how to do that after I show you the stanza from our build file.

As you saw in Chapter 4, the war task has quite a few available options, but we'll use only a few. Listing 8.20 shows our war target. Notice that it depends on compile.

Listing 8.20   *Creating a Web Archive File*

```
<target name="war" depends="compile" unless="testsFailed">
    <war destfile="${build.dir}/${war.name}" webxml="${etc.dir}/web.xml">
        <fileset dir="${src.dir}/jsp" includes="**/*.jsp"/>
        <classes dir="${build.dir.classes}">
            <include name="**/*.class"/>
            <exclude name="**/test/*.class"/>
        </classes>
    </war>
</target>
```

After executing this target, you should have a file called etetest-*20020525*.war with *20020525* replaced with the current date.

As stated earlier, we'll use ${etc.dir}/web.xml as our Web application descriptor. We tell Ant to use this file by setting the webxml attribute of the war task to ${etc.dir}/web.xml.

An important point here is the unless attribute on our target. This attribute says to execute this target *unless* the property specified here is present. You'll remember that if our JUnit tests failed, we would set the property testsFailed. Because we don't want to build or deploy our code if the tests failed, we tell the war and deploy targets not to fire if the tests failed. This is handy.

Notice that we have a fileset that grabs all files ending in .jsp from ${src.dir}/jsp, recursively, and places them in the root of the WAR. This is where you will most often want your JSPs for deployment.

We then have a classes tag that fetches all files ending in .class under ${build.dir.classes}, recursively, and places them under WEB-INF/classes, building appropriate directory structures along the way (except for those class files located in any directory called test). This filters out our test classes, which you normally don't want to go into production anyway. Notice that instead of using the includes and excludes attributes of the classes tag, I chose to use nested include and exclude tags for my filtering. I think this is easier to read in general, and certainly easier to look at in a textbook.

Tip
If you're creating a Web application using the Struts framework from the Apache Jakarta group and you're practicing "JSP hiding," your build file should look slightly different. JSP hiding means instead of your JSP files living in the root of the application, they are located inside WEB-INF. The Servlet specification states that content inside and below WEB-INF is inaccessible to any browser. Thus, the JSPs are hidden. However, servlets and other Java classes inside the Web application do have access to this content. In this way, the Struts framework is able to serve up the JSPs, even though a browser can't directly request them. In this case, your war target would look like this:

```
<target name="war" depends="compile">
    <war destfile="${build.dir}/${war.name}" webxml="${etc.dir}/web.xml">
        <webinf dir="${src.dir}/jsp" includes="**/*.jsp"/>
        <classes dir="${build.dir.classes}" includes="**/*.class"/>
    </war>
</target>
```

Notice that instead of a fileset tag, we're using one called webinf. This tag will place the files specified into the WEB-INF directory, which is exactly what we want to hide our JSPs.

Deploying What We've Built

Now that we have a fully tested and built WAR file, it's time to do something with it. In an actual business development environment, you might need to deploy to a QA machine, an integration test machine, or both. In our example, we'll deploy to a single QA test machine, which we'll access via FTP. This is, of course, not the only way to deploy. If your deployment destination is on the same box that you've been building on, you can simply use the built-in copy task to place the WAR file where it needs to go. Similarly, if you are on a Microsoft Windows network or you are using NFS, copy would also be an appropriate choice for deployment.

If you want to copy files locally, to a Windows share, or to an NFS-mounted directory, you could define a deploy target like Listing 8.21.

Listing 8.21   *Deploying Via copy*

```
<target name="deploy" depends="war" unless="testsFailed">
    <copy file="${build.dir}/${war.name}" todir="${deploy.dir}"/>
</target>
```

Note
If the directory you're specifying in the todir attribute doesn't exist, be sure to add a mkdir task to your prepare target to create it.

Because we want to deploy a WAR file and we have a target that creates a WAR, we should make our `deploy` target dependent on the `war` target. Also, because we don't build the WAR file if our unit tests failed, we should not try to deploy this (nonexistent) WAR file if any unit tests failed. We accomplish this, as before, by using an `unless` attribute to look for the `testsFailed` property.

The `copy` task simply takes our WAR file and copies it to the directory specified by the `todir` attribute. The `${deploy.dir}` property must have been defined to point to the destination directory; this could be a local path (or an NFS mount), or a Windows share that would look something like \\qabox\drops. Your situation, of course, will be different.

`copy` is certainly the simplest solution, but if your destination machine is across the network (or even the Internet) and can't be accessed by mounts or shares, you would need a different solution. The easiest solution would be FTP.

> **Note**
> Ant includes an ftp task in the optional group, so you must have optional.jar installed in
> ANT_HOME/lib. The ftp task has an additional requirement, which is the NetComponents
> library available at http://www.savarese.org/oro/downloads/index.html#NetComponents.
> After you've installed this library, you're ready to use FTP.

Just as in our `copy` example, we'll create a target called `deploy` that will do three things. First, it'll make a copy of our WAR file to the current directory. This might seem odd (because we deliberately created our WAR file inside `${build.dir}`), but it is to get around what I consider an oddity in the FTP task. I'll elaborate shortly. Second, we perform the FTP task itself: Log in to the server, change directories, upload the file, and then disconnect, all of which occurs in one task. Finally, we delete the copy of our WAR file.

Here then, in Listing 8.22, is our `deploy` target.

Listing 8.22   *Deploying the WAR to the Remote Server*

```
<target name="deploy" depends="war" unless="testsFailed">
    <copy file="${build.dir}/${war.name}" todir="."/>
    <ftp server="${deploy.box}" remotedir="/upload"
        userid="${deploy.user}" password="${deploy.pass}"
        binary="yes" verbose="yes" skipFailedTransfers="yes">
        <fileset dir=".">
            <include name="${war.name}"/>
        </fileset>
    </ftp>
    <delete file="${war.name}"/>
</target>
```

Let's go over this target. As I stated, this target depends on the war target, and it won't execute if the testFailed property is set. After we're inside the target, we copy the WAR file to the current directory. We make use of the Ant core task called, as you would expect, copy. We can use the simple form of copy that takes the name of the file to copy as the value of the file attribute and the destination directory in the todir attribute. After we have our copy, we can transfer it.

The ftp task has 17 attributes, but we're only going to use 8 of them. You might need more of these options depending on your particular platforms and servers. Consult Chapter 5 for more details.

Here we're using four properties that we discussed earlier and that we set in our init target. The server attribute is the hostname or IP address of the remote machine to which we will transfer our file. The remotedir attribute tells the ftp task into which directory the files should be placed. As you can probably guess, userid and password are the username and password needed for the remote machine.

I've set binary to be true here to force a binary transfer. Several FTP clients and servers will automatically use binary mode for files that are known to be binary (such as Zip files, Microsoft Word documents, and executables), but this is not guaranteed. Because we know that our Zip file is a binary file, we'll force this mode. If I were transferring text files, I would leave off the binary attribute or include it and set it to no to be explicit.

The verbose attribute causes the task to spit out slightly (and I do mean *slightly*) more information about what is doing than without it. You don't get as much information as I like, but you get the basic idea of what is going on. You'll certainly see whether any failures occurred and the FTP error code will be shown.

Next in line is ignoreNoncriticalErrors, which lets the task continue even if it gets certain errors from the server. An example of this is the WU-FTP server, which complains in certain cases about directory creation. This attribute, and the final one, skipFailedTransfers are critical to keeping your build from dying because of a failed transfer.

The final attribute, skipFailedTransfers, is important to use because without it a failed transfer (for example, a 550 Access denied) will *abort the entire build*, which is not what you want. It would be nice if this task had a property similar to junit's failureProperty attribute to signal failure to any following tasks, but it doesn't. So, if you don't want your entire build to stop dead in its tracks if a transfer error occurs, be sure to include these last two attributes!

Okay, now that we've set up our connection to the FTP server, we need to tell it what to transfer. This is easily accomplished through the use of multiple nested fileset tags. In our example, we have only one file to transfer, so we have only one `fileset` and we specifically tell it which file to send. We could have used a wildcard if we had more than one file, however. Notice that the `dir` attribute is set to ".", which means the current directory. Remember I said there was what I considered to be an oddity in the `ftp` task? This oddity involves creation of directories on the remote machine. If our `fileset` had a `dir` attribute of `${build.dir}`, the `ftp` task would try to create a directory with the same name on the remote machine and place the files in it. This might be what you want in some circumstances, but it is not what we want here. In this example, the task would have tried to create a directory called `build` on the remote server and then transferred the file to that location. I was rather surprised by this, but it makes sense if you remember that the `fileset` builds up a list of files with pathnames based from its `dir` attribute. I couldn't find a way to tell either `fileset` to forget its path and just return the filenames, or the FTP task to forget the paths and just transfer the files. This is not a showstopper, and we easily make up for it with our pre-`copy` and our post-`delete` steps.

Which brings us to the delete step. There's no magic here, just a simple call to the `delete` task and setting the `file` attribute to the name of the copied file.

That's it. With this target defined as shown in Listing 8.24, you should see something like Figure 8.4 after execution.

Figure 8.4
Output from executing our deploy target.

What to Do with Those Reports

So far, we've generated a recording of everything that has transpired and a report from our unit testing (or a directory structure representing the reports from unit testing). Now what should we do with them? Using Ant's built-in `mail` task, we can e-mail these reports to any interested parties. If we have many reports that need mailing, we can use the built-in `zip` task to create a Zip file so that we need to attach only one file rather than several.

As explained in Chapter 4, using the `mail` task requires that you have access to an SMTP server and that you have the JavaMail classes installed for best performance. Refer to Chapter 4 for details on these requirements.

We'll create a target called `sendmail`, which will bundle things up and then send e-mail to those who are interested. For our purposes, let's assume that we need to send the nightly results to our manager John Smith (`jsmith@mycompany.com`) and to a mailing list of quality assurance personnel (`qa@mycompany.com`). We want to combine the output from our record task and the JUnit reports into a single Zip file.

The `mail` task is actually quite simple and straightforward. We'll use only a few of the attributes and nested elements to get these reports mailed out. But first we must zip up the directory structure for our JUnit reports. These files are stored under `${reports.dir}`, but there are some XML files that we don't really want to zip and e-mail. Therefore, we'll filter out `*.xml` files when zipping. We can easily accomplish this as shown in Listing 8.23.

Listing 8.23 *Creating a Zip File from the Report Directory and Filtering Out XML Files*

```
<target name="sendmail" depends="deploy">
    <zip destfile="${name}-${DSTAMP}-reports.zip"
        basedir="${reports.dir}/html"/>
</target>
```

We've now created our `sendmail` target that depends on the `deploy` target. Even if that target doesn't execute because of the `unless` condition on it, `sendmail` will execute unless we use an `unless` condition here as well. We won't do that because we want our reports mailed out regardless of the outcome of the build. So, now that we've created a Zip file with our reports, let's see how to send the file. Listing 8.24 shows the completed `sendmail` target.

Listing 8.24 *How to Send E-mail*

```
<target name="sendmail" depends="deploy, stoprecorder">
    <zip destfile="${name}-${DSTAMP}-reports.zip"
        basedir="${reports.dir}" excludes="**/*.xml"/>
    <mail mailhost="localhost" subject="Build Results: ${TODAY}">
        <from address="joey@joeygibson.com" name="Nightly Build System"/>
        <to address="${manager.email}"/>
        <to address="${qa.email}"/>
        <message src="${name}-${DSTAMP}-log.txt"/>
        <fileset dir=".">
            <include name="${name}-${DSTAMP}-reports.zip"/>
```

Listing 8.24   *(continued)*

```
      </fileset>
   </mail>
</target>
```

The bold sections are what's new. Let's analyze this task and see what it's doing. The `mailhost` attribute specifies an SMTP server to use for sending mail. If you don't specify one, it defaults to using localhost. The `subject` attribute sets the subject line of the e-mail, as you would expect.

Notice that we depend not only on the `deploy` target, but also on the `stoprecorder` target. Remember that we created both start and stop targets for our recorder. We want to stop the recorder at this point because we want to mail the output from the recorder in this target. This keeps us from getting a partial line of output in the report because we would essentially be trying to mail an open file if we didn't stop the recorder first. We could do an `antcall` here and call the `stoprecorder` target, but we achieve the same thing by making this target depend on it.

We then have nested elements that control the source, distribution and the content. First, we have the `from` tag. This tag sets the `From:` line in the e-mail. There are two attributes for this task, `name` and `address`, of which only `address` is required. As you might expect, `address` is the e-mail address of the sender, and `name` is the friendly name of that address, such as `Joey Gibson` or `Nightly Build System`. You need to specify a valid e-mail address here, even if there isn't one for `Nightly Build System`. In that case, you need to provide your own e-mail address or that of an e-mail sink set up by your mail administrator. Most SMTP servers require a valid `From:` in order to send e-mail.

Next, we've included two `to` tags to set the receivers. Each instance of a `to` tag adds a recipient to the `To:` line of the e-mail. You can also use `cc` and `bcc` to add recipients to those lines as well. You can have as many of each of these tags as necessary. Notice that I set the e-mail addresses into properties back in the `init` target. Just as with the `from` tag, `to`, `cc`, and `bcc` support `address` and `name` attributes, with only `address` required. I would think it much more likely to use the `name` attribute only for the sender and not for the recipients.

I could've specified the recipient e-mail addresses as a comma-separated list in a `tolist` attribute of the `mail` task. I chose not to do that because I think the nested format is easier to read. The result is the same: Multiple people will get the e-mail.

Next we have the `message` tag. I chose to use the `src` attribute, which will use the file specified as the message body. In this case, we're telling the `mail` task to use our recorder log as the body of the e-mail. This seems like a good idea because it is a complete record of what went on during the build. We could, of course, have specified some text between open and close message tags, as in Listing 8.25, but there isn't really any text other than the build record that made much sense here.

Listing 8.25   *An Alternative Way to Set the Message Body*

```
<message>Here are the results of the nightly build.</message>
```

If we'd chosen to provide body text inline like this, we would need to attach the build record file as another attachment.

It is extremely simple to attach arbitrary files to an e-mail. You do this with one or more nested fileset tags. In our example, we want to send the one Zip file that we created at the beginning of this target, and we know its name, so we won't really be using any wildcards. We can specify exactly which file we want; we just need to put it in a fileset. If we had more than the one Zip file (including those in a directory structure), our fileset would have looked something like Listing 8.26.

Listing 8.26   *Attaching Multiple Files*

```
<fileset dir=".">
    <include name**/*.zip"/>
</fileset>
```

After you have a working sendmail target, consider making it the default target for your build file. This is accomplished by changing the default attribute in the project tag as in Listing 8.27.

Listing 8.27   *Sets sendmail to Be the Default Target*

```
<project name="etetest" basedir="." default="sendmail">
```

Listing 8.28 presents the entire build file for your perusal.

Listing 8.28   *The Complete build.xml File*

```
<?xml version="1.0"?>
<project name="etetest" basedir="." default="sendmail">
        <target name="init">
                <tstamp/>
                <property file="build.properties"/>

                <path id="classpath">
```

Listing 8.28   *(continued)*

```
                    <pathelement path="${servlet.jar}"/>
                    <pathelement path="${junit.jar}"/>
            </path>
            <property name="classpath" refid="classpath"/>
    </target>
    <target name="startrecorder">
            <record name="${name}-${DSTAMP}-log.txt" action="start"
              ➥append="false"/>
    </target>
    <target name="stoprecorder">
            <record name="${name}-${DSTAMP}-log.txt" action="stop"/>
    </target>
    <target name="prepare" depends="init, startrecorder">
            <mkdir dir="${build.dir.classes}"/>
    </target>
    <target name="fetchCvsSource" depends="init">
            <cvspass cvsroot="${cvsroot}" password="${repo.pass}"/>
            <cvs cvsRoot="${cvsroot}" command="update -P -d"
              ➥failonerror="true"/>
    </target>
    <target name="fetchVssSource" depends="init">
            <vssget recursive="true"
            login="${repo.user},${repo.pass}"
            vsspath="${vss.repo.home}" writable="false"/>
    </target>
    <target name="compile" depends="prepare">
            <javac srcdir="${src.dir}"
            destdir="${build.dir}/classes"
            classpath="${classpath}" debug="on"/>
    </target>
    <target name="war" depends="test" unless="testsFailed">
            <war destfile="${build.dir}/${war.name}"
              ➥webxml="${etc.dir}/web.xml">
                    <fileset dir="${src.dir}/jsp" includes="**/*.jsp"/>
                    <classes dir="${build.dir.classes}">
                            <include name="**/*.class"/>
                            <exclude name="**/test/*.class"/>
                    </classes>
            </war>
    </target>
    <target name="clean" depends="init">
            <delete dir="${build.dir}"/>
```

Listing 8.28   *(continued)*

```
                <delete dir="${reports.dir}"/>
        </target>
        <target name="test" depends="compile">
                <mkdir dir="${reports.dir}/html"/>
                <junit failureproperty="testsFailed">
                        <classpath>
                                <pathelement path="${classpath}"/>
                                <pathelement path="${build.dir.classes}"/>
                        </classpath>
                        <formatter type="xml"/>
                        <test name="chapter8.test.TestAll"
                         ➥todir="${reports.dir}"/>
                        <!-- <test name="chapter8.test.TestClass0"
                                ➥todir="${reports.dir}"/>
                        <test name="chapter8.test.TestClass1"
                         ➥todir="${reports.dir}"/> -->
                </junit>
                <junitreport todir="${reports.dir}">
                        <fileset dir="${reports.dir}">
                        <include name="TEST-*.xml"/>
                        </fileset>
                        <report format="noframes" todir="${reports.dir}/html"/>
                </junitreport>
        </target>
        <target name="deploy" depends="war" unless="testsFailed">
                <copy file="${build.dir}/${war.name}" todir="."/>
  <ftp server="${deploy.box}" remotedir="${deploy.dir}" userid="${deploy.user}"
➥password="${deploy.pass}" binary="yes" verbose="yes"
➥ignoreNoncriticalErrors="yes" skipFailedTransfers="yes">
                        <fileset dir=".">
                                <include name="${war.name}"/>
                        </fileset>
                </ftp>
                <delete file="${war.name}"/>
        </target>
        <target name="sendmail" depends="war, stoprecorder">
        <zip destfile="${name}-${DSTAMP}-reports.zip" basedir="${reports.dir}"
➥excludes="**/*.xml"/>
                <mail mailhost="localhost" subject="Build Results: ${TODAY}">
                        <from address="joey@joeygibson.com"/>
                        <to address="${manager.email}"/>
                        <to address="${qa.email}"/>
```

Listing 8.28   *(continued)*

```
                        <message src="${name}-${DSTAMP}-log.txt"/>
                        <fileset dir=".">
                                <include name="${name}-${DSTAMP}-reports.zip"/>
                        </fileset>
                </mail>
        </target>
</project>
```

Summary

We've covered a ton of material in this chapter. I hope that you'll come away from this chapter with a better appreciation for how much drudgery Ant can automate for you. If you had to do all the steps we performed in this chapter by hand, it would take forever and would be so tedious you'd hate to have to do it. Similarly, if you had to create batch files or shell scripts, it would be easier than the manual method, but still problematic and tedious. Contrast that with the build file we've constructed. Although it might seem like a lot of work to get to this point, after you get used to Ant's build file structure, the common attributes, and your frequently used tasks, this will become old hat. I've been using Ant religiously for about two years now, and I've never looked back.

So, what did we cover? We discussed what constitutes an End to End build: an unattended nightly build that performs the build from beginning to end and then sends out a report to those interested in its work. Although that definition is certainly malleable, it's a pretty good one. We showed the many jobs that need to be performed and the tasks that will do them.

We discussed using the `record` task to keep an exact record of the build process. We also showed how to get the latest version of our source code from both CVS and SourceSafe. After we had the source, we built it using the `javac` task. We then enlisted the help of JUnit via the `junit` task to unit test our classes. Then we used `junitreport` to transform the output from these tests into presentable HTML. Assuming that all the tests passed, we create a Web archive, or WAR, from our files and deployed it to our QA test machine. Finally, regardless of test failure, we created a Zip file of the JUnit reports and sent that, along with the recording of the build process, to both our manager and the QA team using the built-in `mail` task.

CHAPTER 9

Ant in the Real World

In the ongoing battle to maintain their competitive edge, today's businesses are placing more demands on IT departments and vendors to build larger, more flexible and reliable systems in ever-decreasing time budgets. With the demands comes an increase in the complexity of the configuration management (CM) process. If you consider that many (if not all) projects rely on a number of third-party components and products, it's easy to understand why projects struggle with CM issues. It suffices to say that CM is a multifaceted problem that requires a mix of products and procedures to help manage it. Although Ant cannot address all those issues, it can help mitigate the issues surrounding the task of deploying a complex distributed application.

So far, we've seen a number of techniques that demonstrate many of the micro aspects of Ant. The purpose of this chapter is to switch gears to focus on the application of these techniques in large development effort. To aid in this effort, a number of new techniques are introduced. The combination of these techniques enables us to construct a series of build scripts that check out a version of the project from CVS, build, unit test, and then package the application. Let's proceed with a description of our large application.

The Large Sample Application

The large application to be used here is a simple implementation of a chat room. The block diagram in Figure 9.1 illustrates the major components and layers. At the heart of the system is the JMS. A third-party component is used to provide the JMS implementation. The JMS layer is isolated from the application by the `Channel` component. The last two major components are the chat server and clients. The chat server provides the clients with a current list of active topics. Both the server and the client rely on a common set of objects. These objects have been isolated into a common layer.

Even though the application doesn't contain a large number of classes or lines of code, it uses third-party products, components, and layering. This application is a distributed application that has a mix of client/server as well as peer-to-peer-based interactions.

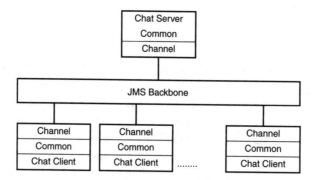

Figure 9.1
ChatRoom block diagram.

At this point, we don't need to know about the implementation details. The general overview of the project shown in Figure 9.1 provides enough information to define the components and identify the dependencies so that we can proceed to building and deploying the application. Let's start the process by defining a physical layout for the build environment.

A Standard Build Environment

Although doing so isn't necessary, it makes sense to develop the application in a project directory that uses a physical layout that everyone agrees on. The layout that most Java developers should be most familiar with is the layout on which the JDK distribution is based. That layout forms the basis for the standard build environment described here.

Note
As my colleagues Mike Boni and Jason Rosso have independently stated, it's best to stick to what's familiar to most developers, otherwise known as the "path of least surprise."

The outermost directory should be named after the end product. For the sample project, the outermost directory is `chatroom`. It is in this directory that we'll drop in the `classes`, `src`, `lib`, `jms`, and `doc` subdirectories. Figure 9.2 shows an expanded view of the layout.

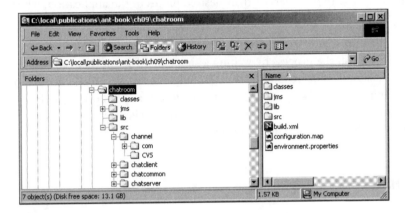

Figure 9.2
Window directory structure.

The target directory for the result of computation is the `classes` subdirectory. The source for each component is placed in the `src` subdirectory. The next common structure is the `lib` subdirectory, which should contain all the project-specific JAR files. The purpose of the `doc` subdirectory is to contain project documentation (which most likely includes `javadoc`).

If you examine the `src` subdirectory, you'll find it contains four subdirectories. Each of these subdirectories contains source for the component or layer that it's named for. For example, the `Channel` component is found in the `channel` subdirectory. From this point on, the subdirectories contain the familiar Java package structure.

Decomposing the Build

Previous sections have hinted that the application should be built in separate small pieces. These pieces can be defined by the natural decomposition of the application into its constituent parts. As with most problem domains, using this divide-and-conquer strategy helps to manage the complexity that accompanies large projects.

Figure 9.1 illustrated how ChatRoom could be decomposed into five components. The directory structure contained in the `src` directory is constructed to match this decomposition. Although this project might not seem large enough to justify such decomposition, it's useful to note that the `Channel` component is readily available for other applications to reuse when it's packaged in this manner.

The downside of this approach is that you must consider dependencies that exist between the packages. You must be careful not to introduce any circular dependencies because that type of coupling forces you to build larger-than-desired pieces of the application, which directly impacts your ability to reuse the component.

At this point, we're ready to create a build file for each component. After that step is completed, we'll finish the process by writing a single build script that calls each of the individual build scripts. This technique is commonly known as *chaining the build* or simply *chaining*. Chaining enables us to compile, test, and deploy an application. Before we start out on this adventure, we must consider the nuances of the declarative nature of properties and how they might affect our ability to chain the build.

Ant Properties

As shown in Chapter 6, "Extending Ant with Custom Tasks, Data Types, and Listeners," Ant properties are declarative in nature. In other words, once set, a property's value can never be changed. Why is this important? If our aim is to chain build files, we must be cognizant that if the `inheritsAll` flag is set on the `ant` task (as described in Chapter 4, "Built-in Tasks"), it is possible that namespace collisions could occur between the various build scripts. Consequently, the results of a build could vary in response to the order in which the Ant targets are executed. Although it's desirable to be able to configure the behavior of a build, we want to be able to do so in a controlled and predictable manner.

One technique that we can use to avoid namespace collisions is to devise a naming convention that guarantees uniqueness. Again, a look at how Java resolves the issue, combined with how the build has been partitioned, can help us.

Naming Conventions

Java comes with a convention that helps it avoid class namespace collisions. The convention is to prefix all classes with a package name. It's generally accepted that a company or organization's Internet domain name prefixes the packages of Java code generated by said company. For our purposes, if we take the idea of a package prefix and turn it into a component prefix, we can use the other ideas offered by this scheme to assist us in our definition of property names.

For the rest of this chapter, all property names will be prefixed by the name of the component for which the build script has been created. For example, consider the following definition for the Channel's source directory: `<property name="channel.src" value="." />`. If we simply used `src` for the name of the property, there's a good chance that another build script in the chain would use the same name. But prefixing by it with `channel`, any attempt to set the variable name is most likely deliberate and the resulting collision will most likely be avoided.

Common Properties Name Suffixes

From the preceding section, it's clear that we must consider that many of the build tasks will want to do the same thing. This leads to requiring us to define a set of properties that will have a common suffix. For example, the common development environment defines the subdirectories `source`, `classes`, `lib`, and `doc`. It follows that each of the build scripts defines values for these properties. Knowing that we're prefixing the property name with the name of the component enables us to predefine a set of suffixes. For example, if we define a common suffix for the source directory to be `src`, it follows that each component will define a property using the template `[component name].src`. Using this (or a similar) notation provides a familiar look and feel to each of the build scripts.

In general, properties fill two purposes. The first purpose is to define resources that are internal to the project's directory structure. The second purpose is to define resources that are external to the project's directory structure. As an example, let's look at how the third-party JMS vendor can be integrated.

When we use a third-party implementation, we can do one of two things. One approach is to embed it into the project subdirectory. The other is to install the product in a separate directory structure and let the build process reference it as such.

Third-party products tend to be fairly static in nature. On the other hand, an application in development changes very rapidly. Based solely on this information, it seems that we should separate the rapidly changing pieces from the more static pieces. Therefore, the JMS implementation will be installed outside of the project's directory structure. What remains in the project's directory structure is the JMS configuration. We're now ready to look for a scheme to name properties for these components.

If we treat the installation directory for the third-party product as we do for our application, we can separate the contents from location. In other words, although the contents might be stable, the location of the installation will likely be unstable. Therefore, we should break our references to these resources into two parts: one that defines the stable component and one that defines the unstable component of the reference. The resulting concatenation of these two components identifies an absolute path to the external resource.

Let's make this real by using an example. The JMS installation is provided at some undetermined location. But we know that the need the provider JARs are found in the `lib` subdirectory. Consequently, we can reference the JAR files using a property named `${jms.home}/lib/${JMS.PROVIDER.JAR}`. The two components of this property are the specification of where the JMS is installed and the specification of a specific resource contained within that installation. Therefore, if we move the JMS installation, all we must do is redefine the value for `jms.home`.

An unexpected benefit of defining common properties is that you can completely change the build simply by redefining the properties. Having third-party dependencies described in this way has the dual effects of enabling an individual user to configure his environment as he sees fit, and enabling the project directory to float freely because the project can specify locations relative either to the project's working directory or a `home` property.

Source

As you saw in Chapters 2, "Preliminaries," 3, "Global Concepts," and 4, the value of a property can be set by a number of different methods. The value of a property depends on which method is used because that determines the order in which the property will be set. This implies that it's important to understand the rules of initialization.

The first rule of initialization is that all properties defined on the command line are processed first. All others are set when the corresponding properties task is encountered. When encountered, a property value may be set or a number of properties may be read in from a properties file. Understanding these rules will help ensure that a property's value is what you expect it to be.

Standard Build Targets

Just as it's advantageous to agree on a standard development environment, properties naming convention, and some common property names, it's also advantageous to define a number of standard targets. Each target should execute a set of tasks required to carry out a logical unit of work. For example, the `compile` task should create its target subdirectory, compile the source, and then move property files and all other resources so that the application is ready to be tested or executed. Let's define some standard targets. Examples of these targets will be provided as we develop the set of scripts needed to build ChatRoom.

The init Target

As you've seen, a property task can exist as a top-level XML attribute. Therefore, it's not absolutely necessary that a property task be contained within a target. Even so, let's introduce an `init` target whose purpose is to contain all the property definitions. Maintaining an `init` target not only works to group the declarations, it also keeps all tasks at the same level.

By placing the `init` block at the top of the build script, we make the definitions easy to evaluate if we ever need to debug the script.

The dependent Target

It's the responsibility of the `dependent` target to fail the build if one of the dependents is missing. It's the responsibility of the `available` tasks in the `init` target to set a common `[component name].dependencies` property. If this property hasn't been set, it implies that at least one of the dependencies is missing. If this property has not been set, The `dependent` target should run. The lone task found in the `dependent` target is `fail`.

The compile Target

One of the responsibilities of the `compile` target is to compile source files to create class files. In addition, it should create the `${[component name].classes}` subdirectory prior to performing a compilation. After completing the compilation, the target copies properties files from the source tree to the class's subdirectory.

The unittest Target

The `unittest` target should trigger the execution of all the relevant unit tests. Under most circumstances, I use the jUnit framework to help me organize, execute, and report on all my unit tests. As described in Chapter 5, "Optional Tasks," an optional task has been developed to support the execution of jUnit.

As previously stated, jUnit is the preferred framework for containing unit tests. But there are occasions when using jUnit creates difficulties. Certainly, GUI testing is one aspect that until recently couldn't be handled without overcoming some difficulties. In addition to this limitation, jUnit imposes an artificial limitation on itself by using a specialized class loader that short-circuits the Java2 delegating class loading model. Although this topic is beyond the scope of this book, the symptom and cure are worth some consideration.

If your unit test receives a class that wasn't loaded by jUnit's class loader, you're likely to experience a `ClassCastException` or a `ClassNotFoundException`. This is most likely to occur in an application such as the example that we developed in this chapter. In the case of our example, classes received by clients have passed through the JMS router. Because the JMS router is run independently of jUnit, the client considers the classes that it receives from the router to be different from those that it has loaded. When the stub object is cast to the appropriate type (typically an interface), a `ClassCastException` will be raised.

jUnit can be configured so that it doesn't short-circuit the loading of any application classes that are to be received from an external source. You can do so by setting the appropriate filters in the `excluded.properties` file found in `junit.jar`. Keep in mind that the developers of jUnit decided to short-circuit class loading delegation to maintain the principle of unit test isolation. By excluding these classes, they'll be loaded once—when they are first referenced. All other classes will be reloaded between tests. Another route is to start the JMS router in a faked-out jUnit test—although this might not always be possible.

The filter Target

The purpose of the `filter` target is to eliminate development artifacts from the final product tree. In most cases, this simply means getting rid of the unit tests before you JAR the classes. As I'll demonstrate shortly, I typically define properties that contain filters as described in Chapter 4. The filters are used by the `delete` task contained in the `filter` target.

The jar Target

The `jar` target creates one or more JAR files. The JARs should contain all the Java-related artifacts (class files, property files, and so on) needed by the application. In a case in which you're packaging a client/server application, it might be prudent to package the client classes separately from the server classes. If, as a result of a compile, all the classes are in a single directory structure, you can use filters to direct artifacts to different JAR files. After the JAR file has been created, you might want to consider deleting the class tree.

Other Targets to Consider

There are a number of convenient targets that you might want to consider adding to your build script. These targets include `all`, `checkout`, `checkin`, `clean`, and `javadoc`.

The `clean` target should remove all the generated artifacts from the development directories. These artifacts include the directory where the class files are contained, any JAR, WAR, or EAR files, and any Javadoc that was generated. The `delete` task (discussed in Chapter 4) is most likely the only task you need to fill out the body of the `clean` target.

The `all` target should use the `depends` attribute to specify the targets defined to clean, compile, test, filter, and finally JAR the classes. Listing 9.1 is one example of what an `all` target could look like.

Listing 9.1   *A Typical all Target*

```
<target name="a" depends="init,clean,compile,unittest,filter,jar" />
```

The `checkout` target should take a set of source files along with other artifacts that the end product is dependent on and drop them in the appropriate location in the project directory structure. Conversely, the `checkin` target should record all the modifications in the source code repository. The mechanics of how this is done vary among different source code control systems.

Last on this list is the `javadoc` target. You can find a complete description of this target in Chapter 4. The most important point to consider is that if you don't build your Javadocs all at once, you must devise an appropriate scheme to avoid overwriting commonly named files, such as `index.html`.

Building the Channel Component

Now that some basic techniques have been covered, we can move on to apply them to our sample application, ChatRoom. From the earlier description, we can see that the application has been partitioned into five primary components. One of the five components is a third-party JMS implementation. Of the four remaining components, the common, client, and server components are domain-specific. The `Channel` component is infrastructure that may be reused by other applications.

The requirements for `Channel` were derived from the requirements for ChatRoom. Although `Channel` may be reused in the future, only ChatRoom is currently using it. Therefore, the task of building and maintaining `Channel` rightfully falls within the realm of ChatRoom. This would most likely change if another project decided to reuse `Channel`. In that scenario, `Channel` should be treated as just another third-party component. This should trigger a refactoring of the build scripts for ChatRoom so that they reflect the new reality. In the meantime, the script in Listing 9.2 illustrates how to build the `Channel` component.

Listing 9.2   *The Build Script for Channel*

```
<project name="channel" default="all" basedir=".">


    <!-- Environmental Specific Properties -->
    <property file="environment.properties" />


    <target name="init" unless="${channel.target.init}">
```

Listing 9.2   *(continued)*

```
        <property name="channel.target.init" value="set" />
        <tstamp/>

        <!-- Project Properties -->
        <property name="channel.src" value="." />
        <property name="channel.classes" value="../../classes" />
        <property name="channel.lib" value="../../lib" />
        <property name="channel.doc" value="../../docs" />
        <property name="channel.javadoc" value="../../${doc}/api" />

        <!-- build properties -->
        <property name="channel.root.package"
                value="com.sams.ant.channel" />
        <property name="channel.root.path"
                value="com/sams/ant/channel" />
        <property name="channel.unittest.package"
                value="${channel.root.package}.unittest" />
        <property name="channel.unittest.path"
                value="${channel.root.path}/unittest" />

        <!-- Project Jar files -->
        <property name="channel.jar" value="${channel.lib}/channel.jar" />

        <!-- entry points -->
        <property name="channel.testcase"
                value="com.sams.ant.channel.unittest.ChannelTest" />

    </target> <!-- init -->


<target name="compile" depends="init">
    <mkdir dir="${channel.classes}" />

    <javac srcdir="${channel.src}" destdir="${channel.classes}">
        <classpath>
            <pathelement location="${jms.provider.jar}" />
        </classpath>
    </javac>

    <copy todir="${channel.classes}" >
        <fileset dir="${channel.src}" >
            <exclude name="**/*.java"/>
```

Listing 9.2   *(continued)*

```
                <exclude name="*" />
            </fileset>
        </copy>

    </target> <!-- compile -->


    <target name="jar" depends="unittest,filter">
        <mkdir dir="${channel.lib}" />

        <jar jarfile="${channel.jar}" basedir="${channel.classes}" />
        <delete dir="${channel.classes}" />
     </target> <!-- jar -->

    <target name="release" depends="compile,jar">
        <delete dir="${channel.classes}" />
    </target> <!-- clean -->


    <!-- Delete classes used for unittest -->
    <target name="filter" depends="init">
        <delete dir="${channel.classes}/${channel.unittest.path}" />
    </target>


    <target name="unittest" depends="init">
        <parallel>
            <java classname="${jms.router}" fork="yes" timeout="15000"
                  dir="${jms.router.config.root}" output="jmsrouter.log" >
                <arg value="${jms.router.config}" />
                <classpath>
                    <fileset dir="${jms.lib}">
                        <include name="**/*.jar"/>
                    </fileset>
                </classpath>
            </java>
            <sequential>
                <sleep seconds="5" />
                <java classname="${channel.testcase}" fork="yes" >
                    <classpath>
                        <pathelement location="${channel.classes}" />
                        <pathelement location="${jms.provider.jar}" />
```

Listing 9.2   *(continued)*

```
                           <pathelement location="${jms.client.jar}" />
                   </classpath>
               </java>
           </sequential>
        </parallel>
    </target> <!-- unittest -->


    <target name="clean" depends="init">
        <delete dir="${channel.classes}" />
        <delete file="${channel.jar}" />
        <delete dir="${channel.javadoc}" />
    </target> <!-- clean -->


    <target name="all" depends="clean,release" />

</project> <!-- channel -->
```

This script contains a number of the concepts that have been conveyed so far. First, note that only one statement resides outside the confines of a target. Furthermore, all the targets perform the steps required to fulfill only a logical unit of work. This structure enables you to selectively execute the targets that meet your specific needs. The importance of this providing the flexibility will become apparent later on as we move to the project-level build script.

The init target

The init target contains a property definition for every attribute used in the build script. The benefits of organizing a build script in this manner are twofold. First, you can replace specific attribute values with meaningful property names. Second, if you were to define a literal value for each attribute, those who need to change a value would be forced to inspect the entire build script. By centralizing these definitions, you not only ease the maintenance issues, you also help reduce the possibility of overlooking attributes that share the same value during maintenance.

One minor drawback of this technique is that every target must now list the init target as a dependency. Although this might not seem like a big deal, without taking the proper measures, it results in the init target being executed more than once. Let's see how this issue is resolved by looking at the init target in Listing 9.2. The first line in the init target sets the property `channel.target.init`. The target attribute `unless` (as described in Chapter 4) is set to check whether the property has been set. Therefore, the `unless` clause ensure that the `init` target is executed only once.

One last observation we can make in the `init` target is that properties have been defined either in terms of the project's `basedir` property or in terms of an externally defined property. The next section completes the discussion of initialization by describing the benefits of using such a strategy.

The Free-Floating Properties Task

As previously noted, there is only one free-floating task. This task loads a set of properties from the file `environment.properties`. You might also recall the discussion of how to handle resources that spill outside of the project directory. Placing a definition for these external references into a properties file enables us to even further separate the stable resources from those that are less stable. Consider that the build script will most likely be stable. We can use the `environment.properties` file to eliminate one more reason for having to edit the build script.

We can see an example of this if we look at the differences in the `environment.properties` files in Listings 9.3 and 9.4. Note that both these properties file support the identical build script.

Listing 9.3 *An environment.properties File for Windows*

```
# Properties used by Ant scripts to build the channel component

#
#Release Number
#
channel.release=v1_0
channel.module=channel

#
# Root directory of JMS installation
#
jms.home=e:/local/opt/java/swiftmq_2_0_1

jms.lib=${jms.home}/jars
jms.provider.jar=${jms.lib}/jms.jar
jms.client.jar=${jms.lib}/smqclient.jar

jms.console=com.swiftmq.admin.explorer.Explorer
```

Listing 9.3   *(continued)*

```
jms.router=com.swiftmq.router.Router
jms.router.config=jms/conf/ChatroomRouter.properties
jms.router.config.root=../..
```

The information contained here defines the name of the component and its release label (referred to as a *tag* in CVS). It then goes on to define properties that identify parameters for using the JMS provider's implementation.

Listing 9.4   *An environment.properties File for Unix*

```
# Properties used by Ant scripts to build the channel component

#
#Release Number
#
channel.release=v1_0
channel.module=channel

#
# Root directory of JMS installation
#
jms.home=/local/opt/jms/swiftmq_2_0_1

jms.lib=${jms.home}/jars
jms.provider.jar=${jms.lib}/jms.jar
jms.client.jar=${jms.lib}/smqclient.jar

jms.console=com.swiftmq.admin.explorer.Explorer
jms.router=com.swiftmq.router.Router
jms.router.config=jms/conf/ChatroomRouter.properties
jms.router.config.root=../..
```

As you can see, the only difference between this properties file and the previous one is the definition of jms.home.

Isolating external properties to environment.properties leads to a couple of benefits. The first major benefit is that the build script can be moved between environments without the need to be edited. If the project structure is maintained, all that's needed is a quick edit of the environment.properties file. Path information is often platform-specific. A side effect of moving the definition of resources external to the project is that these platform specific declarations are now isolated to a properties file. Furthermore, build scripts can be passed between developers without the need for each to share a common image. Finally, reducing the need to edit the build script should also reduce the chances of that errors will be introduced into the build script.

There are other cases in which you might introduce a properties file. One such case is the need to keep user-specific information out of the build and environment.properties file. For example, you might need to store a user ID and password for a source code control or database. Keeping this information separate enables the user to secure it and still have the script be able to access it when the need arises. This example does not end this list of possibilities. It does, however, point out that maintaining a separation of artifacts with some well thought out guidelines can save you time and effort in the long run.

The compile Target

After code has been written, the next logical step is to compile it. The logic needed to perform this step is placed in a compile target. Because Chapter 3 provided a fairly detailed description of this process, let's focus on the enhancements that have been applied to this target.

As you've seen before, the compile task creates class files in a class's subdirectory. The mkdir task ensures that this directory exists. The copy task, performed after the javac task, is intended to copy all other non-Java code artifacts that are needed to support the application. These artifacts might include properties, gifs, and so on.

Note that the property names are prefixed by channel. This prefixing enables us to use a common naming scheme throughout the entire project. The scheme lessens the likelihood that another script will set properties to an inappropriate value.

The unittest Target

The unittest target in Listing 9.2 deserves some additional discussion. The unit test for a component such as Channel involves a number of moving parts. In this case, we must start the JMS process (known as a *router*) that provides the backbone of the messaging layer. The problem is that if we start that process, the build script will block until that process finishes. It is at that point that our tests would be allowed to run. But the test is dependent on the router running. So, it seems that we need a technique that enables us to execute both the router and the unit test at the same time. This is where two tasks—parallel and sequential—come in (refer to Chapter 4 for a complete description).

The parallel task can be used to execute both the router and the unit test at the same time. But beware: Executing the router and the unit test at the same time creates a race condition. If the test executes before the router has completed its initialization process, the test fails. It's then that the `sequential` task comes into play. As you can see in Listing 9.2, the `sequential` task wraps the actual unit test. Preceding the unit test is a `sleep` task. The `sleep` task gives the router a chance to complete its initialization sequence before the unit test fires.

The jar and filter Targets

The `filter` task is responsible for locating and deleting all the class files used to support the unit testing. It's those classes that you most likely don't want to deliver in a final product. Although the `jar` and `filter` tasks generally work in unison, there are some occasions when you might want to filter without creating a JAR. One such case is when you want to include the `Channel` classes in another JAR.

> **Tip**
> It's generally considered to be good practice to place your unit tests in a separate package. This ensures that your tests can touch only the public interface of the target classes. You should be wary of code that cannot be covered from a public interface.

In this project, all the unit tests are contained in a separate package called `unittest`. This simplifies the task of identifying what needs to be deleted. If you decide not to follow this convention, you must devise another scheme to help you identify which classes should be removed before the JAR is created. In many cases, `Test` or `TestCase` is embedded in the class name. In this instance, a list of classes can be created using filters (as described in Chapters 3 and 4).

clean Target

The `clean` target ensures that all artifacts excluding source are removed from the project. The primary artifacts are class files, resources, the component's JAR file, and any Javadoc that might have been generated. The target itself relies on the `delete` task to eliminate these artifacts. I highly recommend that you clean the project directories before performing a complete build because these artifacts can come back to haunt you later.

Other Targets

The earlier descriptions cover a number of essential targets. In addition to these targets, you might also want to consider adding a number of convince targets. These targets include `all`, `release`, `checkout`, and `checkin`.

The `all` target should (as its name suggests) perform all the targets found in the build script in some logical order. Because this can be achieved using the `depends` clause, it's likely that the `all` target doesn't contain any nested elements.

The release target should be nearly the same as the all target. The primary difference is in that the target might want to delete all the class files after they've been JARred.

The checkout and checkin tasks should perform these functions against your source code repository. As was illustrated in Chapters 4 and 5, Ant supports all the major SCCS products. This includes Perforce, CVS, StarTeam, VSS, and a few others.

Building the Common Layer

The common layer represents all classes that are shared between the client and the server. These classes include a number of domain classes that are passed across the wire. Listing 9.5 is the build script for the common layer.

Listing 9.5   *The build.xml Script for the Common Layer*

```
<project name="chatcommon" default="all" basedir=".">

    <!-- Initialize the build and run environments -->
    <target name="init" unless="${chatcommon.target.init}">
        <property name="chatcommon.target.init" value="set" />
        <tstamp/>

        <!-- Project Properties -->
        <property name="chatcommon.src" value="." />
        <property name="chatcommon.classes"
                value="../../classes" />
        <property name="chatcommon.lib"
                value="../../lib" />
        <property name="chatcommon.doc"
                value="../../docs" />
        <property name="chatcommon.javadoc"
                value="../../${chatcommon.doc}/api" />

        <!-- build properties -->
        <property name="chatcommon.root.package"
                value="com.sams.ant.chatroom" />
        <property name="chatcommon.root.path"
                value="com/sams/ant/chatroom" />

        <!-- Project Jar files -->
        <property name="chatcommon.jar"
```

Listing 9.5   *(continued)*

```xml
                          value="${chatcommon.lib}/common.jar" />

        <!-- dependency checking -->
        <available file="${chatcommon.lib}/${channel.jar}"
                   property="channel.classpath"
                   value="${chatcommon.lib}/${channel.jar}"/>

        <available classname="${channel.class}"
            property="channel.classpath"
            value="${chatcommon.classes}">
            <classpath location="${chatcommon.classes}" />
        </available>

        <condition property="common.dependencies">
            <isset property="channel.classpath" />
        </condition>
    </target> <!-- init -->

    <target name="dependents" unless="common.dependencies">
        <fail message="Cannot find classes for channel." />
    </target>

    <target name="compile" depends="init,dependents">
        <mkdir dir="${chatcommon.classes}" />

        <javac srcdir="${chatcommon.src}" destdir="${chatcommon.classes}">
            <classpath>
                <pathelement location="${channel.classpath}" />
            </classpath>
        </javac>

        <copy todir="${chatcommon.classes}" >
            <fileset dir="${chatcommon.src}" >
                <exclude name="**/*.java"/>
                <exclude name="*" />
            </fileset>
        </copy>

    </target> <!-- compile -->

    <target name="jar" depends="init">
        <mkdir dir="${chatcommon.lib}" />
```

Listing 9.5   *(continued)*

```
        <jar jarfile="${chatcommon.jar}" basedir="${chatcommon.classes}" />
    </target> <!-- jar -->

    <target name="release" depends="compile,jar">
        <delete dir="${chatcommon.classes}" />
    </target> <!-- release -->

    <!-- Delete the ${build} and ${dist} directory trees -->
    <target name="clean" depends="init">
        <delete dir="${chatcommon.classes}" />
        <delete file="${chatcommon.jar}" />
        <delete dir="${chatcommon.javadoc}" />
    </target> <!-- clean -->

    <!-- must have a jms router running before this target will work -->
    <target name="all" depends="clean,release" />

</project> <!-- ChatRoom -->
```

The common layer makes reference to the `Channel` component. To build the common layer, we're dependent on the existence of `Channel`. The notion that, for the moment, ChatRoom owns `Channel` implies that a deployment script would most likely bundle `Channel` into the final JAR. As a result, we might find `Channel` in a JAR or in a directory. Taking both cases into account requires only an extra check. These checks are carried out in the two `available` and single-condition tasks found at the bottom of the `init` target in Listing 9.5.

The first `available` task checks for the existence of a JAR that contains the `Channel` component. If it finds a JAR, it sets a property that will be used to help define the classpath. The second `available` task checks for the existence of `channel` classes in a directory structure and if found, attempts to set the property that will be used to help define the classpath. Note that if the corresponding JAR file has also been found, its value is used because it is assigned first.

You might argue that the conditional task is not really necessary at this point and because I'm making this point, I might agree. However, its importance will become more apparent in the next few pages as the dependencies become a little more complicated. In this instance, the single check is used to set the property `common.dependents`. It is this property that is used by the `unless` attribute of the `dependents` target. Because the only task defined in the `dependents` target is `fail`, we certainly want to ensure that this property is set.

Building the Chat Server

ChatServer is the first executable to be delivered. The relevant portion of its build script is illustrated in Listing 9.6.

Listing 9.6   *The build.xml Script for the Common Layer*

```
<available file="${chatserver.lib}/${chatcommon.jar}"
           property="chatcommon.classpath"
           value="${chatserver.lib}/${chatcommon.jar}"/>

<available classname="${chatserver.classes}/${chatcommon.class}"
           property="chatcommon.classpath"
           value="${chatserver.classes}"/>
           <classpath path="${chatserver.classes}" />

<available file="${chatserver.lib}/${channel.jar}"
           property="channel.classpath"
           value="${chatserver.lib}/${channel.jar}"/>

<available classname="${channel.class}"
           property="channel.classpath"
           value="${chatserver.classes}}">
           <classpath path="${chatserver.classes}" />
</available>

<condition property="server.dependencies">
    <and>
        <isset property="chatcommon.classpath" />
        <isset property="channel.classpath" />
    </and>
</condition>

</target> <!-- init -->

<target name="dependents" unless="server.dependencies">
    <fail message="Cannot find one of channel or common." />
</target>
```

Adding the common layer as a dependency results in the need for two more `available` tasks. These dependency checks are performed in the first two `available` tasks. The biggest change is in the `condition` task. It uses the nested and element to check that both properties have been set.

In this example, we can see the value of the condition task. Unlike the `depends` attribute, the `if` and `unless` attributes accept only a single property. The `condition` task combines the two classpath properties into a single `server.dependencies` property. It's the setting of this property that saves the script from failing.

The `environment.properties` file (see Listing 9.7) includes three properties. The first property defines the home directory for the component, the second defines a name for its JAR file, and the third defines a class that's found within the component. The purpose of the last property is to define a class found in the dependent component that can be used for the dependency check. In other words, its existence is an indication of the existence of the source for the entire component. The other properties are to enable you to include the possibility that these components might have been moved to a location outside of the domain of ChatRoom.

Listing 9.7   *The environment.properties File for ChatServer*

```
#Used to build Chatroom Server

#Release Number
chatserver.release=v1_0
chatserver.module=chatserver

#
# Dependency configurations
#
channel.home=basedir
channel.jar=channel.jar
channel.class=com.sams.ant.channel.Channel

chatcommon.home=basedir
chatcommon.jar=common.jar
chatcommon.class=com.sams.ant.chatroom.TopicMessage
```

At this point, it seems prudent to JAR the server because it represents a complete deliverable. We'll use this assumption to help simplify the dependency checking when we build the chat client.

Building the Chat Client

The build script for the chat client is, not surprisingly, not that much different from that used to build the server. Although at first it might seem surprising that building the chat client is dependent on the server being available, the reason for this becomes apparent when we examine the unittest target. First, let's complete our discussion on ensuring that all the dependencies exist. The relevant portion of the build script is illustrated in Listing 9.8.

Listing 9.8   *Dependency Checks for ChatClient*

```
<available file="${chatclient.lib}/${chatserver.jar}"
           property="chatserver.classpath"
           value="${chatclient.lib}/${chatserver.jar}"/>

<available file="${chatclient.lib}/${chatcommon.jar}"
           property="chatcommon.classpath"
           value="${chatclient.lib}/${chatcommon.jar}"/>

<available file="${chatclient.lib}/${channel.jar}"
           property="channel.classpath"
           value="${chatclient.lib}/${channel.jar}"/>


<condition property="chatclient.dependencies">
    <and>
        <isset property="chatcommon.classpath" />
        <isset property="channel.classpath" />
        <isset property="chatserver.classpath" />
    </and>
</condition>
```

At this point in the build process, I require that all the class files be bundled into JAR files. Also note that the nested and element contains the third dependency for the chat server.

Another interesting addition to this script is the comprehensive unit-testing target. The source for this target is in Listing 9.9.

Listing 9.9   *ChatClient Unit Tests*

```
<!-- unit testing
     timeout is set for the task that runs the router because this version
     of swiftmq does always respond to a shutdown command.
```

Listing 9.9   *(continued)*

```
    -->
<target name="unittest" depends="init">
    <parallel>
        <sequential>
            <echo message="Router Started" />
            <java classname="${jms.router}" fork="yes" timeout="45000"
                    dir="${jms.router.config.root}" output="jmsrouter.log" >
                <arg value="${jms.router.config}" />
                <classpath>
                    <fileset dir="${jms.lib}">
                        <include name="**/*.jar"/>
                    </fileset>
                </classpath>
            </java>
            <echo message="Router Stopped" />
        </sequential>
        <sequential>
            <sleep seconds="5" />
            <echo message="ChatServer Started" />
            <java classname="${chatserver.main}" fork="yes" >
                <classpath>
                    <pathelement location="${chatserver.classpath}" />
                    <pathelement location="${channel.classpath}" />
                    <pathelement location="${chatcommon.classpath}" />
                    <pathelement location="${jms.provider.jar}" />
                    <pathelement location="${jms.client.jar}" />
                </classpath>
            </java>
            <echo message="ChatServer Stopped" />
        </sequential>
        <sequential>
            <sleep seconds="15" />
            <parallel>
                <sequential>
                <echo message="Test Client 1 Started" />
                    <java classname="${chatclient.testcase.1.main}" fork="yes" >
                        <classpath>
                            <pathelement location="${chatclient.classes}" />
                            <pathelement location="${channel.classpath}" />
                            <pathelement location="${chatcommon.classpath}" />
                            <pathelement location="${jms.provider.jar}" />
                            <pathelement location="${jms.client.jar}" />
```

Listing 9.9   *(continued)*

```
                    </classpath>
                </java>
                <echo message="Test Client 1 Completed" />
            </sequential>
            <sequential>
            <sleep seconds="5" />
                <echo message="Test Client 2 Started" />
                <java classname="${chatclient.testcase.2.main}" fork="yes" >
                    <classpath>
                        <pathelement location="${chatclient.classes}" />
                        <pathelement location="${channel.classpath}" />
                        <pathelement location="${chatcommon.classpath}" />
                        <pathelement location="${jms.provider.jar}" />
                        <pathelement location="${jms.client.jar}" />
                    </classpath>
                </java>
                <echo message="Test Client 2 Completed" />
            </sequential>
        </parallel>
        <echo message="AdminServer Started" />
        <java classname="${chatadmin.main}" fork="yes" >
            <classpath>
                <pathelement location="${chatserver.classpath}" />
                <pathelement location="${channel.classpath}" />
                <pathelement location="${chatcommon.classpath}" />
                <pathelement location="${jms.provider.jar}" />
                <pathelement location="${jms.client.jar}" />
            </classpath>
        </java>
        <echo message="AdminServer Stopped" />
        </sequential>
    </parallel>
</target> <!-- unittest -->
```

Although the initial length might appear frightening, this listing only uses the combination of sequential and parallel tasks to carry out the testing. The JMS router, ChatServer, and two ChatClient processes must be executed in parallel. Consequently, there are four blocks of sequential elements, one for each process. Within each sequential attribute, an informational message is echoed before the contained tasks are executed. As was previously the case, starting four processes at the same time is a race condition.

Consequently, the `server` target is given a small sleep time that ensures that the JMS router is ready to go. The two clients are given a slightly longer delay to ensure that the server is up and running. Finally, the clients exchange messages to complete the testing.

> **Note**
> In testing an application such as ChatRoom, you must consider how timing issues might interfere with the ability to conduct a test that does not hang. Having the test hang effectively halts the build. Setting the timeout attribute mitigate this issue.

At this point, four Ant build scripts have been developed—one for each of the components used to build the ChatRoom application. Although dependencies between the scripts exist, they're isolated in such a manner that adjusting the build to a new environment should involve only changing properties in the `environment.properties` file. The only remaining task is to develop a script to complete the final integration to complete the process of building ChatRoom. The remainder of this chapter focuses on this final piece of the puzzle.

A One-Shot Build of the ChatRoom Application

All along, we've been building up to the point of having a completely scripted build process for ChatRoom. Now that we're ready to complete the task, let's start with a brief description of the problem.

The overall goal of the project-level build script is to collect and then integrate all the individual pieces of our application. In the process, it should conduct some tests to help ensure the integrity of the final product. Each of the scripts should maintain the degree of separation that we've worked hard to achieve. In addition, there are a few technical questions that should be considered. Where should the project-level script reside? How should it be structured? How will the script interact with each of the component-level scripts?

If we look at the project directory structure, we'll see that it started with a project root directory. As previously described, the `basedir` property is set to the directory in which the build script resides. Therefore, it seems reasonable that the project-level build script should reside in the project's root directory.

Next, let's consider the structure of the project-level build script. We've already spent a considerable amount of time developing a template for component-level build scripts. Let's revisit that template to see whether there are some ideas that can be reused. After the project definition, the first line in the build script loads the `environment.properties` file. As you recall, the purpose of that file is to define properties that are external to the project. It's a safe assumption that this feature can be carried over to the project-level build.

As already mentioned, we can use the `ant` task (refer to Chapter 4) to execute each component-level build script. We could construct a separate task for each component but, for a system of any significant size, this might cause the build script to bloat in size—the very thing we're trying to avoid. One thing is for sure: There's a lot of repetition in the build process—enough that it does seem we should be able to take advantage of it. But Ant doesn't provide any of the programmatic tools (`while`, `for`, and so on) that we normally use to solve this type of problem. We could run through a number of ways to contort Ant into executing the equivalent of a loop, but in the end, a custom task (see Chapter 6) seems like the most sensible approach to take. If we're going make the effort to construct a custom task, let's take some time to see whether we can catch any other requirements in the process. Let's expound on the list to see what can be resolved.

To construct an application, we must be able to retrieve the correct version of each of constituent component used to build the application. Ideally, these components are kept in a version control system. As the build progresses, it's important that we conduct tests to ensure the integrity of each component and the subsequent integrations. How do we know which versions of each component should be used to build a specified version of ChatRoom? Somehow, we need to provide Ant with a blueprint that describes the components and versions to be used.

Because the name and version of each component are well known, we could provide Ant with a list containing these bits of information. By providing a mapping of components and version number to an application, we can solve a number of issues. First and foremost, we now have an accurate description of how to build any version of our application. This information can be preserved in a version control system. Because this information serves a different purpose than what's provided by `environment.properties` and it's also specific enough that we certainly don't want to embed it into the build scripts themselves, we can conclude that this information should be kept in a separate properties file. As such, let's introduce this separate configuration file and name it `configuration.properties`.

Ant doesn't have a task that can process this type of configuration information, so we must write our own custom task to handle it. Let's move on to describe the type of information that should be placed into `configuration.properties`.

A configuration.properties File

Listing 9.10 illustrates a project-level `configuration.properties` file.

Listing 9.10   *A Configuration Description for Channel*

```
#
# A configuration describing the current build of ChatRoom
#
# Version 1.0
#

channel,v1_0,build.xml,clean,compile,unittest,filter
chatcommon,v1_0,build.xml,compile,jar
chatserver,v1_0,build.xml,release
chatclient,v1_0,build.xml,release
```

As you can see in the listing, there's a single line for each component. Each line contains at least four comma-separated columns. The first column contains the name of the component. The next column is the label used to retrieve the source (and other artifacts) from SCCS. The third column specifies the name of the build script. Finally, the remaining columns contain the names of each target to execute.

With this simple definition, we've created a file that completely describes a single version of ChatRoom. Let's move to writing the supporting custom task.

The Supporting Custom Task

The supporting custom task should read and then process each line in the configuration file. The completed task is found in Listing 9.11.

Listing 9.11   *Source for the release Custom Task*

```
package com.sams.ant.taskdef;

import org.apache.tools.ant.*;
import java.io.*;
import java.util.*;
import java.util.Iterator;

public class Release extends Task {

    private static String fileSeparator =
                    System.getProperty("file.separator");
    private boolean failonerror = true;
    private String file;
```

Listing 9.11   *(continued)*

```java
    private File sourceDir;

    public Release() {}

    public void setFailonerror(boolean value) { failonerror=value; }
    public void setFile(String value) { this.file = value; }
    public void setSourceDir(String value) {
        sourceDir = new File(value);
    }

    public void execute() throws BuildException {
        log("Release: " + this.file);
        try {
            execute0();
        } catch (BuildException be) {
            if (failonerror)
                throw be;
            else
                log(be.getMessage());
        }
    }

    public void execute0() throws BuildException {
        try {
            this.createSourceDir();
            BufferedReader configuration = new BufferedReader(new FileReader
                                                     (this.file));
            String configComponent;
            while ( ( configComponent = configuration.readLine()) != null)
                processConfigComponent( configComponent);
        } catch (Exception e) {
            throw new BuildException(e);
        }
    }

    private void processConfigComponent(String component) throws BuildException {
        if ( ( component.length() == 0) ||
             ( component.charAt(0) == '#') ||
             (component.indexOf(",") < 0))
            return;
```

Listing 9.11   *(continued)*

```
    StringTokenizer st = new StringTokenizer(component,",");
    if ( ! st.hasMoreTokens())
        return;

    String moduleName = st.nextToken();
    String version = st.nextToken();
    String buildFile = st.nextToken();
    this.getSource(moduleName, version);

    while (st.hasMoreTokens()) {
        this.perform(moduleName, buildFile, st.nextToken());
    }

}

private void executeTask(Task task) throws BuildException {
    task.setProject(this.getProject());
    task.setLocation(this.getLocation());
    task.setOwningTarget(this.getOwningTarget());
    task.init();
    task.execute();
}

private void getSource(String moduleName, String version)
throws BuildException {
    Cvs task = new Cvs();
    task.setCommand("checkout");
    task.setPackage(moduleName);
    task.setTag(version);
    task.setDest(this.sourceDir);
    this.executeTask(task);
}

// make the output directory
private void createSourceDir() throws BuildException {
    if ( ( sourceDir.exists()) && ( ! sourceDir.isDirectory()))
        throw new BuildException(sourceDir.toString() +
                                 "is not a directory");

    Mkdir task = new Mkdir();
    task.setDir(this.sourceDir);
```

Listing 9.11 *(continued)*

```
        this.executeTask(task);
    }

    private void perform(String componentName,
                         String buildFile,
                         String taskName)
    throws BuildException {
        Ant task = new Ant();
        task.setInheritAll(false);
        task.setTarget(taskName);
        try {
            task.setAntfile(this.sourceDir.getCanonicalPath() +
            this.fileSeparator + componentName +
            this.fileSeparator + buildFile );
        } catch (IOException e) {
            throw new BuildException(e);
        }
        this.executeTask(task);
    }
}
```

The custom task was constructed according to the strategy set out in Chapter 6. The discussion that follows focuses on the functionality of the execute0() method.

The execute0() method is responsible for reading and triggering the process of each line in the configuration file. To achieve this, it makes use of the processConfigComponent() method. This method performs a cursory assessment of the validity of the line. As per generally accepted conventions, comment lines begin with a # character and are ignored. As described earlier, the first field is the SCC label that locks down this version of the component, and the second field is a version number. This information is passed along to the getSource() method.

The getSource() method is responsible for configuring a CVS task to retrieve all the source code. Note that the methods used to configure the task map directly to their equivalent XML-specified attributes. It should be no surprise that the mapping between the attribute and the field names follows the JavaBeans specification. One other thing to note is that this task assumes that the target directory source directory exists. This is accomplished by Ant's mkdir task. Again, you can see that the attributes and field names map using the JavaBeans specification. The last two lines in each of these methods (as well as the perform() method) makes a call to executeTask().

The `executeTask()` method sets the technical parameters for the task. Those parameters include the project, the base directory, and finally, the owning target. Because these items are identical to those currently being used by the custom task, the references are transferred using a simple get/set method combination. The last two lines first initialize the task and then execute it (refer to Chapter 6 for the complete details).

When the `getSource()` method has completed, the `processConfigComponent()` method moves on to execute each of the specified targets in the specified build file using the `perform()` method. The `perform()` method in turn configures and then delegates the execution of the target to the `ant` task. The three parameters set are `inheritsAll`, `taskName`, and, finally, the complete path to the component's build script. It's quite conceivable that you might not always want `inheritsAll` to be `false`. If this is the case, you could easily parameterize this setting as well.

Every method in the class throws a `BuildException`. The task supports the standard `failOnError` setting, so the decision of how to react to the exception is now up to the person most likely to know how to handle it. That person is you, not me. As such, the exception handling follows the principle of "throw, don't catch."

Now that the custom task is complete, the next step is to use it.

A Build Script for ChatRoom

As was the case before, the build script for ChatRoom contains some familiar targets: `init`, `clean`, and `all`. The difference between these targets and the one used to support component-level builds is that these are focused at the project level. Starting with the `init` target, let's look at some of the features of this script as illustrated in Listing 9.12.

Listing 9.12   *The Build Script for ChatRoom*

```
<project name="chatroom" default="all" basedir=".">

    <!-- Environmental Specific Properties -->
    <property file="environment.properties" />


    <target name="init" unless="${cr.target.init}">

        <property name="cr.target.init" value="set" />
        <tstamp/>
        <property name="chatroom.src" value="src" />
        <property name="chatroom.classes" value="classes" />
        <property name="chatroom.lib" value="lib" />
```

Listing 9.12 *(continued)*

```
    <taskdef name="release" classname="com.sams.ant.taskdef.Release" >
        <classpath>
            <pathelement location="${ant.extn.path}" />
            <pathelement location="${ant.path}" />
        </classpath>
    </taskdef>

</target> <!-- init -->

<target name="release" depends="init">
    <release file="configuration.properties" sourceDir="src" />
</target>

<target name="clean" depends="init">
    <delete dir="${chatroom.lib}" />
</target> <!-- clean -->

<target name="all" depends="clean,release" />

</project> <!-- channel -->
```

As is the case with the component-level build scripts, the `init` target here is used to parameterize all the properties that are considered to be internal to the project. These include the `source`, `class`, and `lib` directories. External properties are set in the `environment.properties` file (see Listing 9.13). These properties include the JMS implementation, the JAR containing the custom task, and Ant itself.

The `taskdef` task is used to define our custom task (for more details, refer to Chapter 4). The custom task is not part of ChatRoom; consequently, it isn't contained within ChatRoom's project directory. As a result, the property that identifies the JAR that contains the class used to support the custom `release` task is specified in the `environment.properties` file.

Listing 9.13 *The Build Script for Channel*

```
# Properties used by Ant scripts to build ChatRoom

#Version Number
chatroom.version=v1_0

#
```

Listing 9.13   *(continued)*

```
# Root directory of JMS installation
#

ant.home=/local/opt/apache/jakarta-ant-1.5
ant.path=${ant.home}/lib/ant.jar
ant.extn.path=/local/opt/java/lib/releasetask.jar
```

Finally, we're ready to look at the unfamiliar `release` target. Although it's deceptively simple, we can see that the target contains a very powerful and complex task. The task specifies the source directory and the configuration information to use. The output in Listing 9.14 shows the task flowing through the process of retrieving source and then compiling it. Sets of unit tests are run against the two final products, `channel` and the ChatRoom client. While testing the ChatRoom client, we also test the ChatRoom server.

Listing 9.14   *The Build Script for Channel*

```
C:\ chatroom>ant release
Buildfile: build.xml

init:

release:
[release] Release: configuration.properties
     [null] Created dir: C:\chatroom\src
     [null] cvs checkout: Updating channel
     [null] U channel/build.xml
     [null] U channel/environment.properties
     [null] cvs checkout: Updating channel/com
     [null] cvs checkout: Updating channel/com/sams
     [null] cvs checkout: Updating channel/com/sams/ant
     [null] cvs checkout: Updating channel/com/sams/ant/channel
     [null] U channel/com/sams/ant/channel/Channel.java
     [null] U channel/com/sams/ant/channel/ChannelException.java
     [null] U channel/com/sams/ant/channel/ChannelListener.java
     [null] U channel/com/sams/ant/channel/Content.java
     [null] U channel/com/sams/ant/channel/ReadChannel.java
     [null] U channel/com/sams/ant/channel/WriteChannel.java
     [null] U channel/com/sams/ant/channel/channel.properties
     [null] cvs checkout: Updating channel/com/sams/ant/channel/unittest
     [null] U channel/com/sams/ant/channel/unittest/ChannelTest.java
     [null] U channel/com/sams/ant/channel/unittest/TestMessage.java
```

Listing 9.14   *(continued)*

```
init:

clean:

init:

compile:
    [mkdir] Created dir: C:\chatroom\classes
    [javac] Compiling 8 source files to C:\chatroom\classes
     [copy] Copying 1 file to C:\chatroom\class
es

init:

unittest:
     [java] Test good
     [java] Timeout: killed the sub-process
     [java] Java Result: 1

init:

filter:
    [delete] Deleting directory C:\chatroom\classes\com\sams\ant\channel\unittest

init:

filter:
     [null] cvs checkout: Updating chatcommon
     [null] U chatcommon/build.xml
     [null] U chatcommon/environment.properties
     [null] cvs checkout: Updating chatcommon/com
     [null] cvs checkout: Updating chatcommon/com/sams
     [null] cvs checkout: Updating chatcommon/com/sams/ant
     [null] cvs checkout: Updating chatcommon/com/sams/ant/chatroom
     [null] U chatcommon/com/sams/ant/chatroom/ChatResources.java
     [null] U chatcommon/com/sams/ant/chatroom/ChatRoomMessage.java
     [null] U chatcommon/com/sams/ant/chatroom/TopicMessage.java

init:

dependents:
```

Listing 9.14   *(continued)*

```
compile:
    [javac] Compiling 3 source files to C:\chatroom\classes

init:

jar:
    [mkdir] Created dir: C:\chatroom\lib
      [jar] Building jar: C:\chatroom\lib\common.jar
     [null] cvs checkout: Updating chatserver
     [null] U chatserver/build.xml
     [null] U chatserver/environment.properties
     [null] cvs checkout: Updating chatserver/com
     [null] cvs checkout: Updating chatserver/com/sams
     [null] cvs checkout: Updating chatserver/com/sams/ant
     [null] cvs checkout: Updating chatserver/com/sams/ant/chatroom
     [null] U chatserver/com/sams/ant/chatroom/AdminMessage.java
     [null] U chatserver/com/sams/ant/chatroom/AdminServer.java
     [null] U chatserver/com/sams/ant/chatroom/ChatServer.java
     [null] U chatserver/com/sams/ant/chatroom/chatserver.properties

init:

dependents:

compile:
    [javac] Compiling 3 source files to C:\chatroom\classes
     [copy] Copying 1 file to C:\chatroom\classes

jar:
      [jar] Building jar: C:\chatroom\lib\chatserver.jar

release:
   [delete] Deleting directory C:\chatroom\classes
     [null] cvs checkout: Updating chatclient
     [null] U chatclient/build.xml
     [null] U chatclient/environment.properties
     [null] cvs checkout: Updating chatclient/com
     [null] cvs checkout: Updating chatclient/com/sams
     [null] cvs checkout: Updating chatclient/com/sams/ant
     [null] cvs checkout: Updating chatclient/com/sams/ant/chatroom
     [null] U chatclient/com/sams/ant/chatroom/ChatClient.java
     [null] U chatclient/com/sams/ant/chatroom/ChatMessage.java
```

Listing 9.14   *(continued)*

```
[null] U chatclient/com/sams/ant/chatroom/ChatRoom.java
[null] U chatclient/com/sams/ant/chatroom/ChatRoomException.java
[null] U chatclient/com/sams/ant/chatroom/ChatRoomListener.java
[null] U chatclient/com/sams/ant/chatroom/chatclient.properties
[null] cvs checkout: Updating chatclient/com/sams/ant/chatroom/unittest
[null] U
chatclient/com/sams/ant/chatroom/unittest/TopicClientTestCase1.java
[null]
U chatclient/com/sams/ant/chatroom/unittest/TopicClientTestCase2.java

init:

dependent:

compile:
    [mkdir] Created dir: C:\chatroom\classes
    [javac] Compiling 7 source files to C:\chatroom\classes
    [copy] Copying 1 file to C:\chatroom\classes

unittest:
    [echo] Router Started
    [echo] ChatServer Started
    [java] Starting Topics: ant.developer ant.user.
    [echo] Test Client 1 Started
    [java] Received message from user1.
    [java] Entered room ant.developer
    [echo] Test Client 2 Started
    [java] Received message from user2.
    [java] Entered room ant.developer
    [java] user2 : Hello World.
    [java] user1 : Hello
    [echo] Test Client 1 Completed
    [echo] Test Client 2 Completed
    [echo] AdminServer Started
    [java] Shutdown Server @localhost:4001
    [java] Shutdown complete
    [java] Received message from AdminServer.
    [echo] AdminServer Stopped
    [echo] ChatServer Stopped
    [java] Timeout: killed the sub-process
    [java] Java Result: 1
    [echo] Router Stopped
```

Listing 9.14   *(continued)*

```
filter:

jar:
     [jar] Building jar: C:\chatroom\lib\chatroom.jar

release:
   [delete] Deleting directory C:\chatroom\classes

BUILD SUCCESSFUL
Total time: 1 minute 19 seconds
```

Some Benefits of Chaining Builds

Finally, I want offer some thoughts on the benefits of decomposing and relinking each of the pieces using the technique of chaining the individual build scripts in the manner described in this chapter. Although much can be said about the benefits of component-based development, that topic is well beyond the scope of this text. Even so, there's an assumption that a project can be clearly delineated into separate components. From experience, you should recognize that this is not always the case.

Even if the project cannot be delineated into separate components, using the techniques described in this chapter can still help simplify the build process. One such case is when an automated build process replaces a manual process. This can have the dramatic effect of reducing build times from several hours to a couple of minutes. Many builds are plagued with problems that result from changes in the build, configurations, and procedures. Having these procedures captured in the form of a build script can help ensure that these changes are captured and distributed. It also reduces the possibilities of finger problems causing delays.

Decomposition of the build helps other team members to easily share their efforts in an IDE-independent manner. This strategy also can help with multiteam development efforts in which a consistent environment might be impossible to agree on, let alone enforce. Divorcing yourself from the IDE enables your developers to choose the tools that they're most comfortable with. As will be demonstrated in Chapter 11, "Tool Support for Ant," many IDEs support the integration of Ant. After you can build an application with Ant, everyone (including QA, production, and so on) can share the benefits that would be locked away if you didn't use build scripts.

The stressor for using component-based builds is granularity. If things become too granular, you start to lose the benefits of decomposition. So, as in other aspects of life, you must strike a balance between a level of decomposition that's too high and one that's too low. The level of granularity that should be used will most likely be self-evident once a design has been arrived at.

Summary

As we've probably all experienced, there's a real need to maintain tight control over how your build or development environment is configured. But having said that, we must also inject some flexibility because the build and development environments will be different. It's also advantageous for both the developers and the people responsible for the build to be able to leverage each other's work. Being able to fragment the build into small pieces is one step toward these goals.

Another step is the introduction of configuration files. These configuration files help to externalize parameters so that individual environments may be configured as desired without the need to edit the build script.

Finally, having a project-level build script that ties together all the individual scripts enables the build team and others to leverage the work of the individual developers—they are the people who'll author the component-level scripts.

The custom task `release` is at the heart of the project-level build script. This script enables the build team to reduce the step of scripting the entire build to one of authoring a description of the configuration. Because these artifacts represent a specific version of the application, they can be locked down in source code control with all the other artifacts. This facilitates the ability to rebuild any version of your application at any time in the future.

Tips

The following list summarizes the main points introduced in this chapter:

- Use a divide-and-conquer strategy to decompose your build into smaller more manageable pieces.
- Use the natural architecture of the application to help define components.
- To build an entire project, chain the individual build scripts.
- Parameterize the attributes so that their values can be changed without the need for someone else to edit the build script.
- Specifying the configuration in a file helps to clearly define the current and past versions of the project.
- Resources that aren't part of the project should be defined outside of the build script.
- Use a standard set of targets.

- Use a standard naming convention to reduce the possibility of having different properties sharing the same name.
- Complex unit testing can be conducted using combinations of the parallel and sequential tasks.
- Use a standard project directory structure.
- Automating the build process helps to reduce the number of errors.
- Adding a custom task to your build process can help solve problems that are specific to your environment.
- Ant artifacts should be stored along with the source code. This includes the source for the version of Ant that you're currently using.

CHAPTER 10

The Future Direction of Ant

Since its beginnings in the arms of James Davidson, Ant has grown immensely, and it is very much still growing. Ant has come from offering facilities designed to build one specific project to a tool that meets the demands of many projects. As Ant grows, it lends itself to more tasks, although its primary focus has always been as a build tool. This chapter looks at the plans in place to bring Ant to the next level of maturity, giving you—the Ant user—a taste of what is to come.

In this book, we've addressed the data types and both core and optional tasks. These are accurate for version 1.5, but chances are that from the time this chapter was written until the time you read it, more tasks will have been added, bugs will have been fixed, and Ant will have been further enhanced. Improvements and bug fixes to Ant are made daily, the results of which are available as nightly builds to those who want *the* most up-to-date version. (Chapter 2, "Preliminaries," gives details for installing nightly builds.)

The evolution is very evident in Ant. The differences between 1.4.1 and 1.5, for example, included the addition of new data types and tasks, and attributes to existing tasks. The `<input>` task, for example was introduced in 1.5, and the `<condition>` task was extended to allow more complex conditions to be expressed. A comparison to even earlier versions of Ant will show that they offer a small subset of what Ant offers now. This trend will probably continue, so what will future versions offer? Although there will be some arbitrary number of 1.*x* versions to come, the most excitement stems from the promise of what Ant 2.0 will bring.

Ant 2

Ant 2 will be a minor revolution in Ant's short history. At the time this book was written, the basis for what Ant 2 will be has been defined. To be more precise, the main requirements have been decided on, but it is not clear when Ant 2 is expected. Discussions will be ongoing and undoubtedly things will change as Ant 2 is implemented.

The first point to be made about Ant 2 is that there won't be any drastic changes in the goals of Ant. Ant 2 will build on the original design goals of simplicity, understandability, and extensibility. What does this mean? Well, in addition to being simple to use, Ant should be easy to understand no matter the level of user experience, and it should also be easy to extend via the API. You might think that Ant already does this pretty well, but Ant 2 promises to try to do an even better job of achieving these goals. So, what can you expect?

Backward Incompatibility

The first major point about Ant 2 is that it will not be backward compatible. The Ant team has decided that to make the headway planned for Ant 2, it could not maintain support for backward compatibility.

As much as possible, you can expect that things will be kept the same, but it's unlikely that build files for 1.*x* will work with the new version without modification. Custom tasks will also suffer this burden. It is anticipated that there will be changes to the API that will render current custom tasks incompatible. On the bright side, there probably will be facilities to ease the transition. The first will be in the form of a tool to convert build files to an equivalent Ant 2–compatible version. In all likelihood, the second facility will be adapter and utility classes to help the task writer use existing custom tasks with minimal changes.

Consistency

One of the reasons that 1.*x* build files won't be compatible with Ant 2 is because attributes will be renamed so that task attributes that share similar functionality will share a common name. For example, in Ant 1.5, the `earfile`, `jarfile`, `warfile`, and `zipfile` attributes of the `ear`, `jar`, `war`, and `zip` tasks were renamed "`destfile`". This is in addition to some underlying changes in the code structure to make things more consistent for the developer. Needless to say, a more consistent Ant can only be a good thing.

Removal of Deprecated Tasks and Attributes

Unlike the management of deprecated methods in Java, Ant 2 will see the removal of all deprecated tasks and attributes. So, for example, you won't be able to use the `<copydir>` task. An alternative is usually provided when a task or attribute is deprecated, so it should be easy to find and replace them. By not using them now, you can ease the transition when it comes along.

New Tasks

Ant 2 will bring with it new tasks that extend the scope that Ant can be used with. New tasks that will be added include

- A task for obfuscating class files

- A task for creating RPMs

- A JSP compilation task

New Features

There will be some nice new features included in Ant 2. Here's just a subset of the features that will be included:

- Dynamic properties; that is, it will be possible to reassign property values.

- The capability to include other XML files into a build file, thus allowing portions of XML such as common targets and paths to be easily reused.

- The facility to set default values for attributes. For example, you could set the default compiler in the <javac> task to "jikes" rather than set the attribute every time you use the javac task.

- Antidote will provide a GUI front end to Ant, with a servlet front end also expected.

- A richer set of events for BuildListeners.

- Internationalization. Error messages will be internationalized with the provision of utility classes to enable task writers to use them also.

A more comprehensive list of the requirements for Ant 2 containing the features listed earlier, as well as a few more, can be found on the Ant Web site (`http://jakarta.apache.org/ant/`). It provides the latest news on Ant 2.

One thing Ant will not bring is further tasks that move Ant closer to being a scripting language. Ant is not now and will never be a scripting language. Although tasks that facilitate iteration, for example, will not appear in the core of Ant, tasks such as `<foreach>` and `<if>` exist in the ant-contrib project (`http://sourceforge.net/projects/ant-contrib/`).

These are just a few of the treasures to look forward to in Ant 2, but they probably will not stop there.

What Can I Do to Help?

Much like any other open source effort, the drive behind bringing Ant forward is the user community and the developers. Much respect is due the developers who continue to make Ant what it is. These are people who have given their spare time to produce a tool that is pretty darn cool, to say the least! Shaping the future of Ant is very much a team effort and, as an Ant user, you can have a role to play. By participating and possibly even contributing code to the Ant project, you can help build an even better tool.

Full details of how you can get involved with Ant (or any other Jakarta project for that matter) can be found at `http://jakarta.apache.org/site/getinvolved.html`. But for the purposes of this chapter, I'll summarize the main ways you can get involved.

With a user's experience of Ant, there is undoubtedly at least one thing you would change or add to Ant. Perhaps it's something that would be useful to a substantial section of the Ant user community or maybe to just a few. Proof of how much the user community can affect Ant's future can be seen in the requirements gathering for Ant 2. Users were invited to suggest requirements for it and these were voted on in the finalization of the actual requirements. Got an idea already and are anxious to have your say? The main port of call is the mailing lists. There are two mailing lists (as referred to in Chapter 7, "Troubleshooting Ant Build Scripts"):

- The ant-user list—Subscribe by sending an empty e-mail to ant-user-subscribe@jakarta.apache.org with the subject Subscribe.

- The ant-dev list—Subscribe by sending an empty e-mail to ant-dev-subscribe@jakarta.apache.org with the subject Subscribe.

The ant-user list is aimed at providing a place for users to make comments and discuss problems with the use of Ant. It is the ideal place to make suggestions as to how Ant can be improved. The ant-dev list, on the other hand, is for Ant source code–related questions and comments for the developers. You can contribute code and patches to Ant via this list.

There are guidelines you should follow in using the mailing lists. Generally speaking, messages should be short and to the point, but with enough information for the reader to understand your point or problem. Looking at the mailing list archives can help you judge whether your message is reasonably put. When posting to either of these lists, it's important to observe etiquette. For example, cross posting (posting the same message to both lists) is frowned upon even if you feel the question is appropriate for both lists.

Another way to help is in the reporting of bugs. There is a database for Ant bugs reporting (`http://nagoya.apache.org/bugzilla/`), but it is important to check whether the bug really is a bug. Second, make sure that it does not already exist as a recorded bug. If you're unsure, it's advisable to post to the user list to confirm.

If you're still searching for a reason why you should help, think of the satisfaction you'll get from taking part in the maturation of a software tool that is fast growing in stature.

Summary

Ant is open source, and to that end, it requires a community to maintain interest and keep it progressing. The Ant community is very much alive and the next big step, Ant 2, will bring an improved version of a great tool. The compromise of backward incompatibility must be faced, but it is for the benefit of a more mature Ant. Ant is still very young in comparison to `make`, for example, but with the help of the user community and an excellent team of developers, Ant will evolve with bugs fixed and improvements made. As part of that community, you can make a difference.

CHAPTER 11

Tool Support for Ant

Evidence of the adoption rate by the development community is provided by the support for Ant added to many other existing development tools. This chapter looks at some of the tools that provide support for Ant, including a tool that is basically a wrapper for Ant. Use this chapter primarily as a quick start if you want to integrate Ant with your current development environment.

Ant Farm for jEdit

One of the more popular open-source development tools available is jEdit, which is freely available from

```
http://www.jedit.org/
```

jEdit is a complete source code editor, written entirely in Java. It's primarily for developing Java, although it's fair to say that jEdit isn't restricted to only Java development. Although jEdit doesn't claim to be an IDE, its very powerful Plugin Manager makes adding features to jEdit very easy.

The open-source community has been busy building a wealth of downloadable plug-ins for this editor. To that end, there are very few tasks that haven't been covered, including one that enables you to have a chat window within your editor!

Naturally, the support for Ant is very prolific. One of the more popular plug-ins is Ant Farm, which is available at

```
http://plugins.jedit.org/plugins/AntFarm
```

Alternatively, one of the great strengths of jEdit is the Plugin Manager that enables you to easily add features to the software without ever going anywhere near a Web browser.

Installing Ant Farm via the Plugin Manager is a very simple process. Just choose the Plugin Manager menu from the top pull-down menu, click on Install Plugins, and select Ant Farm. When you click Install, Ant Farm and other required plug-ins will be downloaded and installed. After a quick restart of jEdit, you're just about ready to go.

The last step is to configure Ant Farm. Via the Global Options menu under Utilities, you can choose to configure Ant Farm's options by expanding the Plugin Options branch of the menu. There are two main options screens for Ant Farm. The first screen, Build Options, specifies how you want to run Ant: within the same JVM as jEdit or using an external script. From here, you can also set options such as the logging level you would like Ant to be executed with, and the properties you want to be set globally throughout builds.

To get started using Ant Farm, just select it from the Plugins menu. This will bring up the window shown in Figure 11.1.

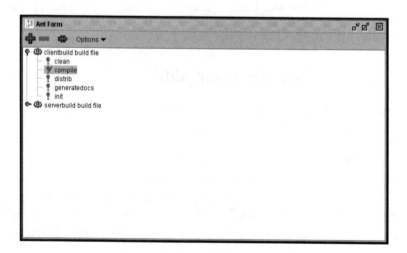

Figure 11.1

The Ant Farm window with the build files clientbuild.xml and serverbuild.xml loaded.

Tip

Use of the Ant Farm and Console windows as floating windows (as they are by default) is slightly erratic in that the focus switches between windows, and you must bring the Console window back into focus to see the result. But with the ability to dock windows pretty much anywhere in the editor space you can imagine, this won't be a problem.

The Ant Farm window displays a list of build files; in this case, `clientbuild.xml` and `serverbuild.xml`. Build files are added and removed using the plus and minus buttons at the top. The build files are organized as a tree in the interface. Each main branch is a build file. When the branch is expanded, it shows the executable targets within that particular build file. After you've loaded your build file, executing it is as easy as double-clicking the target. (Clicking the double-arrow icon also executes the currently selected target.) On execution, another window—the Console, which acts like a terminal and displays the output from the build—pops up as shown in Figure 11.2.

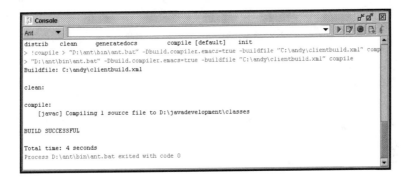

Figure 11.2

The Console window displaying output from a target execution.

The console also provides another way to load and run build files. This is a neat feature for the more command-line oriented users. More details on this, and Ant Farm as a whole, are provided in the documentation that comes with the installed Ant Farm JAR.

jEdit also can be used to create and edit build files, and this is nicely integrated with Ant Farm. When you save a build file that has been edited in jEdit, the Ant Farm window automatically updates the list of available targets for that particular build file. This is particularly useful because Ant Farm provides immediate feedback about errors in the edited build file (as it does on the initial load of a build file).

Full details of the errors in the build file are listed via the ErrorList plug-in. (If it's not already installed, ErrorList is one of the required plug-ins that's downloaded with Ant Farm.) This makes your life easier when you're creating and editing build files.

Ant Farm has some other nice features that make it a well-tuned plug-in. For example, you can choose to save all opened files in jEdit prior to any target execution, and also display a prompt for runtime properties on target execution. One particular feature of note is the capability to integrate with the project viewer. If you use the project viewer plug-in—which enables you to group a set of source files as a project—the projects you set up can include a build file(s). Subsequently, when you load a project that includes build files, you'll load the `build.xml` file from the root of any project. In fact, you'll also automatically load any `build.xml` file that has been opened for editing.

Other nice features include setting the logging level throughout builds, displaying a prompt for runtime properties, and the capability to set global properties that will be applied to all build files.

jEdit is not an IDE, but the installation of Ant Farm brings jEdit a step toward that feeling, at least in the sense that you are one double-click away from saving, compiling, and running your files. But, of course, because it's Ant, you're one double-click away from anything the power of Ant will enable you to do.

AntRunner for JBuilder

One of the oldest and most widely used Java IDEs still available is, of course, JBuilder from Borland:

```
http://www.borland.com/jbuilder
```

Borland presently maintains a number of versions and editions of JBuilder, but only the Enterprise edition from version 7 onward supports Ant as part of the core package. For early versions as far back as version 4, or for non-Enterprise editions, help is at hand thanks to Dieter Bogdoll (although now actively supported by Kirk Schnelle), who developed the AntRunner plug-in for JBuilder. AntRunner is freely available at

```
http://antrunner.sourceforge.net/
```

This very lightweight addition (weighing in at only approximately 67KB) is freely available and will enable you to trigger any Ant target from any Ant build file. In addition to providing this basic interaction with Ant, some nice touches have been integrated into this plug-in to allow Ant and JBuilder to co-exist. Namely, if an error is found, you can simply double-click on the error line in JBuilder's Console window and you'll be taken to the originating file for that error.

The installation of AntRunner is not straightforward, but it's painless if the following steps are followed:

1. After you've downloaded the Zip file, open it. You should see at least four files: antrunner.jar, antrunner.config, antrunnerdoc.jar, and antrunnerlogger.jar.

2. Place the antrunner.jar and antrunner.config files in the /lib/ext/ directory within your JBuilder home directory. Place the antrunnerdoc.jar file in the /doc/ directory within your JBuilder home. Finally, the antrunnerlogger.jar file goes into the /lib/ directory of your Ant installation.

3. You must modify the antrunner.config file with the details of the location of your Ant installation. Locate the line

```
addjars <your path to ANT_HOME goes here>/lib
```

and replace <your path to ANT_HOME goes here> with your real path location to Ant so that it reads something like this:

```
addjars c:/ant/lib
```

If you're running version 4.0 of JBuilder, you must add the following additional line:

```
vmparam -DJBuilder.version=4
```

After completing these steps, start JBuilder and you'll notice the addition of three new icons to your toolbar. These icons enable you to control access to the Ant targets.

Before you begin, you must tell AntRunner which build file it should use. You do this by bringing up the configuration window from the Project Properties menu as shown in Figure 11.3.

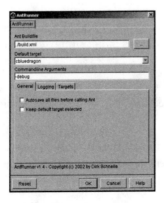

Figure 11.3
The configuration window for AntRunner.

This window permits you to chose a single build file and redefine the default target for that file. In addition, you can pass through some command-line arguments to Ant, while also instructing JBuilder to save all the files before an Ant script is run.

From here, it's business as usual; you can use all the features of JBuilder to build your application. When you come to the point at which you need to trigger an Ant target, you can simply click the Ant icon with the play symbol on it, as shown in Figure 11.4.

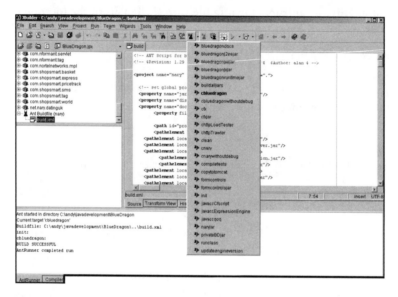

Figure 11.4

Selecting a target to run and observing the output.

This will run the target, with the entire output going to the standard JBuilder console window. Should you want to cancel this build, simply click the Stop Ant icon in the toolbar.

If the Ant target was compiling source files and an error was found, you can simply double-click in the Console window to be taken to that point in the source code. At present, there is a small bug in AntRunner that requires you to have that particular source file already open within JBuilder.

AntRunner is primarily used for the execution of Ant scripts, with only a "reload build file" available to aid in the development of Ant scripts. This isn't a major issue and shouldn't discourage the usage of this excellent addition to JBuilder.

Sun ONE Studio (AKA Forte for Java)

The official Java development environment from Sun Microsystems is Forte, or what is now known as Sun ONE Studio (to fall in with Sun's view of Web services). This platform is built on top of Netbeans (http://www.netbeans.org/) technology and has a very impressive integration with Ant. Sun ONE Studio is available at

http://wwws.sun.com/software/sundev/jde/index.html

Version 4 of this software supports Ant features up to 1.4.1. The good news is that Sun ONE Studio comes with Ant already available, so there's no need for a separate installation if you're already running this IDE.

Integration with Ant has been a well thought out process, and you definitely feel that Ant belongs within the IDE. The easiest way to get started is simply to browse to an existing Ant file using your Project Explorer, as shown in Figure 11.5.

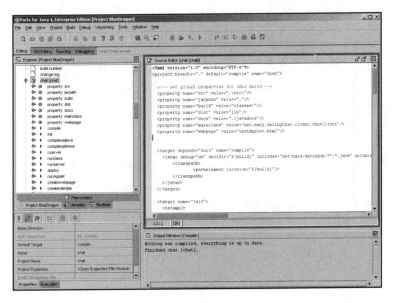

Figure 11.5

A typical view of an Ant script within Sun ONE Studio.

As you can see, the Explorer view knows all about Ant and the structure the file takes. If you expand the name of the build file, the drop-downs represent that target and properties of your Ant script. By selecting any one of these, you'll discover that the property panel changes to reflect the attributes you can change, including easy-to-use drop-downs. In fact, you can edit the whole Ant script without going near a single line of XML, which is very handy for those who prefer a much more structured way of dealing with Ant.

This facility is not lost when creating new Ant scripts, with a couple of quick start methods to begin your scripting. You can choose to start with a plain file or edit a standard template to suit your purposes.

After your Ant script is ready, you'll want a quick-and-easy way to trigger a particular target. Sun ONE Studio makes this very easy by enabling you to add a shortcut to either the menu or toolbar for a particular Ant target, as shown in Figure 11.6.

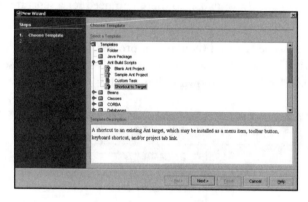

Figure 11.6
Creating new Ant scripts or shortcuts.

As with all the other IDEs, Sun ONE Studio integrates the output of Ant within its own console window, which gives you quick and easy access.

The integration of Ant within this IDE is so good that you can easily forget that Ant is an entirely separate package.

Eclipse

The Eclipse project is a fairly new integrated development environment that can be used with Java code. It's written in Java and it has a very nice Java editing environment, but it was designed as a platform for hosting different types of tools. The current version is 2.0, and it runs on multiple platforms. Eclipse is available from www.eclipse.org, but be sure to get the 2.0 version because it is far better than the 1.0 distribution. It supports color syntax formatting and highlighting, code completion, incremental builds, and easy access to JavaDoc. Eclipse doesn't have a GUI builder, so if you want to easily build Swing applications, you might need to find a different IDE.

Eclipse comes with its own incremental compiler, but it understands Ant build files and will allow you to execute arbitrary targets on demand. After you've created a project, Eclipse will detect a file called `build.xml` (the standard Ant build file) and attach a Run Ant item to its context menu. Selecting this will pop up a dialog box showing all the targets defined in your build file, as shown in Figure 11.7.

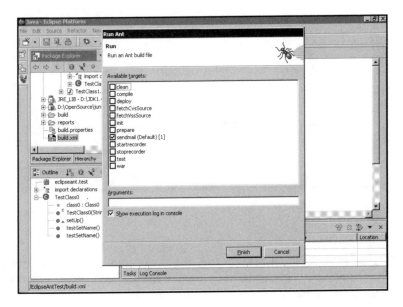

Figure 11.7
Run Ant dialog box.

Notice that in this case the `sendmail` target is selected and marked as the default target (as indicated by the default attribute in the project tag). You can select as many targets as you want, with their order of execution determined by the order in which you selected them. After you've selected the target(s) you want executed, you can provide any command-line arguments that you need in the text field, and then click on the Finish button. Unless you unchecked the Show Execution Log in Console check box, the results will show up in the Eclipse Log Console.

Assuming that all goes well, that's it. If something breaks, you'll not only see the output in the Console, but Eclipse will also pop up a message box to warn you that the build failed. You'll need to consult the Log Console for full details. Figure 11.8 shows the Log Console window with Ant errors displayed.

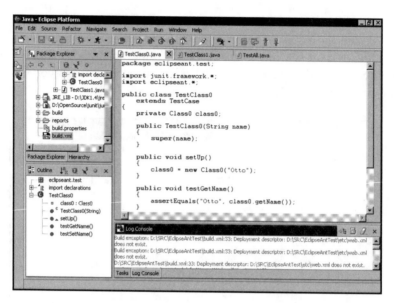

Figure 11.8
The Log Console window with Ant errors.

One neat feature of Eclipse's Ant support is that after you've run an Ant target for the current project, Eclipse will add an item to the Run, External Tools menu with the text being the path of the build file; for example, /EclipseAntTest/build.xml. (It also appears on the Run drop-down menu on the toolbar.) You can then re-execute Ant with the same target selections and parameters simply by selecting the menu item; you don't have to keep selecting targets.

Note
Be certain that your Eclipse build output folder is the same as your Ant output directory. If you make these paths point to the same directory, they will mutually support each other by not recompiling files that the other compiler has already handled. When you think about it, there really is no reason *not* to have them point to the same directory. The same goes for the source paths.

One thing you need to be aware of is that Eclipse 2.0 still ships with Ant 1.4.1, which is the previous stable release. The current version is 1.5, and that is the version upon which this book is based. If you want to use Ant with Eclipse and you plan on using this book as a reference (I hope you do!), you need to replace the version of Ant that Eclipse uses. You couldn't do this in Eclipse version 1.0, but 2.0 makes it easy. Navigate to the Ant configuration screen by selecting Window, Preferences, External Tools, Ant, which will bring up the window shown in Figure 11.9.

Figure 11.9
The Ant Properties window.

Remove the two JAR files relating to Ant 1.4.1: `ant.jar` and `jakarta-ant-1.4.1-optional.jar`. After you've deleted these files from the window, click on Add Jar, navigate to your `ANT_HOME/lib` directory, and add `ant.jar`. Then go back and add `optional.jar`. That's it! You're now using Ant 1.5 (or later) with Eclipse.

CruiseControl

CruiseControl (obtainable from `http://cruisecontrol.sourceforge.net`) is a new open source tool from ThoughtWorks (Martin Fowler's company) for performing continuous integration of your project. *Continuous integration* is a concept from the eXtreme Programming (XP) world, which says you want to execute an integration build several times each day. An integration build is just what its name implies: a build that integrates changes to the system from everyone on the team. The reason for performing these builds is to make certain that no one, mistakenly thinking he/she was changing code in a vacuum, breaks the system. By continuously performing these builds, the time between broken code being checked into the source code repository and team members becoming aware of the problem is greatly reduced. It works by periodically getting the latest version of all the code for your project from the source code repository and executing a build. All changes that have been checked in to the repository will be reflected.

The beauty of this setup is that it quickly exposes problems in integration that didn't show up on a particular developer's local box. Consider this scenario: You write your own test cases for some code and when those tests pass, you consider yourself done. You check in the new code and prepare to start on something else. But, unbeknownst to you, a coworker changed the interface of some code upon which your code depended and checked it in to the repository. Your code is now broken. By running CruiseControl frequently, this problem will be detected in a matter of minutes, not hours, weeks, or months later.

So, how does Ant fit in with CruiseControl? A better question is, "How does CruiseControl fit in with Ant?" You can't use CruiseControl without Ant. CruiseControl provides a set of Ant tasks that you add to your working build file. These tasks tell CruiseControl what it needs to get updates from the source code repository, execute a build, update logs, and send out e-mail alerts to team members and/or management. These e-mails are sent on completion of a build, whether success *or* failure.

To fully take advantage of CruiseControl, you also must have a strong set of JUnit test cases that are executed by your build file. The simple fact that a project compiles is not a measure of whether the project works correctly, or even at all. Having tests for everything will help CruiseControl, and you, quickly discover newly introduced problems.

After you've installed and configured CruiseControl (topics that are far beyond the scope of this book), you start it using the supplied batch file or shell script. It will then run continuously, checking for updates in the repository and executing builds as updates become available. The visual output from the running CruiseControl instance is just standard Ant output, but CruiseControl also provides a Web application that enables your team to view the logs of previous builds. This is a very nice feature that enables you to review previous logs to help track down a problem. Figure 11.10 shows an example of the log viewer.

The e-mails mentioned earlier that are sent out at the end of a build will contain a link to the Web application for viewing the log for that build. There is also a menu of previous builds that you can select from to review older builds.

Just to give you an idea of what you'll have to do, Listing 11.1 shows a target that incorporates the `modificationset` task. This task controls the CruiseControl processing. It can contain a handful of subtasks, tailored for whichever SCM system you are using. In this example, I'm using CVS. Listing 11.1 shows a target with the `modificationset` task.

Listing 11.1   *modificationset Task in Action*

```
<target name="modificationcheck" depends="init"
    description="Check modifications since last build">
    <taskdef name="modificationset"
        classname="net.sourceforge.cruisecontrol.ModificationSet"/>
```

Listing 11.1   *(continued)*

```
<modificationset lastbuild="${lastBuildAttemptTime}"
    quietperiod="30" dateformat="yyyy-MMM-dd HH:mm:ss">
    <cvselement cvsroot="${cvs.repository}"/>
</modificationset>
</target>
```

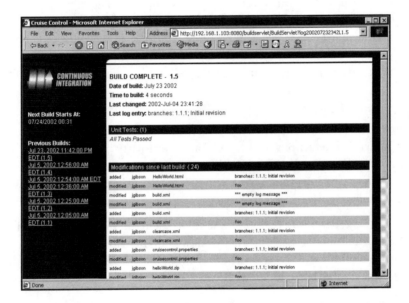

Figure 11.10
The CruiseControl log viewer.

The `cvselement` tag is obviously for interfacing with a CVS repository, but CruiseControl comes ready to work with Visual SourceSafe, StarTeam, PerForce, and ClearCase, so your SCM system should be readily supported.

Some complexities are inherent with CruiseControl, but there is excellent documentation and an active user community available to help out. The URL for CruiseControl is `http://cruisecontrol.sourceforge.net`.

> **Note**
> Martin Fowler has a paper about continuous integration available at http://www.martin-fowler.com/articles/continuousIntegration.html.

Control Center

TogetherSoft's Control Center 6.0 (CC) (`http://www.togethersoft.com`) is a unique IDE in that it has the capability to generate a significant portion (if not all) of a project's code base. So, it comes as no surprise that CC also can generate its own Ant scripts. Although these scripts might be overly simplistic, they work! With the capability to generate its own Ant scripts, you'd expect that Ant is well supported within CC. Happily, the level of integration meets these expectations, although you don't get it straight out of the box. The advantage of the strategy is that the user has more control over how much memory is consumed by CC because she can load only the tools that she needs and isn't forced to load tools that she won't use. To see how it all fits together, let's explore how CC and Ant interact.

Configuring Control Center

To configure CC to use Ant, you must use the activate/deactivate feature. This feature enables you to define interactions between CC and third-party products such as Ant. As is the case with other IDEs (such as IntelliJ), Ant version 1.4.1 comes bundled with CC. This bundling, along with the integration work with CC's API, reduces the job of activating Ant to a few simple mouse clicks.

Selecting the activate/deactivate option on the Tools menu on the main menu raises the Activate/Deactivate Features window. The window contains three tabs, as shown in Figure 11.11. At the time of this writing, the activation check box for Ant was found in the Early Access tab. Checking this box tells CC that you want to load Ant.

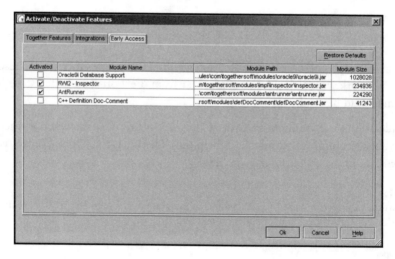

Figure 11.11

The Activate/Deactivate Features window.

If you mouse over the Run selection in the main menu, you'll find that an AntRunner selection has been added to the bottom of the drop-down. Place your mouse over that selection, and you'll find three subselections: Run Ant, AntRunner Configuration, and Generate Buildfile for Project. Selecting AntRunner Configuration pops up the window shown in Figure 11.12.

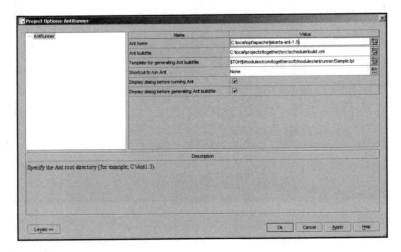

Figure 11.12
Project Options: AntRunner.

The window contains six configuration options as well as a handy context-sensitive help panel at the bottom. Although the documentation claims to support only Ant version 1.4.1, as you can see in Figure 11.12, CC is configured to use Ant 1.5. CC seems to cope with 1.5 without demonstrating any apparent difficulties. It's interesting to note that in the Template for Generating Ant build file, the setting begins with TGH. This handy macro, which is one of several, is set to the installation directory for CC. In that directory, you'll find a default template that is used in the generation of a build file. The last two check boxes will cause a display to pop up when either Ant is executed or an Ant build file is generated. It seems sensible to have this guard against accidentally running either the run or generate option because each of the panes contains an option to cancel the operation. Imagine how you'd feel if you accidentally ran `generate` after you spent some time customizing the build file.

A Generated Build File

Figure 11.13 shows a build file that was generated for a sample project using the settings shown in Figure 11.12. As shown in the listing, the attributes are parameterized to the head of the file, whereas the targets contain only references to parameters. As stated before, the script is simplistic but effective.

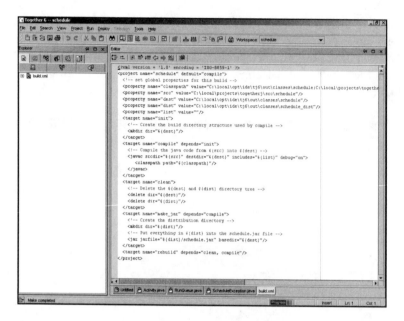

Figure 11.13

A generated build file.

Navigating the Run menu down to AntRunner and then to Run will cause a settings window to pop up (assuming that you set the check box option as described in the previous section). From this window, you can choose the build file that you want to work with. CC will parse the build file and present you with a drop-down menu filled with the targets that it has found in the build file. Figure 11.14 shows that we're almost ready to run the `execute` target. Clicking on the OK button triggers AntRunner to run.

What happens next depends on whether the build is successful. In either case, you'll start by having the output from Ant collected into a message pane (as demonstrated in Figure 11.15).

Note that in the upper-left portion of the main window, there is a collapsed view of the `build.xml` file. Mouse clicks in this window affect the movement of the cursor in the editor view of the `build.xml` file. If errors occur, they're displayed in red in the message pane. Clicking on an error has the effect demonstrated in Figure 11.16.

Figure 11.14

The Run dialog.

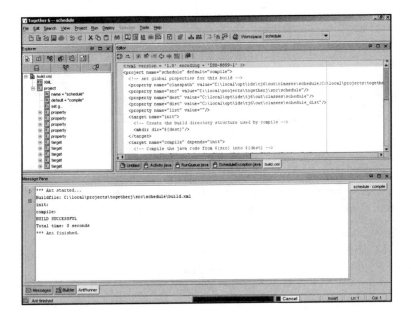

Figure 11.15

A successful compile.

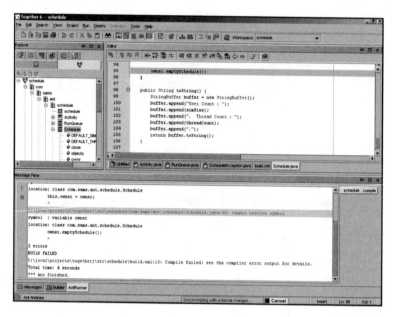

Figure 11.16
Compile errors.

In this figure, the offending line is highlighted in the editor. The project view highlights the class in question. This feature should significantly aid developers in fixing syntax errors.

As has been demonstrated, Control Center offers little or no resistance to you when replacing the build aspect of its native project management with Ant. You can navigate between the build file, output, and source with ease. The capability to generate build files is the icing on the cake.

IntelliJ IDEA 2.5

IntelliJ Software LLC (http://www.intellij.com) produces IDEA. As is typical with many Java IDEs, it has its own proprietary means by which you define and interact with a Java project. Parameters for this interaction are defined in a Project Properties GUI interface. The GUI enables you to define run and debug targets that include jUnit tests. It also enables you to define interactions with either CVS or SourceSafe. However, it does not include any support for Ant. Instead, you must right-click on either a target or an Ant project name in the Ant Build window, and then select the property item. Performing this action causes an Ant configuration window to pop up (see Figure 11.17). In this window, you supply a customized configuration that includes a classpath and properties for each build defined in the Ant Build window.

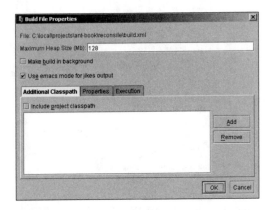

Figure 11.17

Setting the Ant configuration.

A menu running down the right side of the IDE contains a tab to pop up the Ant Build window (see Figure 11.18). There is a toolbar at the top of the window that contains four widgets—one each for adding and removing an Ant build. The green arrow runs the default target in the selected Ant build. The last widget opens a help window. Selecting the plus sign pops up a file browser that enables you to select the Ant build file. It's interesting to note that the same Ant build can be added several times. The advantages of this feature will become more apparent later. As soon as a build file is included into a project, IDEA parses it. Each of the build's targets is displayed in a tree-like structure. IDEA does not report on any structural errors that it finds in the build file. Although the parsing fails silently, the Ant Build window will not display any target that follows the offender.

As is the case with most modern IDEs, XML documents are a recognized file type by IDEA. The editor recognizes and colorizes XML tags, attributes, comments, and other elements that make up a document. Because an Ant build script is an XML document, the IDEA editor treats it as such. But it is also linked to the Ant Build window in interesting ways. As is the case with Java source, IDEA continuously parses the Ant build file as you are editing it. But, unlike continuous Java parsing, which places a red tick in the margin on any line containing a syntax error, the Ant parser does not provide this type of feedback to the user. Instead, the Ant Build window adjusts its list of targets as they become visible.

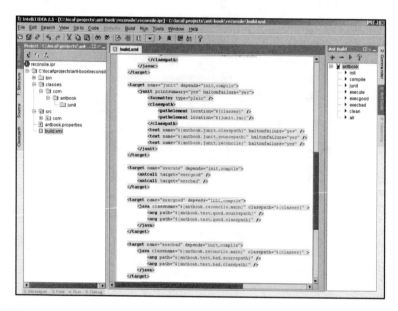

Figure 11.18
Main edit window.

Executing an Ant build target is as easy as double-clicking it in the Ant Build window. Ant targets also appear in the Build pull-down on the main menu bar. If that's not enough, clicking on the green arrow in the Ant Build window also will cause the execution of the selected target. Selecting the build will cause the default target to be executed.

In addition to the project configurations, the Ant build properties are used to configure the execution environment. The one point of confusion that I found was how IDEA treats the Ant variable `basedir`. This point is important if you use relative pathing (which I always recommend). IDEA sets `basedir` to that of the project's root directory. When running Ant by itself, `basedir` is set to where it finds the build script. This important difference caused me to move my `build.xml` files into the directory specified by the project path.

IDEA provides a framework to collect output from any compilation or execution activity that occurs, and to use that output to support interactions with other components contained within the IDE. Ant is nicely integrated in this framework. The first point of integration is the collection and organization of output from executing a target. Messages from Ant are displayed in an expanding tree. The upper level of the tree is the target that generated the output. The next level is the task that was executed. The next layers are the logged messages themselves. These messages might be *hot*; in other words, double-clicking them will cause the editor to navigate to the line in the source file that generated the message. For example, double-clicking on a compiler error originating from the `javac` task will cause the editor to go to the offending line in the Java source file. Other messages might cause the editor to display the build file as shown in Figure 11.19.

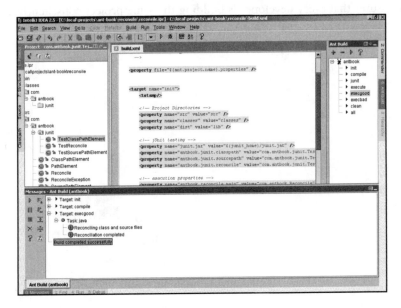

Figure 11.19
IDEA Messages window.

Note
In summary, aside from configuration, Ant uses all the standard frameworks found in IDEA. The only hiccup I encountered was the minor confusion with basedir. Although you cannot entirely replace IDEA's proprietary project management scheme, the level of integration with Ant enables you to come really close to doing so.

Summary

The tools covered in this chapter are just a subset of the growing number of development tools that integrate with Ant. With this level of support available, we as developers can take advantage of the fact that Ant creates a level playing field in terms of project management. Whether you're utilizing the most complex integrated developer tool or the simplest text editor, Ant ensures that every developer is building the same project consistently and accurately, irrespective of his platform.

Index

A

errorproperty, 207

errorreporting, 199

<excludepackage> element, 138

<excludepackagenames, 136

excludes

    <cab> task, 184

    <chmod> task, 101

    <delete> task, 113

    <ear> task, 116

    FileSet data type, 233

    <fixcrlf> task, 122

    <jar> task, 128

    <javac> task, 132

    <replace> task, 155

    <rmic> task, 157

    <style> task, 163

    <tar> task, 165

    <war> task, 175

    <zip> task, 178

excludesfile

    <cab> task, 184

    <delete> task, 113

    <ear> task, 116

    FileSet data type, 233

    <fixcrlf> task, 122

    <jar> task, 128

    <javac> task, 132

    <replace> task, 155

    <rmic> task, 157

    <style> task, 163

    <tar> task, 165

    <war> task, 175

    <zip> task, 178

<exec> task, 93-94, 118-119

executable, 118

expression, 164

extdirs

    <javac> task, 132

    <javadoc> task, 136

    <javadoc2> task, 136

    <javah> task, 202

    <rmic> task, 157

extension

    <formatter> element, 209

    <style> task, 163

<fail> task, 120

failifexecutionfails, 118

failonerror

    <apply> task, 94

    <copy> task, 107

    <delete> task, 113

    <echoproperties> task, 188

    <exec> task, 118

    <execon> task, 94

    <java> task, 130

    <javac> task, 132

    <javadoc> task, 136

    <javadoc2> task, 136

    <jspc> task, 203

    <loadfile> task, 141

    <mail> task, 143

    <sleep> task, 160

    tasks, 225

    <xmlvalidate> task, 219

failthrowable, 194

failureproperty, 207

Family, 104

file

    <available> task, 96

    <basename> task, 97

    <buildnumber> task, 98

    <checksum> task, 99

maxwait attribute, 174

maxwaitunit attribute, 174

memoryinitialsize attribute, 133

memorymaximumsize attribute, 133

merge mapper, 59

message attribute

    <echo> task, 117

    <fail> task, 120

    <input> task, 126

    <mail> task, 143

message tags, 302

<message> element, 144

messagefile attribute, 143

Messagemimetype attribute, 143

messages

    error, 260

    levels, 264-267

    log, 252

Messages window (IDEA), 373

methods

    classFiles(), 234

    execute(), 227-229

    execute0(), 336

    executeTargets(), 223

    executeTask(), 337

    getSource(), 336

    perform(), 337

    processConfigComponent(), 336

    sourceFiles(), 234

millis attribute, 168

milliseconds attribute, 160

mimetype attribute, 144

minutes attribute, 160

mkdir command, 190

<mkdir> task, 146

mode attribute

    <manifest> task, 144

    <tarfileset> element, 166

Modern compiler, 133

<modificationset> task, 364

<move> task, 146-148

multi attribute, 200

multiple files, attaching, 303

multiple targets, 40

N

name attribute

    <attribute> element, 145

    <batchtest> element, 209

    <bcc> element, 144

    <cc> element, 144

    <doclet> element, 139

    <from> element, 144

    <os> element, 104

    <package> element, 138

    <excludepackage> element, 138

    <param> element, 164

    projects, 13

    <property> task, 152

    <record> task, 153

    <section> element, 145

    <tag> element, 139

    <taglet> element, 140

    targets, 15

    <taskdef> task, 167

    <test> element, 209

    <to> element, 144

    <typedef> task, 171

name property, 31

V

validargs attribute, 126

validate attribute, 177

validity attribute, 123

value attribute

<attribute> element, 145

<available> task, 96

<compilearg> task, 134

<condition> task, 103

<entry> element, 197

<env> element, 119

<filter> task, 121

<istrue> element, 105

<isfalse> element, 105

<jvmarg> task, 208

<property> task, 151

<replace> task, 155

<replacefilter> element, 156

<sysproperty> element, 208

<uptodate> task, 173

variables

basedir, 372

environment

ANT_HOME, 8, 26

installation, 26-27

JAVA_HOME, 9

PATH, 26

verbose attribute

<cab> task, 183

<copy> task, 107

<delete> task, 113

<ftp> task, 189

<genkey> task, 123

<get> task, 124

<javac> task, 133

<javadoc> task, 137

<javadoc2> task, 137

<javah> task, 202

<jspc> task, 202

<signjar> task, 159

verbose flag, 264-265

verbose option, 86

verbosity attribute, 195

verify attribute, 157

verifyproperty attribute, 99

version attribute

<javadoc> task, 137

<javadoc2> task, 137

<os> element, 104

<sql> task, 161

visitor attribute, 201

visitorexception attribute, 201

vmlauncher attribute, 94, 119

W

<waitfor> task, 173-174

WAR (Web Archive) files

creating, 295

deploying, 298

listing, 296

war target, 47, 51

<war> task, 175-176, 296

warn attribute, 219

Web applications, 45-46

Web archives. *See* **WAR files**

Web sites

alternative Web-based interface, 271

Ant, 349

Ant Farm, 354

X – Y - Z

Other Related Titles